the world of

DJS

and the

turntable
culture

Todd Souvignier

the world of DJs

and the
turntable culture

Todd Souvignier

HAL•LEONARD® CORPORATION

Published by Hal Leonard Corporation
7777 West Bluemound Road
P.O. Box 13819
Milwaukee, WI 53213, USA

Trade Book Division Editorial Offices:
151 West 46th Street, 8th Floor
New York, NY 10036

Visit Hal Leonard online at www.halleonard.com

Library of Congress Cataloging-in-Publication Data:

Souvignier, Todd.
    The world of DJs and the turntable culture / by Todd Souvignier.
        p. cm.
Includes index.
    ISBN 0-634-05833-9
    1. Disc jockeys—Vocational guidance. I. Title.
    ML3795.S66 2003
    791.44'3—dc22

                                        2003015098

Printed in the United States of America
First Edition

10 9 8 7 6 5 4 3 2 1

Contents

Preface

About this Book

Welcome to *The World of DJs and the Turntable Culture*, a hands-on field guide to the art, science, and history of disk jockeying. The purpose of this book is to take you behind the wheels of steel and teach you the tools, techniques, and traditions of professional DJs.

We'll trace the evolution of the turntable as it has grown from a consumer playback device into a professional musical instrument. We'll learn about other types of DJ gear, such as mixers and effects. And we'll explore how the possibilities for DJs have expanded – DJing can lead into remixing, production, even a performance career.

To put things in perspective, we talked to some of the biggest names in the business and got exclusive, full-length interviews with a cross-section of superstar DJs. We also rounded up some of the latest, hottest gear for DJs; we emphasize state-of-the-art equipment and their cutting-edge features.

Naturally none of this happens in a vacuum. Today's DJ is part of a disruptive tradition that stretches across the entire 20th century. From the inception of commercial radio, to this very minute, DJs have precipitated a series of showdowns over property rights. Having some understanding of that historical backdrop—and the DJs place in it—will hopefully put the turntable culture in context. This book is a nuts-and-bolts gear reference that also tells the story of how DJing evolved, and it discusses the significance, aesthetics, and social implications of the DJ's practice.

In entering this territory we'll encounter some slightly complicated technical and legal bits. We've tried to keep it all simple and clear and to spell out anything that isn't common knowledge. If you encounter something you don't quite understand, read on; the most important topics and themes are touched on repeatedly in the course of these pages.

You don't have to read this book sequentially, from front to back. We expect that you'll jump around, perusing the parts you find most applicable or interesting. The table of contents and the index will help you locate what you're looking for. For those who do read cover-to-cover we've tried to pace things; technical chapters, narrative, and interviews are interspersed for variety's sake.

Beginning, entry-level DJs may want to start at the end of the book and do the tutorials in the appendices. Then have a look at the sections on turntable anatomy and mixers. Long-time, expert DJs might wish to start with the chapters on CD decks and computer tools; this is the first reference guide to survey those product categories.

By the time you're done with this book, you'll be familiar with the tools that a DJ uses. You'll know the fundamentals of what to do with those tools. You'll understand how DJing developed, and you'll have a clearer view of some of the directions you can take it.

The World of DJs

The world of DJs is filled with real beauty, excitement, creativity, and innovation, yet is also fraught with conflict.

The DJ's world is very much the real world, where it's all about money. As frontline musical emissaries, DJs repeatedly find themselves in the crossfire of major industrial disputes. DJs drove the early adoption of radio, but were treated like heretics by the record business, thrust into a twenty-year battle over spinning records on the airwaves. When the music industry was called to task for shady promotional practices, it was a DJ who took the fall. DJs and community activists asked for small slices of the radio spectrum and wound up in a decade-long hassle with the federal government and corporate broadcasters. And when DJs took to the Internet, playing music to listeners across the globe, it sparked another series of conflicts involving huge media companies, giant technology firms, the courts, Congress, and the Copyright office.

Beyond the business milieu, DJs were at the flashpoint of some of the century's biggest social transformations. DJs went to war periodically, often at great personal cost. DJs broke the color barrier in racially segregated America, brought black music into the mainstream, and helped pave the way for the civil rights movement. Freeform FM DJs provided the counter-culture soundtrack for the late 1960s and early 1970s. From the birth of gay pride, through the AIDS crisis and beyond, DJs have been there every step of the way with the gay community. And, of course, the DJ is the foundation of hip-hop. Throughout the turmoil of each decade, for each successive generation, the DJ is the one who kept the party rolling and who plugged kids into the zeitgeist.

The Turntable Culture

As for the turntable culture, it exists on a number of levels:

At the most prosaic level is the culture of the turntable itself. Turntable phonographs, in the home, in public places, and at radio stations, were the primary means of music delivery for most of the last century. The very existence of the turntable, and the DJ, fostered the archiving and promulgation of every type of music around the world. The success of the turntable drove innovations in electronics and led to the digital technologies that would replace it. When the turntable became obsolete, the DJ rescued it and transformed it from a consumer entertainment device into a professional audio tool.

There is also the post-modern level. Grandmaster Flash and his precursors in Jamaican music spearheaded a recombinant approach to record making, constructing hits from segments of other recordings. The turntable culture presupposes that innovation depends on plagiarism; the most effective (and quickest, and cheapest) way to make something new is to build on previous achievements. That idea existed in the art world for a long time, guys like Duchamp and Warhol made careers out of selecting and juxtaposing "stolen" elements. DJs, initially using turntables, eventually with digital samplers and computers, made direct, wholesale copying a predominant mode of music production.

As sampling became a widespread practice, the DJ was thrust to the center of (yet another) fight for control over sound recordings. While the courts and the music industry eventually built fences around sampling, nagging questions about fair use, intellectual property, the real intent of copyright laws, and the rights of artists and listeners remained unsolved. Those issues have a direct impact on all of society.

The turntable culture doesn't assume that everything's been done before; lots of new things are possible. It recognizes the enormous value and usefulness of our vast legacy of recorded music. It understands how innovation works: through selection, juxtaposition, modification, and synthesis. Nearly every sound ever recorded is available somewhere, and inexpensive audio technology makes it easy to appropriate and modify those recordings. In the turntable culture, seizing that opportunity is the only sensible response.

The turntable culture succeeds (in part) because its methods are forms of brainwashing. Humans are highly sensitive to audio cues and especially responsive to familiarity. A familiar song may evoke any number of conscious and unconscious reactions in a listener. When a song has been embedded in one's mind it takes just a few notes to push the button of recognition, evoking all the associated memories and emotions.

Even a small fragment, a drum loop or stray sound, can recollect the full inner experience of the complete source song. DJs play with familiarity and context. They also work with repetition and monotony, another brainwashing staple, which can induce trance-like states. The commercial upshot is that the DJ-driven practice of sampling, and the DJ-led migration toward repetitive, linear song constructions, enhanced the industry's ability to prefabricate and regenerate hits. Consumers not only accept monotonous, heard-it-before grooves, they have come to expect them.

The turntable can be a metaphor for popular culture, which since the 1970s has become a repetitious parade of recycled retro movements. All prior underground movements have been thoroughly co-opted and commercialized; the culture industry tries to anticipate and suppress new undergrounds by overexposing and colonizing them as soon as they appear. In the post-modern world subcultures are reduced to consumer styles; one can try on, and discard, any number of them. The major styles are revived and trotted around every few years.

The DJ is part of the larger, social culture. A culture where "what goes around, comes around." The DJ's quandary is that DJs play other people's records. Whether sequencing discs at a party, or creating the most Byzantine scratch assemblages, it's all built from prior work, crafted from borrowed or stolen goods. Branded by that core illegitimacy, wherever DJs go, whenever DJs succeed, somebody is always there to stop them, and shake them down for money.

Although we now see a small number of superstar celebrity DJs, much of the world does not recognize, or value, the DJ's creative and facilitative contributions. Like their allies the musicians, DJs are on the fringes of society, weird outcast bastards, routinely exploited, usually tolerated, but rarely accepted or thanked. They're rebels, hustlers, rabble-rousers, mad scientists, and the leaders of the pack.

DJing, and its corollary activity, obsessive record collecting, are stereotypical bastions of male geekdom. Nevertheless, women disk jockeys have always been part of the picture, more now than ever. We'll encounter a number of pioneering woman DJs in the course of this book, including one who remains the most infamous name in radio. While most DJs are men, we try to use gender-neutral terminology in this book for the sake of accuracy and fairness.

Many people helped create this book, including John Cerullo, Brad Smith, Kallie Shimek, Tim Bigonia, Nicole Julius, and others too numerous to mention at the Hal Leonard Corporation. Jeff Feinman, the Horizons Unlimited DJ Project, and Joe Hornof, provided key early assistance. Christie Z-Pabon (Tools of War) was fantastically generous with fact-checking, hip-hop consulting and celebrity wrangling. Mark Prince and Sara Hughes at Numark, Brian Dowdle at American Audio, Ron Neilson at Neilson Clyne, Debra Lind at Denon, Bill Oakley, Greg Riggs, and Cory Lorentz at Shure, Ken Ninomiya at Stanton, Jerry Kovarsky at Korg, Karl Detken, Nick Hahn, and Aaron Levine at Pioneer, Dan Brown, Mate Galic, and Omar Torres at Native Instruments, and Darlene Rattan at Yamaha all helped out with gear and fact-checking.

Yogafrog, Megan Meade, Sue Harbottle, Nick DeCosemo, Dan Ross and Rachel Matthews graciously assisted with the interviews. Anne, Nancy, Blake, and Vic Souvignier, plus Evelyn "Cybernana" Mitchell, kept the home fires burning. Special thanks to Uncle Buddy, Scott Aiges, Mister Tim, and Steve Oppenheimer at *Electronic Musician* magazine.

A DJ's basic job is to spin some tunes for partying. In doing so DJs create the soundtrack for our culture, indeed the very soundtracks for our lives. This book is a tribute to those practitioners, and a map to their world.

Welcome aboard, and keep your hands on the wheels.

Chapter 1

Understanding Music

The DJ's core task is selecting music. You don't have to be a trained musician to DJ, but knowing some basics will help immeasurably. At least understand how music is described and organized, so you can choose and mix intelligently. This chapter provides the fundamentals; it's Music 101, from the DJ perspective.

The Beat

Most music has a steady rhythmic pulse, or "beat." One can certainly find examples of music with irregular rhythmic patterns or with no discernable beat. Nonetheless, a prominent, repetitive beat is the central, defining feature of all dance music and most popular music, worldwide.

The beat has a direct physical corollary in the rhythms of heartbeat and breath, which are the very proof of human life. Indeed, there is much anecdotal and scientific evidence demonstrating the direct effects of music on breathing and heart rate.[1]

1 Such as Davis and Cunningham's "Physiologic Responses of Patients in the Coronary Care Unit to Selected Music," Heart and Lung 14(3), 1985. Or consider the calming effect of a soap opera's theme music on newborns, reported by PG Hepper in "Fetal 'Soap' Addiction," Lancet, June 11, 1988.

Dancers and listeners like to hear a steady beat, one that's easy to find, easy to move with. Changing tastes and the evolution of music production techniques brought the beat front and center. The beat became the main sonic aspect of most popular music, probably because records with a big beat sell better and get played more.

To get a feel for the beat, turn on some music and walk around the room in time to the rhythm. Clap your hands or bang your head while walking with the music. Focus on instruments that are playing the most rhythmically, typically the drums and bass.

Next, count to four as you walk, counting "one-two-three-four, one-two-three-four," in time with the beat. Rhythmic patterns and musical phrases usually start on a specific beat, called "the one." Do this experiment with several records, of any style. You'll quickly see that musical passages are frequently arranged in units of four, eight or sixteen. This idea of counting the beat leads to the concept of "time signature."

Time Signature

The beat or pulse of music is represented by the time signature. The time signature is a part of traditional music notation that indicates the number of beats in a measure and the number of notes in each beat. Most popular music is in a 4/4 time signature, meaning there are four beats per measure and each quarter note is one beat.

The numbers at the beginning of a score indicate time signature.

Music is thought about and notated in terms of measures. A measure is a building block, a moment in time containing a certain number of beats. Those beats are represented as notes. A whole note lasts one entire measure that's usually four beats. A half note sounds for half the measure, two beats. A

quarter note's duration is one-fourth the time of the measure, one beat. An eighth note lasts one-half a beat.

Music note shapes denote their time value. A whole note lasts for one full measure, then you have the half note, quarter note, eighth note, and sixteenth. There are also thirty-second notes, as well as other note shapes and note time symbols, but we're going to gloss over all that.

As we said before, most music you'll encounter has four beats in each measure, and each beat is the equivalent of a quarter note.

There are, however, many "alternate" time signatures. Artists such as Frank Zappa and King Crimson are noteworthy (in part) for their use of unusual time values such as 5/4 and 7/8, which have five and seven beats per measure, respectively. The result can be a fairly bizarre rhythmic feel within a rock/pop context. And you have the waltz, a dance that relies upon a 3/4 time signature, imparting a pronounced "swaying" feel. But by and large, most popular or commercial music—from the Top Forty to the underground—makes use of the steady walking rhythms of the 4/4 time signature.

Accents

Some beats are louder than others. The most prominent beats are called "accents." Accents play a big role in determining the feel or musical impression of a beat. Drummers typically use the snare drum to provide the accent. An accent is sometimes called a "downbeat;" the term downbeat also sometimes means the first beat in the measure, the one. An unaccented beat is called an "upbeat." Lots of popular music puts the accent on the two and the four, the second and fourth beats in a measure. That's called a "backbeat."

Tempo

The pace or speed of music is called the "tempo." Music's mood and urgency is partly determined by the tempo. Tempo is measured in beats per minute or BPM.

You'll encounter a broad spectrum of tempos as you explore the range of recorded music. Most drum machines start up, by default, at 120BPM. That's a good pace for dance music—many disco classics are at or around 120BPM. Tempos ranging from 60 to 100BPM are common in hip-hop and R&B. And you'll find tempos of 135BPM and faster in certain dance styles like drum & bass or speed garage.

Tempos are generally described as "down-tempo" (slow), "mid-tempo" (medium), or "up-tempo" (fast), but these terms are imprecise. To create smooth transitions between songs, we must deal with exact tempo values.

Determining Tempo

Some dance records have the tempo printed right on the label, but with most recordings you'll have to figure out the tempo. There are a number of ways to determine the tempo of a piece of music.

The most low-tech approach is to use a watch, any watch with a second hand or digital readout of seconds. Play a section of the song and count the number of beats you hear during one minute.

A slightly more accurate approach is to use a metronome or a click track from a drum machine. Metronomes are the original click tracks used by musicians to find a particular tempo and maintain a steady beat. The traditional metronome is a small wooden pyramid, containing mechanical clockwork, with a weighted swinging arm that sets the tempo. Most models today use digital electronics; one can find stand-alone digital metronomes or metronomes built-in to tuners and signal processing effects.

To derive the tempo of a recording, play the song, and start the metronome or drum machine. Adjust the tempo until the clicks synchronize with the beats of the music. Once you're in the neighborhood restart the metronome or drum machine, so that it's beginning right on the One (the first beat of a measure.) Fine-tuning the tempo, down to tenths or hundredths of a beat per minute, may be necessary to get a precise lock. You'll know you have the right tempo when the clicks no longer drift out of step with the beat. Like beat counting, it's a lot of work.

Fortunately beat detection technology has come a long way. Many devices marketed to DJs, including certain turntables, CD decks, and mixers, have built-in BPM meters. We've also seen stand-alone devices, which can be added to any sound system, that measure and display the BPM. Beat meters have two basic modes of operation: tap tempo and automatic.

A tap tempo device has a button, key, or pad, which the user must tap or press in time with the music. After a few taps the device will have enough timing information to determine the tempo. This method is only as accurate as your own ability to tap in time.

Beat meters are a godsend, telling you the tempo in beats per minute (BPM) at a glance. This one has a tap mode. Photo: Linda Monson

Automatic beat meters monitor the volume level of the audio signal and assume that the loudest moments are the beats. This works really well with sparse dance tracks, but can run into trouble with complex arrangements or recordings that don't have slamming percussion. Despite the shortcomings, beat detection devices usually work well, are a real time saver, and can be indispensable for DJs who want seamless mixes. Some beat detection products include both tap and automatic modes, offering the best of both worlds.

Key

All tonal music, any song that includes pitched tones, melodic parts, or singing (as opposed to rapping), is in a certain key. The key is the main note of the song, the tonal center.

We'll avoid any long tangents about music theory. DJs need to know that the key provides the foundation or root for all the other notes used in the song, which collectively are called a "scale." Most Western music since the Renaissance has been based on a seven-note scale. Notes are referred to by letter, hence the keys of A, B, C, D, E, F, and G. In addition, there are some in-between notes available, most easily envisioned as the black keys on a piano keyboard. A note that is half a tone higher is called a "sharp"; half a tone lower is called a "flat." The ♯ is shorthand for sharp. The ♭ symbol indicates flat.

The key and scale help determine the tone color and musical sound of a composition. Certain keys are frequently used in particular styles of music. A lot of rock music is in the keys of E and A, because those keys are easy to play on electric guitar. Much folk and country music is in C or G, which lend themselves to the open fingerings preferred by acoustic guitarists. While drums and drum machines can be tuned to a degree, percussion instruments are generally atonal, meaning they sound like noise. Percussion parts are not usually thought of as having a particular key. But add a bass part or synthesizer line, and you're dealing with a key.

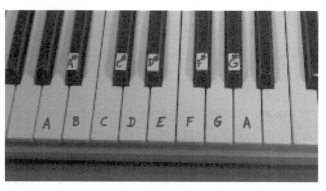

The piano keyboard offers the easiest way to visualize the names of notes. Note that the black keys all have two names; A♯ (A-sharp) is the same thing as B♭ (B-flat). Photo: Linda Monson

Determining Key

If you want to create a transition in which the pitched melodic portions of two songs overlap or segue nicely, you'll want to match the keys of the two songs.

It's very unusual for a record or CD to include any indication of a song's key. And while pitch detection technologies do exist, they're only useful on monophonic (one-note) musical parts. A chord, or a multi-part musical arrangement, will render pitch detection utterly useless. Pitch detection technology is found in all electronic tuners and certain music software packages, but is almost never included in gear marketed to DJs.

Determining the key of a recording requires ears and a little musical know-how. The easiest method is to use a piano or electronic keyboard. Play the recording and hold down individual notes on the keyboard until you find the one note that sounds best with the main part of the song. That note is very likely the root tone or key. If you're having trouble finding it, listen for the bass note in the main part of the song.

A piano or electronic keyboard works best for this, because each note is at a fixed pitch. One could use a guitar or other instrument, but make sure it has been tuned correctly or you'll never be sure you've found the right key.

Some people are said to be "tone deaf" and may have difficulty finding the key of a song. Others seem to have a natural gift for pitch detection and can pick out the key almost instantly. Most people with normal hearing and access to a musical instrument can develop and improve this skill with time and practice.

The point to finding the key is to mix parts of a song with other records in the same key. Musical phrases like melodies and bass lines, which are in the same key may go together nicely. It can create a very appealing segue. While many DJs never bother with key matching, some such as DJ Shadow have made it a part of their art. For remixers and mash-up artists like The Freelance Hellraiser, key matching is an essential technique.

Frequency

The pitch of any note is determined by that note's frequency. Understanding frequency and its relationship to pitch and key requires knowing a little about the physics of sound, hearing, and music.

All sound is vibrations. These vibrations are transmitted by the air and travel away from the sound source until they lose energy (due to the friction of air molecules). Those airborne vibrations induce vibrations in the eardrum and are transferred through the machinery of the human inner ear, allowing us to hear the sound.

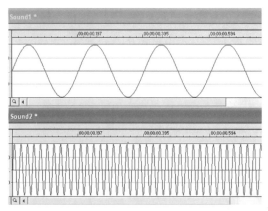

Frequency is easiest to visualize in a waveform display. The top waveform is at a lower frequency (5Hz, or five cycles per second) than the bottom waveform (50Hz). The top waveform sounds lower in pitch than the bottom.

The perceived pitch or tone of a particular sound is determined by the number of vibrations per second, also called the frequency. A sound source that vibrates at a slow frequency, say around fifty cycles per second, produces a very low pitched, bass tone. A sound source that vibrates at a high frequency, perhaps at ten thousand cycles per second or higher, is perceived as being a high pitched, or "trebly" sound.

Audio engineers and musicians use the term Hertz (abbreviated Hz) as shorthand for "cycles per second" when talking about frequency. Average human hearing is arguably able to detect sounds that range from 20Hz to 20,000Hz. Another shorthand term is used when talking about higher frequencies: Kilohertz (kHz) means "thousand Hertz"; 20kHz is the same thing as 20,000Hz.

While pitched (musical) sound sources vibrate at a steady rate, many sound sources are aperiodic and have no single frequency. An explosion, a drum hit, or radio static, are just three examples of un-pitched, aperiodic waveforms. They have no repeating waveform pattern, no discernable frequency. Vibrating at many different frequencies, they all pretty much sound like noise.

As musical instrument manufacturing became standardized, piano tuners came to an agreement about the relationship between frequency and note value, so instruments could be tuned to exactly the same frequencies. The middle A note on a keyboard is usually tuned to 440Hz.[2] The A note one octave (eight steps) below is tuned to 220Hz; the A one octave above is at 880Hz.

We'll sidestep the long discussion of how tunings are achieved and the mathematical relationships between notes in a scale. The important takeaway for DJs is simply this: Human hearing and all music operate within a frequency range from roughly 20Hz to 20,000Hz (20kHz). The frequency of a sound source's vibration determines its pitch or note value.

Later in this book we'll talk about tools such as filters and equalizers that can be used to increase or reduce the volume level of specific audio frequencies. And later in this chapter we'll discuss the correlation between turntable speed and musical pitch.

---

2 A=440Hz is the typical point of reference, although some composers and orchestras prefer to tune middle A to 442Hz. Better electronic tuners and instruments can calibrate to either 440 or 442.

Amplitude

Amplitude is a fancy word for volume or loudness. Amplitude refers to the energy level in a signal, indicating the maximum value of a periodic waveform.

To envision amplitude, think about a guitar string. Before it is struck, the guitar string is at a zero-energy state; it's at rest and not vibrating. A weak pluck will transfer a small amount of physical energy to the string, displacing it slightly from the zero-state. The weak pluck creates a low-amplitude vibration and results in a low-volume sound. A heavy pluck on the string transfers a larger amount of energy, causing a greater displacement, a higher-energy vibration, resulting in a louder sound.

As mentioned earlier, air molecules have friction. This friction reduces the energy level in a sound wave as it travels through air. The result is a decrease in the amplitude or volume of a sound as it moves away from the sound source.

Electronic sound systems increase the amplitude of audio signals by using amplifiers, which boost the energy level and therefore increase the signal's volume. Amplitude and loudness are measured using a scale called decibels, abbreviated as dB. Decibels represent relative differences in power, using a logarithmic ratio. That may sound rather complicated, because it is.

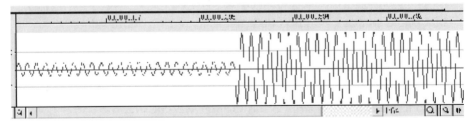

A low-amplitude signal (left) sounds soft or weak; a high-amplitude signal (right) is louder, because there's more energy in the sound wave.

You might have seen hand-held decibel meters in use at concerts or public events; these devices can't measure the actual volume of a sound, merely the relative volume at a particular distance from the sound source. As a rule of thumb 0dB is essentially silence, and 130dB is sound that causes pain.

The important points to remember are: When someone talks about amplitude, they mean volume or loudness. The amount of energy in a vibrating sound source is what determines the loudness. Decibels (or dB) are used to measure amplitude. Electronic circuits called amplifiers are used to increase the amplitude of audio signals so that they may be transmitted and heard.

Speed and Pitch

As mentioned earlier, the pitch or tone of a note is determined by its frequency, meaning the sound source's number of vibrations per second. Now consider an audio waveform that has been recorded to a phonograph record. A vinyl LP normally rotates at a rate of 33 and 1/3 revolutions per minute (RPM). Slow down the turntable, and you'll immediately notice two things: The tempo of the music has decreased. And the pitch or tone of the music has been lowered.

By the same token, increasing the speed of the turntable will raise the tempo and pitch of the music. Take a 33 and 1/3 RPM record that contains singing, and play it at 45RPM. You'll hear the classic "chipmunk" effect on the vocals. This effect is not isolated to vinyl LPs; the same phenomenon can be witnessed by altering the speed of any analog tape recording, like a cassette or reel-to-reel. Or check out any digital sampler, which allows you to map a sound across the entire piano keyboard, each key playing the recording at a slightly different speed.

This is frequency at work. Changing playback speed causes the music's vibrations to reach the needle (or tape head, or digital converter) at a slower or faster pace than normal. Since the frequency has changed, the perceived pitch or tone changes.

Most professional turntables have a slider called the pitch slider. It's a speed adjustment determining the turntable's number of revolutions per minute. Adjusting the pitch can help you match the tempos of two records that were originally recorded at different BPMs. Pitch adjustments also shift the key of a musical performance up or down.

The pitch slider changes the turntable's rotation speed. Photo: Linda Monson

In a traditional mechanical turntable that relationship between speed and key are inexorably linked. You can't speed up or slow down the tempo without changing the key. However, thanks to advances in digital signal processing (DSP) technology and the advent of realistic time shifting processes, some current turntables can change the tempo without affecting the key. We'll discuss this further in Chapter 3.

Drums and Percussion

As mentioned earlier, the purpose of drums and percussion instruments is to keep the beat. Each drum in a trap kit or drum machine has a different sound and they each serve different functions within the beat. There are many different drums, but there are three that every DJ must know:

The bass drum, also called the kick drum, makes a low, deep thud. It's usually used for an unaccented part, often as a "heartbeat" for the song.

Snare drums usually sound like a sharp crack or shot in the upper-mid-range frequencies. Snare drums often provide the accented beat.

Most rhythm tracks are built from simple bass-and-snare patterns. The other instruments fill in the rhythm part, adding variance and sonic interest.

The third important percussion sound is the high hat, two cymbals that are held together or apart by a pedal mechanism. It has a high-pitched, sometimes hissy sound. The high hat can create movement within a drum part; one frequently hears repeating eighth- or sixteenth-note high hat patterns in dance music.

Of course, there are many different drums and a whole world of electronic percussion sounds. Latin music had an especially profound effect on today's drum sounds; Latin players brought in a whole cast of distinctive percussion instruments, and a complex fluid rhythmic style.

If you have access to a drum machine, sit down with it and listen to each drum sound. Learn their names and their distinctive characteristics. If you can't get hold of a drum machine, at least learn to identify the kick, snare, and high hat or cymbal in a recording. Have someone point them out if you aren't sure. Identifying and locating the kick and the snare is an essential DJ skill.

Gibson Les Paul bass guitar.
Photo: Linda Monson

Other Instruments

The bass plays a big role, working with the drums to carry the rhythm, and establishing the basic notes for the song. Bass once meant the bass guitar or violin. With the advent of synthesizers and samplers, bass parts are commonly played by keyboards. Bass lines are usually low frequency, single-note passages. Bassists often play simple repeating patterns or just hold on the main note. Since the bass and the drums are the instruments that maintain the beat, they're sometimes referred to as the "rhythm section."

Guitars, keyboards, violins, horns, and all the other instruments of the orchestra can be brought to bear on a recording. But most productions are pretty simple. In general, the instruments in a song are either accenting the beat, or accompanying and embellishing on top of the beat. Guitarists, for example, have two basic modes, "rhythm" and "lead." Rhythm guitar means playing chords that accent the beat. Lead means playing melodic parts that may be untethered from the beat.

Roland SH-101 synthesizer, a vintage one-note synth. Photo: Linda Monson

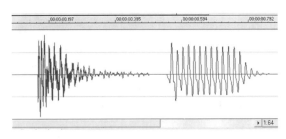

Waveform envelopes for a drum hit (left) and a bass note (right). The bass note sustains before its release.

While all musical instruments have their value, a lot of music can be made with just the bass and drums. Or just a one-note synth and a drum machine. Bass and drums are the sonic foundation of all popular music.

Note Envelopes

The "envelope" is a note's shape, its volume characteristics over time.

The easiest way to visualize envelopes is to look at a waveform display, as seen in most computer audio software.

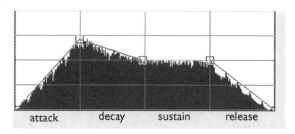

Envelope shapes are described using terms including "attack," "release," and "sustain."

Synth players usually think of envelopes as having four parts: attack, decay, sustain, and release.

Drum hits have a quick attack. As the stick displaces the drumhead, the volume level goes from zero to maximum almost immediately. Some instruments like violins and horns can play with a slow attack, producing notes that go from soft to loud very slowly.

Drum sounds usually have a quick release, meaning they diminish quickly. Other instruments, like a guitar, can "ring out" after a note is played, hence a longer release time.

Pitched instruments (instruments that create repeating, periodic waveforms) can usually sustain a note, holding it at a constant volume level over a period of time.

Envelopes really come into play with scratching. Moving the vinyl beneath the needle, one can easily locate drum hits and other instrument sounds, and compare the differences in attack and release. Some scratches might suggest a sound with a fast attack, like a snare drum. Others might entail a sustained sound, like a guitar power chord, or a synthesizer tone. Sometimes a complex envelope, like human speech, is the best thing. Scratching allows one to "feel" and manipulate note envelopes in a way that's very tangible.

Song Parts

Although one can find some wild sub-genres like free jazz and noise music, most popular music is heavily structured. The beat is the foundation of that structure, providing a rhythmic underpinning. Pitched instruments usually play in the same key, and note patterns or riffs are often repeated to some degree. Adding another layer of structure is the concept of song, meaning a pre-meditated musical composition, typically accompanying singing or rapping.

Songs are put together in some traditional ways. There are a couple of common formats, a verse/chorus or A/B structure would be one of the most simple.

The verse contains the main words of a song, often the storytelling part. The chorus is usually a repeated melodic or vocal part, often containing the song title. Song writers talk about "hooks" meaning a catchy, repeatable, musical phrase or vocal bit, and often try to put such hooks in the chorus.

With two parts to work with, one could make a song that went A/B/A, A/B/A/B, A/B/A/A/B, or any number of permutations.

Obviously you can branch out from the simple A/B structure. One might add a third part, sometimes called a "bridge," and have an A/B/C structure, or A/B/C/A, A/B/A/C/B, or some variation thereof.

Another common template is call-and-response in which singers or instruments trade off, the call being mimicked, or elaborated upon, by the response. Call-and-response is said to derive from African music, and evidently came into pop through slave songs and spirituals. There are many ways to do call and response, and this archetype is easily combined with other songwriting methods.

One of the most successful formats is the blues. Songs in the blues tradition are usually based on three chords, which are called I, IV, and V (one, four and five).[3] Blues songs are categorized by the number of bars, or measures, contained in each verse/chorus cycle. Eight-bar and twelve-bar blues patterns are two of the classic frameworks.

Most songs have introductions, or intros, meaning opening notes before the main body of the song. In dance music the intro is often just a drumbeat, making it easier for a DJ to mix the record. Songs also have endings; how one mixes out of a song depends on the nature of the ending, be it an abrupt stop, a fade-out, a vocal or instrumental rave-up, or some other type of outro.

Hip-hop and dance music have contributed to the erosion of old "Tin Pan Alley" models of heavily formatted pop songwriting. Dancers want long grooves and don't mind great passages of repetitious instrumental music. That emphasis on the beat leads to expansive grooves, linear constructions, minimalist arrangements, and a sparse, fragmented vocal style, perhaps consisting of just a word or phrase. At the other end of the vocal spectrum, an MC may go on for any length of time over the same beat, although most commercial rap recordings opt for a more formatted verse/chorus approach.

---

3 A chord is a group of notes that sound good together. There are many types of chords—major, minor, augmented, diminished—all of which are beyond the scope of this book. The I, IV, V designation comes from the chord's relation to the song's key – a I chord is based on the first (or root) note of the scale, the IV is based on the fourth note, and the V built from the fifth note of the scale.

Breaks

Another hip-hop innovation is the practice of extracting and extending the "break." Some records have passages where the pitched instruments drop out, leaving just the drums. It's called a drum break. Hip-hop DJs seek out such passages, often located after a chorus, or in the introduction.

With two copies of the record, a skillful DJ can use a "breakbeat" to create an extended, uninterrupted groove. The DJ plays the break sections back-to-back, one after another, while quickly repositioning the records and manipulating the mixer.

To understand the purpose of this, it helps to know a little about hip-hop culture: In the 1970s dance forms called breaking and uprocking developed in New York City. A sort of modern tribal war dance, breaking and uprocking were literally forms of battle and had roots in teen gang life. Dancers would compete to see who had the best moves. It was a safe alternative to violence or sometimes a prelude.

Kool DJ Herc knew that the dancers waited for the drum breaks in certain records such as "Apache" and "Bongo Rock," busting their wildest moves during those segments.[4] Herc decided to repeat the breakbeat, to extend the dancing. Grandmaster Flash seized upon this concept of extending the break, and perfected the quick mix technique, constructing seamless ongoing grooves. We'll talk more about this evolution in Chapter 4.

---

4 "Apache" and "Bongo Rock" by the Incredible Bongo Band are on the *Bongo Rock* LP, released on the Pride label in 1973.

Genre and Style

"Genre" means kind, species, or type. We use genre to refer to the main musical movements such as classical, jazz, the blues, rock, and dance music. It's an inexact term, as is "style," which we take to mean sub-genre. Within any genre one can find multiple styles. Rock has fragmented into variants like punk rock, progressive rock, heavy metal, funk rock, and a hundred other styles. Likewise the dance genre has been split into styles such as house, techno, jungle, drum and bass, trance, and a multitude of others.

Such definitions and categorizations are very slippery. Some might have once dismissed hip-hop as a sub-genre of pop or dance music. Today hip-hop is a genre unto itself, encompassing a host of divergent styles.

Stylistic innovation usually occurs by borrowing from other styles and genres. Artists frequently cross-pollinate, taking elements from one tradition and recasting them in a new context. When they succeed we wind up with ongoing trends, like country-rock or trip-hop.

Music marketing has come to depend on a continuing succession of new, recombinant styles and formats, accompanied by periodic retro/nostalgia movements. One sees it most starkly in the U.K., where the British music press and record labels manufacture a new "next big thing" each season, then declare the whole trend dead soon after. This cycle churns more slowly in the States, but is evident wherever you find popular culture.

In some cases musical styles grow out of (or become connected to) youth subcultures or larger social trends. The elements of hip-hop (rapping, DJing, graffiti, and dancing) grew primarily out of street gang life. Punk rock, a Manhattan in-crowd scene that became a fabricated British trend, inspired a legitimate, worldwide, youth subculture, now in its 25th year. House music was exported from America's gay nightclubs and adopted by the European rave scene, where it splintered into a host of variant styles.

Musical styles derive authenticity, subject matter, and audience from their associated subcultures. The subculture gains an outlet, artifact, and advertisement. Music can cross cultural, economic, or geographic boundaries, carrying the message of the subculture that spawned it.

The task of categorizing music into styles and genres reached its apotheosis with the advent of radio formats. Music programming on radio is controlled by formats, each format consisting of musical styles and repertoire proven to appeal to certain groups of consumers. The core of each format is the playlist, a groups of songs that has been thoroughly market-tested by a broadcasting chain or consulting firm. Artists that don't test well within tightly defined segments, such as Urban Contemporary, Classic Rock, or a limited assortment of other radio formats, won't get much airplay.

For radio DJs the playlist is simply a fact of life. College or community stations might let DJs pick music, but too much money is at stake in commercial radio to let the DJs make all the decisions. While there are some exceptions, the days of the commercial radio DJ as musical curator are long gone. The more accurate job description would usually be "on-air personality" or "announcer."

One might say there are only two types of music: good and bad. And there may be some truth to that approach. Nonetheless DJs should be aware of, and conversant in, matters of genre and style. Surely every seasoned DJ has at least one story about putting on the wrong record, for the wrong crowd.

In point of fact, the DJ is normally expected to have a thorough understanding of the genres and styles in which he or she operates, to know what's hot within those styles, and to actively set the trend. Achieving that level of understanding is a life-long pursuit, because music is constantly changing. The only way to keep up with it is to live in it.

Read the music trade magazines, listen to radio, go places where music is played. Keep up with your favorite artists, and look for new ones. Stay in touch with your audience, make sure you're up on the hits of the day, and consider the ongoing discovery of new music a normal, essential, part of your routine.

In the final analysis, the type of music one plays, and how one plays it, define the essence and personality of any DJ. Some DJs play strictly out of a certain musical style. Other DJs are all over the map. Deciding what to play to satisfy and excite your audience, is the real core of the DJ's art.

Chapter 2

The Turntable
Century

This chapter focuses on the invention and popularization of the phonograph. We'll blast through a century of history, covering all the technological fundamentals along the way. We'll also discuss the telephone, radio, and AC power—related technologies that played important roles in the turntable's development. And we'll talk about some of the legendary individuals who made it happen.

The record industry has a longstanding reputation for being a colorful, backstabbing, and highly litigious field. As you'll learn in this chapter, that pattern was established during the earliest days of the business.

Edison tin foil phonograph. Photo courtesy of National Parks Service, Edison Historic Site.

Edison's Phonograph

American inventor Thomas Alva Edison gets credit for inventing the phonograph.[1] Best known for inventing the light bulb and motion pictures, he devised a way to record sound by drawing a representation of sound waves onto a physical medium. Although there were some precursors, Edison was the first to build and patent a working model.[2]

Edison noticed that whenever he talked or sang into a paper cone, or drumhead, its surface would vibrate. So he rigged a way of transferring these vibrations to a needle (or "stylus") and making an inscription of the vibrations on a piece of tin foil.

Edison's early designs had a diaphragm (much like a small drumhead or a human eardrum) connected to a needle, which passed over a cylinder of wax or tinfoil. One spoke or sang into the diaphragm while turning the cylinder. The vibrations were transmitted to the needle, which etched a spiraling indentation in the recording surface. This groove made by the vibrating needle was a direct model of the sound waves.

Thomas Edison, 1878. Photo courtesy of National Parks Service, Edison Historic Site.

1 "Phono" means sound or voice, and "graph" means "something written, printed, drawn or incised" according to New Webster's Encyclopedic Dictionary.
2 Thomas A. Edison "Improvement in Phonograph or Speaking Machines" U.S. Patent no. 200,521 granted February 19, 1878.

The principle was applied in reverse to play back the sound – dragging a different needle through the groove would make that needle vibrate. Those vibrations were transmitted to another diaphragm. A cone was attached to the apparatus to reflect and amplify the sound. Thus was born the phonograph.

Edison's original model was completely mechanical; it didn't rely on electrical power. The only amplification was the cone, and one turned a crank by hand to rotate the cylinder. Edison's invention caused a huge stir. Two months after his patent was issued he was called to Washington D.C. to demonstrate the phonograph for Congress. President Rutherford B. Hayes got a private demo at the White House. Ironically, Edison became almost totally deaf in his later years.

Bell's Graphophone and Berliner's Gramophone

Other inventors raced to improve the Edison design. One of the first was Edison's rival, Alexander Graham Bell, inventor of the telephone. Bell and his partners found that wax cylinders with cardboard cores worked much better than tinfoil. The wax offered superior sound reproduction, easier handling, and longer playing time.

Bell also added an improved stylus design, a spring-wound motor, and other innovations, to his "Graphophones."[3] Edison copied Bell's ideas, and vice-versa, as the phonograph became a battlefield in the ongoing feud between these two legendary inventors.

An investor eventually merged the competing Edison and Bell phonograph companies into a single firm, the North American Phonograph Company. Focused on the business dictation market, (as opposed to home entertainment) their expensive recorders and players were huge flops, distributors lost their shirts, and the firm was out of business by 1894.

---

3 Graphophone is "phonograph" with the syllables reversed, a name reportedly chosen because it would annoy Edison.

Meanwhile, a German immigrant named Emile Berliner had worked up a design for a disc phonograph. Berliner already had a reputation for innovation. He'd invented a carbon microphone and sold it to Bell's telephone company, which wished to circumvent Edison's patent on a similar mouthpiece. Bell reportedly paid Berliner $100,000 for the rights to the mic, plus a $5000 annual retainer, just to keep Berliner around.[4] The money allowed Berliner to focus on the Gramophone.

Berliner's rotating turntable held a flat disc with a spiraling groove. Instead of Edison's linear-tracking carriage, the needle on Berliner's Gramophone was held by a pivoting lever, which evolved into the tone arm.

Berliner also pioneered the disc replication process, recording sound onto a wax-coated zinc disc. The inscribed disc would be plunged into an acid bath, that ate away the wax and burned the grooves into the zinc surface. Berliner then made a mold from the zinc "master" which could be used to press a nearly unlimited number of copies.

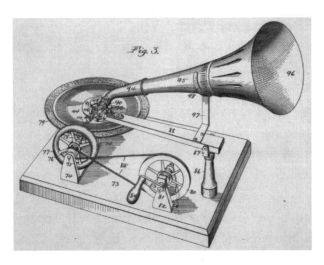

Berliner hand-cranked Gramophone, diagram from U. S. patent 534,543 Feb 19, 1895.

---

4 Other sources say the purchase price was $50,000; still big bucks in an era when the average family income was about six dollars a week.

Unfortunately the early Gramophones did not have electric or spring-wind motors, and had to be hand-cranked continuously during playback. They were inexpensive compared to Edison and Bell models, but very primitive. It took one person to turn the lever, and a second person to stabilize the machine's base, so the record wouldn't skip from the cranking motion. With later improvements Berliner's turntable concept eventually prevailed, but in the 1890s cylinders were still the dominant format.

The Rise of the Record Labels

Following the bankruptcy of the North American Phonograph Company, Thomas Edison took on a barrage of lawsuits as he scrambled to regain rights to his invention, eventually re-emerging as the National Phonograph Company. Meanwhile, Alexander Graham Bell and his partners teamed up with the District of Columbia Phonograph Company, and became the Columbia Graphophone Company. Both new firms focused on marketing the phonograph as a music entertainment device.

In 1895, Columbia introduced the first inexpensive spring-wound cylinder player. It used a simple mechanical spring motor to rotate the cylinder and move the playback needle. The product was a hit and Columbia was on its way.[5] Edison responded the following year with his own cheap, spring-wound model.

Emile Berliner saw the writing on the wall and hooked up with a New Jersey machine shop owner who designed a simple, reliable, and cost-effective spring motor. Introduced in 1897, the spring-wound Gramophone was affordable, easy to use, and established the disc as a mainstream format.

5 **Columbia Graphophone Company eventually morphed into the Columbia record label (now part of Sony Music Entertainment) and the Columbia Broadcasting System (CBS).**

The Berliner Gramophone Company quickly ran into trouble. Their exclusive distributor, a sharp operator named Frank Seaman, went into direct competition with Berliner. Seaman began marketing a similar player called the Zon-o-phone, and refused to purchase, or distribute, any more Berliner machines. Seaman's contract, which forbade Berliner from selling phonographs to any other party until 1911, was held up in court. Berliner was screwed, but Seaman didn't stop there...

After secret meetings with Columbia in 1899, Seaman began alleging that the Gramophone infringed on a Bell patent. Although the claim was far-fetched, Columbia followed up with a lawsuit against Berliner Gramophone. Unable to sell his machines, and battered by the legal hassles, Berliner closed shop and retired in 1900. Seaman's Zon-o-phone company eventually merged with Columbia.

Motorized Gramophone, circa 1897. Photo courtesy of Library of Congress, American Memory Project.

The wealthy Berliner could simply walk away from the business, but the machinist who designed his spring motor and manufactured his players faced financial ruin. With everything invested into expanding Gramophone production, Eldridge Johnson had little choice but to enter the phonograph business on his own, so he launched the Consolidated Talking Machine Company.

Johnson had redesigned the Gramophone sound box during the course of his work with Berliner. Johnson has also improved the disc replication process, using electroplating instead of acid etching to create a master disc. Armed with these innovations and the Berliner customer list, Johnson made Gramophone owners an offer they couldn't refuse: send in the serial number of your Gramophone to receive a free record that sounds better than any heard before.

The promotion worked. As Consolidated records and phonographs started selling, Frank Seaman appeared, dragging Johnson into court. Seaman argued that Consolidated Talking Machine was a front for Berliner interests, marketing products that should only be distributed through Seaman. Johnson prevailed, although he had to stop using the term "Gramophone." Since Johnson had beat Seaman and Columbia, he began labeling his disks as "Victor Records." Johnson eventually changed his firm's name to the Victor Talking Machine Company, and his phonographs became known as Victrolas.[6]

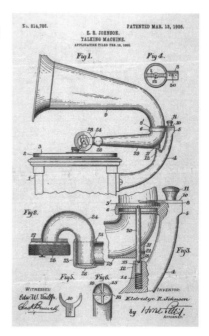

Eldridge Johnson patent diagrams, from U.S. patent number 814,786 March 13, 1906.

Louder, more durable, easier to handle, more convenient to store, and cheaper to transport than cylinders, disks became the dominant format over the course of time. Columbia quit manufacturing cylinders in 1912. Another major cylinder maker, United States Phonograph Company stopped production the following year, leaving Edison as the only American cylinder manufacturer. Accepting the reality that the public preferred disks, Edison introduced the Edison Disc Phonograph in 1913, but continued issuing cylinder releases until his record label tanked in 1929.

6 Radio Corporation of America (RCA) bought the Victor Talking Machine Company in 1928.

Telephone transmitter (microphone) circa 1876. Photo courtesy of Smithsonian.

The Telephone

Although some early phonographs had battery-powered electric motors that rotated the cylinder or turntable, those units were cumbersome, expensive, and did not fare well in the marketplace. For the most part, early phonographs and the sound recording and reproduction processes, were entirely mechanical affairs.

Electronic sound recording and playback grew out of the telephone. Alexander Graham Bell was an educator who taught deaf mutes to communicate. He was also an electronics enthusiast, with some wealthy friends willing to sponsor his research. Bell wasn't the only guy working on a "talking telegraph" idea. Another inventor named Elisha Gray applied for a patent on the telephone the very same day as Bell. But Bell had filed two hours earlier, and his invention was more developed. [7] Three days after the patent was granted, Bell finally got it to work, transmitting his famous request "Mr. Watson, come here, I want you" on March 10, 1876.

A telephone has a microphone and a speaker, both based on the diaphragm. Microphones and speakers are transducers. That means they transfer one form of energy into another. Microphones convert the air movements of sound waves into voltage fluctuations in an electrical current. Speakers do the exact opposite, converting voltage fluctuations back into air movements.

7 Alexander Graham Bell, "Improvement in Telegraphy" Patent No. 174,465, dated March 7, 1876, application filed February 14, 1876.

Turntable cartridges (the needle and its mounting) are another type of transducer, transferring the physical vibrations of a record groove into electrical current fluctuations.

Basic speakers, microphones, and phonograph cartridges make use of "electromagnets." An electromagnet is simply a piece of metal wrapped in wire. Applying a charge to the wire makes the metal magnetic.

Bell attached a small permanent magnet to a diaphragm, so when the diaphragm moved back and forth, the permanent magnet moved as well. The movement of the permanent magnet's magnetic field created a fluctuating current in the wires of a nearby electromagnet. The voltage would vary into positive current, then negative current, according to the position of the magnetic field. This voltage fluctuation could be amplified and transmitted. Thus was born the microphone.

Speakers convert voltage changes back into sound. Simple speakers are very similar to microphones; a permanent magnet is suspended next to an electromagnet and attached to a diaphragm (or cone) made of paper or cloth. Voltage fluctuations in the wire wrapping change the polarity of the electromagnet. This fluctuating magnetic field makes the permanent magnet move back and forth. The vibrations are transmitted by the diaphragm or cone to the air and produce sound waves.

Alexander Graham Bell, in 1876. Photo courtesy of AT&T.

Western Union, the dominant telegraph company, was threatened by Bell's invention and hired Thomas Edison to develop competing technology. Edison's innovations, including an improved microphone design, made the phone much more practical, and sparked the Edison/Bell feud mentioned earlier. Bell eventually sued Western Union, and won the first of a long series of courtroom victories. The Bell Company (which became AT&T) went on to prevail in more than 600 legal challenges to Bell's original patent.

Not all of Bell's inventions turned out that well. After Bell's friend President James Garfield was shot in 1881, Bell invented a rudimentary metal detector and attempted to find the bullet. It didn't work, and Garfield had a slow, painful death.

Radio and AC Power

Radio and household electrical current are two more fundamental technologies that arose in the last years of the 19th century. When combined with the phonograph, they allowed the DJ to come into existence.

A Scottish physicist named James Clerk Maxwell first predicted the existence of electromagnetic "radio" waves in the 1860s. A physics teacher named Heinrich Hertz proved Maxwell's theory in 1886.

Hertz was the first person to generate and receive radio waves, using a device called a spark oscillator. Ironically, Hertz couldn't envision any practical application for his discovery; he reportedly said "it's of no use whatsoever." Hertz's name is memorialized as the unit of measurement for frequency (abbreviated as Hz). He died a month before his 37th birthday, in 1894.

That same year, the twenty-year-old son of a wealthy Italian land-owner came up with a practical use for radio waves: wireless telegraph. Guglielmo Marconi studied Hertz's work and improved on Hertz's apparatus. By 1895 he was able to send and receive signals across a distance of about a mile. Unable to interest the Italian government in this invention, he relocated to England. In June 1896 Marconi applied for a British patent on the technology and a month later demonstrated radio for officials from the British Navy, Army, and Post Office.

Marconi's early "wireless" sets didn't transmit speech or music. They sent a series of on/off pulses called Morse code, which was already familiar to telegraph operators. Marconi's first important market was maritime signaling; before his invention, ships at sea were completely isolated. Ships with radio onboard could signal for help when in distress, and lives might be saved.

In fact there were some legendary sea rescues thanks to Marconi wireless, including the Titanic. Marconi became world famous, got the Nobel Prize in physics in 1909, and founded a company that still exists today. Privately, Marconi was a love man, with a bevy of mistresses in Manhattan, and a team of messengers who carried them notes and flowers. One of Marconi's errand boys was a fifteen-year-old named David Sarnoff, who we'll encounter again in Chapter 4.

Marconi got the credit for radio and enjoyed the benefits. But another person, named Nikola Tesla, may have actually invented it first.

A disgruntled former Edison employee, Nikola Tesla devised the Tesla Coil in 1891. A type of high-frequency transformer, the Tesla Coil became a key component of radio transmitters. Tesla built various types of radio circuitry and by 1895 was doing broadcast experiments in New York. He filed his first U.S. radio patent in 1897, and the following year demonstrated a radio-controlled boat at Madison Square Garden. The U.S. Trademark and Patent Office granted Tesla a patent on radio in 1900, and subsequently refused Marconi patent applications, citing Tesla's prior work.

Meanwhile, Tesla had hooked up with industrialist George Westinghouse, and designed the electrical generators and distribution system that harnessed Niagara Falls in 1896. Within a few years that power system was lighting up New York. Those achievements established alternating current (also known as AC power) as the standard electrical system used everywhere today.[8]

Batteries provide direct current (DC), a continuous positive voltage. Alternating current fluctuates back and forth between positive and negative. This fluctuation, much like a sound wave, allows AC to travel better through a distribution system and do more work with lower voltages, compared to DC power.

It was all Tesla's idea and he could have been a rich man. He had a lucrative deal with Westinghouse that gave him $2.50 for every horsepower of electricity sold. But George Westinghouse wound up in a financial bind in 1902. J. P. Morgan was trying to take over his company, Westinghouse couldn't raise money, and investment bankers urged him to rescind Tesla's royalty agreement. When Westinghouse explained his predicament, Tesla said "you have stood by me as a friend," and tore up his contract.

Then, in a surprise decision, the U.S. Patent Office reversed itself in 1904, and awarded Marconi the patent on radio. The reasons were never made clear; historians have speculated that the wealthy, socially connected Marconi or his associates, which included Edison and Andrew Carnegie, may have wielded some influence. Tesla tried suing the Marconi Company for patent infringement at one point, but couldn't afford to litigate against them. It was a big setback for Tesla, but he went on to design a system for delivering electricity without wires, as well as a "death ray." It's unclear whether those two inventions ever worked or not.

---

8 Tesla and Westinghouse's success with alternating current infuriated Edison, who had been pushing for direct current. Edison even embarked on a publicity tour, electrocuting animals onstage to prove the deadliness of AC. In truth DC was far more dangerous, requiring much higher voltages for transmission than AC.

Tesla was quite an inventor, at one point he came up with a scheme for reversible clothes. But he died poor and alone at the Hotel New Yorker in 1943. Within days of his death government agents had combed his hotel room and confiscated his notes on weapons and energy research.

Ironically, six months later, the U.S. Supreme Court overturned Marconi's U.S. radio patent in favor of Tesla (and others), citing evidence of prior work. The Marconi Company was suing the U.S. government at that time, claiming the government had infringed its patents during World War I. The Supreme Court didn't want to hear that case, so they simply restored the priority of Tesla's patent over Marconi's, and dismissed the whole affair.

Nikola Tesla. Photo courtesy of the Tesla Museum.

While Marconi and Tesla were colorful originators, many individuals contributed to the development of modern radio. The invention of the vacuum tube diode by J. Ambrose Fleming in 1904, and the triode vacuum tube amplifier by Lee de Forest in 1906, were key milestones in the evolution from Morse code beeps to actual audio (sound) transmissions. De Forest's "audion" tube made it possible to amplify audio signals, which became a big deal for phonographs as well as radio.

There is some debate about who first transmitted human speech over radio; many sources point to a 1906 experimental broadcast by one Reginald A. Fessenden. Fessenden talked and played music on phonograph and violin, which was heard by radio-equipped ships within several hundred miles. From the very inception of broadcast audio, the phonograph was radio's natural partner and Fessenden had inadvertently become the first DJ. We'll talk more about Fessenden in Chapter 4.

Commercial radio broadcasting got rolling in the 1920s. KDKA in Pittsburgh broadcast the 1920 U.S. presidential election results, considered by some the beginning of professional radio. Network radio, with stations connected by phone lines, began with a World Series baseball broadcast in 1922. The Radio Corporation of America (RCA) launched the National Broadcasting Company (NBC) in 1926, establishing the first permanent national radio network.

Just as most early phonographs were entirely mechanical, many early radios were crystal sets, which required no electricity and allowed listening through an earpiece. Over time, radios that used AC power became the norm, and the phonograph became electrified as well.

While the technologies of radio and phonographs might go together like bread and butter, the record industry did not immediately embrace radio. They viewed it as a threat. It was essentially illegal to play records over the airwaves, and DJs were the musician's enemy. We'll examine that situation in Chapter 4.

Electrical Recording and Playback

Researchers at AT&T, formerly the Bell Telephone Company, devised the first electrical sound recording and reproducing system in 1924. Phonograph recording and playback had been an entirely mechanical process until that point. By applying new technologies such as microphones and amplifiers, plus electromagnetic disc cutting heads and phonograph cartridges, one could achieve much better sound quality. The recording industry quickly adopted electrical recording, licensing the system from AT&T. Victor popularized AT&T's technology under the brand name "Orthophonic."

Electrical recording offered tremendous advantages compared to the old mechanical techniques. Suddenly one could capture and magnify the smallest sounds using microphones and amplifiers. Performers no longer needed to be clustered in front of the cone in order to be heard. Realistic concert hall recording became a possibility. Although most phonographs were still all-mechanical affairs, electrically recorded disks sounded much better than their predecessors.

Columbia hired Art Gillham, "The Whispering Pianist," to make the first commercial electrical recording, "You May Be Lonesome," in February of 1925. Victor made its first Orthophonic electrical recording the following month.

In 1926 Victor debuted the Electrola phonograph, which featured an electromagnetic needle assembly, amplifier, and loudspeaker, and might be considered the first modern phonograph. Brunswick made its own version, using the same RCA parts. Amplification was a key selling point—families no longer needed to gather around the phonograph horn—now the music could fill the room. The next year Victor introduced the first phonograph with a record changing mechanism, called the Automatic Orthophonic.

One artist who really took advantage of electrical recording was a young singer named Bing Crosby. Crosby didn't "belt" or shout into a horn like his mechanical-recording predecessors. He realized that he could get close to the mic and sing softly, "crooning," letting the amplification project his voice. That was a sensational new sound in the 1930s, listeners went wild for it, and Crosby became the biggest star of his era. Nearly every singer that followed, including Sinatra, Presley, and the Beatles, used Bing's microphone technique. Crosby went on to finance the development of audiotape and videotape recording in conjunction with the Ampex Corporation.

Speeds and Formats

The turntable's rotation speed, meaning the rate at which it goes around, is expressed as "revolutions-per-minute" or RPM. There were a number of competing standards over the years. Some early acoustically recorded disks would spin between 60 and 75 RPM. Pathé put out records with speeds anywhere from 90 to 120 RPM. Victor settled on 78 RPM as the standard for its records; Edison discs turned at 80 RPM, and others used 82 RPM. Then, as now, most phonographs had pitch (speed adjustment) controls, allowing a range of RPM settings.

The AT&T electrical recording system established 33 1/3 revolutions-per-minute as a standard speed for professional use, initially in the film industry. Hollywood wanted "talkies," so AT&T's Western Electric division set out to synchronize phonograph records with motion pictures. They decided to use simple motors that spun at 60 cycles per second, which is AC current's rate of fluctuation (60Hz). They could get 33 1/3 from 60 with a simple gearing ratio. To match the length of film reels, the system used a 20-inch disc. Marketed as "Vitaphone" sound, it had a brief heyday, although Hollywood eventually settled on optical soundtracks printed along the edge of the film.

A twelve-inch, 33 1/3 RPM Microgroove LP. Photo: Linda Monson

In the late 1940s, the record labels started pressing records out of vinyl, replacing shellac and other formulations that had been used previously. Vinyl, a type of plastic, provided better durability, longer life, and cheaper maufacturing. Combined with better phonograph cartridges and cutting heads, vinyl made it possible to squeeze more grooves on a record with less space between them. Thus was born the "microgroove" records, better known as the LP and 45.

Columbia issued the first microgroove records, in the twelve-inch long playing (LP) format, in 1948. Long-playing records had been tried before, by others including Edison, but failed for various technical and economic reasons. Rotating at 33 1/3 RPM, the microgroove LP made it possible to release longer symphonic pieces, which were impractical on short-playing 78 RPM ten-inch disks.

The following year, in 1949, Victor introduced the seven-inch format, adopting the 45 RPM speed. LPs and 45s competed for a couple of years. But the record buying public was getting confused and sales started to sag. So in the early 1950s the record industry reached a consensus on the concept of LPs for albums, meaning collections of songs, and 45s for singles.

Stereo

The next major advance came in 1958 when the labels began releasing records in stereo. Although they continued making monophonic (one-channel) records for the next decade stereo records became the industry standard. Stereo takes advantage of the fact that most people have two ears. By presenting slightly different recordings to each ear, stereo records can convey a realistic sense of space and direction.

Stereo was invented in 1931 by Alan Blumlein, a former Bell Labs researcher who worked for the EMI record label. Labels had grown tired of paying royalties to AT&T for their electrical recording system, so Blumlein devised an improved record cutting head that allowed EMI (and others) to circumvent AT&T's monopoly.

But Blumlein had something bigger in mind, as he wrote in his patent application: "The fundamental object of the invention is to provide a... true directional impression." Blumlein worked on microphone designs and stereo mic techniques; he even placed mics in the ears of a mannequin head, a practice known today as binaural recording. Blumlein went on to design circuits for television and radar systems. He died in 1942 during a airplane radar experiment, at age 39.

The Twelve-Inch Single

Although recording techniques improved with the introduction of multi-track recording, the vinyl LP hasn't changed much since stereo came into vogue.[9] Quadraphonic (four-channel) LPs hit the market in the 1970s, but surround sound didn't catch on with consumers at the time, primarily because it was expensive.

The seven-inch single hasn't changed much in the last half century either. But there was one further milestone in the development of the vinyl record: The twelve-inch single was introduced in the mid-1970s, to meet the demands of dance music DJs.

Played at 45 RPM, the twelve-inch single format allows lots of room for extended musical passages and alternate "remixes," compared to seven-inch singles. A twelve-inch single's sound quality can be vastly superior to an LP. There's less music, so the grooves are more widely spaced. Mastering engineers can cut the record with more bass signal, giving a louder, bottom-heavy sound. DJs also found the twelve-inch easier to handle and cue.

Promotional twelve-inches started cropping up in 1975. The Salsoul label released the first commercial twelve-inch single in 1976, "Ten Percent" by Double Exposure.

---

9 Guitarist Les Paul was the originator of multitrack recording, pioneering the use of overdubs to craft records as layers of sound.

Twelve-inch singles made a lot sense for dance music, which is mostly a singles market. Punk and new wave artists also experimented with the twelve-inch 45 format, giving rise to the EP or extended play release.

And then everything changed. The phonograph reached its technological half-life and lost its consumer application.

The Death and Rebirth of the Turntable

The recording and consumer electronics industries adopted the compact disc (CD) format during the 1980s and abandoned the turntable and vinyl records. The compact disc is a digital technology, meaning it represents the audio signal as a series of numbers. Phonographs are an analog technology, meaning they represent audio using a continuous signal, such as the wavering groove on a record, or fluctuations in an electrical current.

The principles behind digital recording had been around since the 1930s. But they didn't really get pressed into service until the early 1970s, when researchers at Philips started using lasers to burn streams of numbers onto glass disks. Manufacturers experimented with several analog and digital disc formats as the decade progressed, most notably Laserdisk. In 1979 Phillips teamed up with Sony to establish a specification for the compact disc. By 1981 Sharp began producing tiny semiconductor lasers, and competitor Matsushita accepted the CD standard proposed by Philips and Sony.

Launched in the U.S. market in 1983, CDs were adopted slowly at first. They cost twice as much as LPs and early players were pricey. Then, around 1988, all major record labels stopped accepting wholesale returns on LPs, so most retailers quit stocking vinyl records.

Because they could no longer get the latest hits (or anything else) on LP, most record buyers quickly migrated to CDs. Some put their vinyl collections out on the sidewalk with the trash, having re-purchased their favorite music in the new digital format.

It was a good time for the record business. Consumers had resisted paying more than ten dollars for a vinyl LP; the usual price was around seven or eight bucks. Labels could price CDs much higher, fifteen dollars or more. As manufacturing ramped up, CDs became cheaper to produce than the old LPs. They were also lighter and smaller, less expensive to warehouse and transport. Record labels even paid artists less; royalties on CDs were lower than LPs, offsetting purported new technology costs, or other such doubletalk.

By the 1990s one could no longer buy a turntable or LP at any major retailer and most people seemed fairly content with that. But one group held on to their records and phonographs: DJs.

Commercial radio disk jockeys had long since moved to playing tape cartridges ("carts") instead of records. But mobile disk jockeys, club DJs, and hip-hop DJs all stuck with their turntables. The reasons were pretty simple. DJs need to cue songs, beginning them at specific points. The first several generations of CD players were so simplistic and cumbersome that cuing was easier with vinyl. Some DJs like to tempo-match, adjusting the speed of one record to match another; that technique was impossible with CDs until fairly recently. The same held true for hip-hop DJs; techniques like scratching and cutting just couldn't be done with CDs.

Thanks to the DJ, vinyl never completely died out. Labels that wanted club play continued to issue twelve-inch singles because DJs demanded it.

As for the turntable, development essentially stopped when the CD came along. By the time the 1980s were finished, the downsizing of the phonograph business had left few participants. Needle makers Shure and Stanton had diversified product lines, and continued serving turntable owners even as the market declined. The Matsushita Corporation was another

Technics SL-1200M3D turntable. Photo courtesy of Panasonic.

important holdout. Their Technics SL-1200 was a high-end professional turntable. Originally introduced in 1972, it had become a perennial favorite among disk jockeys.

Built from steel and diecast aluminum, the SL-1200's weight was a distinguishing feature, all of 27 pounds. That mass makes it less sensitive to outside vibrations and more stable. A direct-drive turntable, the SL-1200 allowed DJ's to backspin and scratch without breaking the belt found in belt-drive turntables.

The Technics SL-1200 was the turntable Grandmaster Flash and practically every other noteworthy DJ relied on. It became the only game in town. Matsushita didn't have to advertise the SL-1200 much, demand from professional DJs was always there. Nor were they under pressure to improve or alter the design; they just kept stamping out turntables and selling them. The SL-1200MK2 turntable debuted in 1978, but the SL-1200MK3 didn't arrive until 1989, followed by the SL-1200M3D in 1997. That's roughly one upgrade per decade. Technics continued tinkering slightly with their other turntable models throughout the eighties, but the SL-1200 design was essentially frozen.

The turntable had changed roles. No longer a consumer device, it had turned into a professional tool. A musical instrument. As changing music tastes brought dance sounds and hip-hop to the forefront, the DJ equipment market began to expand. Newer companies such as Numark, Gemini, American Audio, and Vestax moved to address the demand; older concerns like Technics, Pioneer, and the needle makers likewise devoted more energy to the burgeoning DJ segment.

Competition is fierce in the pro audio business and innovation is one of the best ways to compete. So by the end of the 1990's the art and science of turntable design was progressing again after years of neglect. Digital electronics could now be used to augment a turntable's capabilities. The needs of scratch DJs in particular helped drive the most recent advances in turntable design and manufacture.

We'll take a deeper look at the state-of-the-art in turntable design in just a few pages. But first pause to reflect how this soulful piece of hardware, a part of daily life for a century, was so quickly cast aside when something better came along. And consider how DJs clung to this archaic technology, because it helped them to conduct their business and craft their art.

In doing so they took the phonograph to a higher level, elevating the turntable to the status of musical instrument, complete with its own set of virtuosos. We'll meet one of the original virtuosos next.

GrandWizzard Theodore

Theodore Livingston, better known as GrandWizzard Theodore, is the inventor of needle dropping and scratching. Theodore told us that it's actually skratch, spelled with a "K," which we duly note, although we use the more conventional spelling.

At what age did you start DJing?

About twelve, thirteen years old. I got started through my brother, Mean Gene. Him and Grandmaster Flash had their own little group together. Then Flash went and formed his own group and my brother Mean Gene formed his own group, that's when we became the L Brothers. That's when I really started getting into it. I didn't realize that I had a gift until I actually got on the turntables.

Flash and Gene were big influences on you?

Oh yes, definitely, they were the ones that introduced it to me.

What other DJs influenced you?

Kool Herc and Afrika Bambaataa. I was fortunate to become a DJ at the stage where hip-hop was still being developed into the culture that it is today.

What types of things did you do to build your reputation?

Making tapes, doing parties. Being that I had a talent, people were always out to listen to me play, because they had heard about me. That was one good thing that worked in my favor.

You're credited with inventing the scratch...

Yeah, and the needle drop.

Can you explain to the reader, who might not be familiar, what a scratch and a needle drop is?

A needle drop is picking the needle up and dropping it back on the vinyl. When you're doing that the record is still on-beat. You can snap your fingers and tap your feet as you're picking up the needle and dropping it back down. You can still dance to it, it's being done in the rhythm, where it sounds like you're looping the beat. It sounds like a loop.

As far as a scratch is concerned, letting one record play and using the remaining turntable. Moving it back and forth in a rhythmic position. Making your own rhythm from just one part of the record. Holding one part of the record on the needle and moving it back and forth to make a rhythm.

Scratching has become an important sound in music. How did you run into this technique?

I can thank my mother for that. I was in my room playing music too loud. My mother banged on the door, and when she opened the door she was pointing her finger at me, telling me I had to turn the music down, or turn it off. While she was in the doorway screaming at me, I had one record playing, and was moving the other record back and forth. In a rhythmic motion. And didn't realize what I was doing until she left the room. Once I realized what I was doing, I experimented with different records. It became the scratch, and the rest is history.

Do you have any tips for people who are learning to scratch?

Make sure they learn how to hold the record...Look at the turntable as if it's a clock. Hold your hand at nine o'clock on the turntable. And learn how to move the record back and forth without skipping the record... Make sure to learn what a snare is, what a kick is, what a high-hat is...

The average record has writing on it. Put the needle on the record, and watch the record go around. When you get to the part of the record that you really like, you can get a pen or magic marker, and mark the part of the record that you want to scratch. And just keep moving the needle back and forth where that mark is at, while you're pushing the mixer (crossfader) back and forth. That will give you a pretty good idea of how to exercise at the first stages of scratch...

I go by ear. I'll stop the record at the snare drum, or the kick drum, or the high hat, or any sound that's in the record.

Just try to be yourself. Don't try to be like any other DJ, try to get a style that's all your own. There are so many DJs out here today, that you have to make sure you have your own style, so you can stand out from all the other DJs.

What type of gear do you use?

Right now I'm using a Rane TTM-56 mixer and Vestax turntables.

What should people look for, or avoid, when putting together their first DJ setups?

They should find out what feels comfortable for them. Some DJs get into it because they want to be a disco mix DJ, mixing disco or house records back and forth. Scratch DJs should look for a smaller mixer, mixers these days are in so many different sizes. For me a small mixer is good, because it's compact, you don't have to move very far when moving from one record to another. Find equipment that's small and compact so you don't have to go to much trouble when moving it, being mobile.

Between you, and people like Flash and Herc, you guys invented the turntable as a musical instrument. Are you pleased by its evolution?

I can only speak for myself. I feel good that people see it as a musical instrument. When we first started doing this, it was something that we loved to do.

Today a lot of people get into the art form for different reasons, other than love. If anybody out there is getting into this art form, the first thing they should do is make sure they get into it for the love. The fame and fortune and everything else is going to come in due time. But...you have to make sure that you love the art form, before you get into the art form. So that people can take you seriously when they see you doing it.

It's a struggle to be an artist. If you don't love it, it's going to be a hard road.

Exactly. Some people just get into it for different reasons, you know?

What's your goal with DJing now? What do you want to achieve?

I want to achieve the notoriety. I want people to know that GrandWizzard Theodore was the creator of scratch, the needle drop. The blood, sweat and tears that he put into this art form. So that all these DJs today can do what they do, and be able to travel around, and make careers out of what they do. I don't want people to forget where it came from. I feel that if you're going to be into the art form, you should know who the key players are, who put the blood, sweat and tears into it, who put the blueprint together, so that the people today are able to do what they do.

You're not as well known to mainstream audiences as others in the DJ business. Why do you think that is?

I always catered to the people in the streets, because that's where hip-hop came from. There's nothing wrong with catering to the record buying public, but the people in the streets made the culture what it is today. The people of the streets made me who I am today.

It seems like the DJ is no longer the focus in hip-hop, the emphasis has been placed on producers and MCs. Do you think that's a fair assessment?

I can say yes, and I can say no. People have to understand that the DJ is the one that sets the tone for the culture. The DJ is the first element of hip-hop. They play the music so that the b-boys can get their groove on. They inspire the graffiti artists. And the MCs spit their rhymes through what the DJ plays. It's very important. The DJ sets the tone for hip-hop, period.

Scratch DJing has become its own musical genre, separate and apart from hip-hop per se. We see DJs showing up with rock bands and jazz groups and other configurations...

It's a musical instrument. By people recognizing it as a musical instrument, there are so many other different directions that you're able to go in. It's going to go even further than it is now.

Tell us about your experiences with the record business.

There are a lot of companies that wouldn't have anything to do with hip-hop. Now that hip-hop has become a multi-billion dollar business, I see people jumping on the bandwagon, trying to profit from it. When they didn't want to have anything to do with it in the first place. A lot of these record companies today are confusing people as far as hip-hop and rap are concerned. Hip-hop and rap are two different things. I feel that rap music today is giving hip-hop a really bad name.

Back in the days when you could hear MCs from the true school, the MC was talking about having fun, and partying, and dancing. Today you have the rappers talking about "I'm going to shoot this person, and that girl's a bitch..." And I think that's totally wrong. It didn't start out as girls being bitches and ho's, and "I want to shoot this person, I'm selling crack and I'm smoking weed." It wasn't all about that. That's not hip-hop.

Do you think gangster rap has any value as social commentary?

These people have to realize that they are role models. Yes this stuff goes on in the streets, and I believe that some of these rappers today really do go through the things that they say on their records. But in order for it to be right, they have to talk about the problem, and then at the end of the song, let there be a solution. I would like to hear at the end of the record "well, I used to do all that, but right now I'm just writing rhymes and being an MC." You never hear about none of these MCs trying to give these kids a solution. They have to remember that these kids today are going to be running our country tomorrow. You don't want kids to grow up with violent thoughts in their minds.

What became of the Fantastic Five MCs?

They're still around. Whipper Whip moved to San Diego. Rubie Dee moved to Florida. Master Rob was incarcerated. Dota Rock is a family man now. Waterbed Kev is a family man. They're just doing their own thing.

And you're still DJing.

Yes, I never stopped. Since the first day I touched a turntable, I never stopped DJing. (Laughs.) Right now I got my own company, GWT Music. I'm going to have my new CD out this summer, called Hip-Hop Hits. I'm getting artists from all over the country that haven't been heard yet. I'm tired of hearing the same old recycled MCs all the time. I want to give people a chance to hear some new talent.

Are there particular MCs that you work with, or are you a solo act at this point?

I'm basically a solo act. I've been doing a lot of touring. I just came off the *Skratch* Tour. Pretty soon we're going to be holding a twentieth anniversary tour for the movie *Wild Style*. I've been traveling around, holding seminars and DJ classes.

Anything else you want to tell the people?

Learn the history of the art form of hip-hop. It's very, very important to learn the history. People who are not interested in learning about the history, shouldn't get into the culture.

It doesn't even matter what color you are. You can learn about the history of hip-hop, and somewhere along the line you could learn more stuff about yourself.

Chapter 3

Turntable Anatomy

As we saw in the last chapter, turntables have undergone more than a century of development. In the course of that evolution their role changed from consumer entertainment devices into professional music production tools. While the basics are still the same, modern turntables are built for DJs, and they've come a long way from the hi-fis our parents and grandparents used. Professional turntables are built to rigorous standards, are rugged, durable, and have been optimized for scratching and back spinning.

We invited Technics and Vestax to participate in this book; they declined. Fortunately Numark sent over their new TT-X1 turntable for our use, and both Shure and Stanton provided cartridges and other assistance.

The Numark TT-X1 feature set and controls are much like any professional turntable you'll ever encounter; it also has a few twenty-first century features that we'll point out along the way. It's comparable to any contemporary high-end turntable and has some distinguishing characteristics.

Numark TT-X1 turntable with Stanton Trackmaster II SK cartridge.
Photo: Linda Monson

How Does It Work?

• The stylus (the diamond tip of the needle) traces the ridges in the record's groove, which causes the stylus to vibrate.

• Those vibrations move through the cantilever (the large part of the needle).

• The cantilever is attached to a magnet, which is suspended between two pole pieces. The cantilever's movements are transferred to the magnet.[1]

• As the magnet moves, its magnetic field also moves. Movements of the magnetic field create an electrical signal in the coils around the pole pieces. The signal is called a flux current.

• The electrical signal is passed through the lead wires to the turntable's outputs.

• Signals at the turntable's outputs are connected to a mixer or amplifier, which boosts their strength, then sent to speakers so they can be heard.

---

1 This chapter focuses on moving magnet cartridges, which are the type most often encountered by DJs. The other variety would be moving coil cartridges, which have a coil around the end of the canti-lever. Delicate and pricey, moving coil cartridges are for audiophiles, or archiving.

General Features

Power Button – Turns the phonograph on and off.

Stop/Start Button – Starts and stops the turntable motor. In the example here, the TT-X1 has two stop/start buttons for convenience.

Motor – Although not usually visible, the motor is a core feature of any turntable. There are two basic models, belt-drive and direct-drive.

Belt-drive works like a car's fan belt. Running a belt between the motor and platter is a cheap solution for motor noise; the belt insulates the platter and cartridge from the sound of the motor. Many old, inexpensive turntables were belt-drive. Most belt-drive models couldn't be back spun without damaging the mechanism, so DJs sought out direct-drive turntables.

The Technics SL-1200 led the direct-drive trend; the Numark TT-X1 shown here is another example. Direct-drive is exactly as the name implies, the motor rotates the platter directly. This requires a quieter motor that can spin at several different speeds. As a result, direct-drive turntables are generally more expensive than belt-drive. Direct-drive also requires a heavier housing to minimize vibration.

A central attribute of any turntable motor is its torque, meaning the strength of the drive on the platter. More torque is better, allowing faster start-ups and more precise handling.

Platter – The round metal platter can usually be lifted off the base, allowing you to see more of the motor below. When replacing the platter make sure it's securely seated. The marks around the edge of the platter are for use with the strobe light. Weight helps rotational stability so big, heavy platters are called for.

A slip mat allows the turntable to rotate freely while the record is held. Photo: Linda Monson

Slip Mat – DJs place a soft felt sheet called a slip mat between the platter and the record. The slip mat allows the record to be held in place while the turntable continues to rotate below, reducing the friction.

Speed Selection (33/45) Control – After World War II the record industry settled on two rotation speeds, 33 1/3 RPM and 45 RPM. Some turntables, including the TT-X1, offer 78 RPM as well.

Pitch Slider – Fine-tunes the platter's rotation speed. The speed is increased or decreased by moving the slider above, or below, the center point. On the TT-X1 the pitch range is adjustable from +/- 8% to 50%.

Strobe Light – The strobe light flashes against the marks on the platter's edge, providing a visual reference of the platter's speed. When the marks appear stationary, the platter is at the full play speed. If the dots appear to be crawling, the platter is above or below play speed.

Reverse – The Numark TT-X1 and some other models will go in reverse, changing the direction of the platter's rotation. It's ideal for finding satanic "backward-masking" on heavy metal albums.

Start Time/Brake Time – Start and brake time controls determine how quickly the motor starts and stops. Specifically they set the amount of time requred to get the platter up to full speed, or to a full stop.

Dust Cover – Some models including the TT-X1 simply omit them. If your decks do have dust covers, remove them completely before doing any mixing or scratching. They just get in the way.

Needle and Cartridge

As mentioned in Chapter 2, the phonograph cartridge is a transducer; it changes one form of energy into another, in this case from movement into an electrical signal. Movement is derived from the groove of a record.

The Groove – A record's groove is a physical representation of sound waves. The V-shaped groove has ridges etched into its walls; tracing those ridges re-creates the waveforms of the recording.

The ridges are essentially a graph, drawn in the master disc by a disc cutting head. Amplitude is represented by modulation along the vertical axis; frequency is represented by lateral modulation on the horizontal axis. That means up-and-down movement, the depth of the groove, is loudness. Sideways movement is pitch. The two walls of the groove have different ridges, representing left and right stereo channels.

Stylus and Cantilever –The stylus is the tiny tip of the needle, usually made of an industrial diamond. The stylus traces the walls of the record's grooves; the ridges in the grooves cause the stylus to move up, down, and laterally.

The larger part of the needle is called a cantilever. The cantilever keeps the stylus in place; a magnet is attached to the other end of the cantilever. The cantilever transfers vibration from the stylus to the magnet. The stylus movements make the cantilever vibrate, creating proportional movement in the magnet.

Cantilever Guts

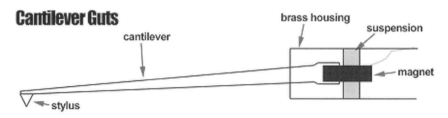

Cantilever diagram courtesy of Shure.

Tone arm height and cartridge position determine how the stylus sits in the record groove. This is a concept called "overhang," more on it later.

The shape (or "geometry") of a stylus is directly related to its sound quality and record wear. Larger surface contact causes less record wear. Smaller surface contact means more accurate high frequencies, but increased wear. Spherical styli are recommended for DJs, they have a circular footprint within the record groove; the large contact area transfers less pressure per square inch. Elliptical styli (and other designs) have thinner, football-shaped footprints. They offer greater fidelity and are recommended for archiving, not scratching.

The stylus should be cleaned occasionally with a small soft brush and warm water. Pull the brush from the back to front only. Never brush from side to side, that can damage the cantilever.

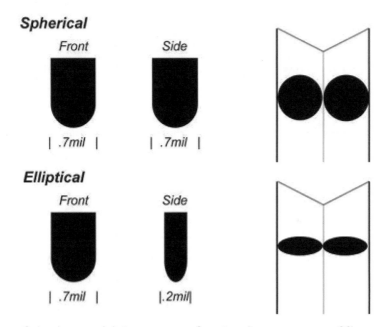

Spherical

Front   Side

| .7mil | | .7mil |

Elliptical

Front   Side

| .7mil | |.2mil|

Stylus shapes and their contact area footprints; diagrams courtesy of Shure.

Cartridge – As the stylus traces the ridges of the record's groove, its movements are transferred by the cantilever to the magnet. The magnet is suspended by bearings between two pole pieces, which are pieces of metal wrapped with coils of wire.

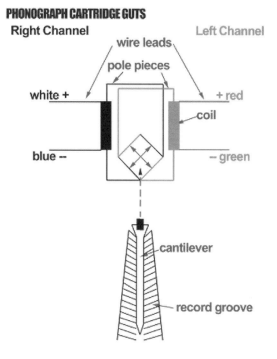

PHONOGRAPH CARTRIDGE GUTS

Cartridge diagram courtesy of Shure. Note the error in this diagram—the artist got the left and right channels mixed up! See page 63 for the correct pin-out.

When the magnet moves back and forth, its magnetic field creates an electrical signal, called a flux current in the coils of the pole pieces. The flux current travels through the lead wires to the turntable's outputs, is boosted by the mixer and amplifier, and sent to the speakers, which convert it to sound waves.

Some cartridges are integrated with a head shell; simply snap it onto the end of the tone arm and secure the lock cuff. Other cartridges have a separate head shell; the cartridge is held in place by screws.

A cartridge's center of gravity is a consideration; cartridges perform more accurately with the center of gravity forward, toward the stylus. "Forward mass" cartridges require less tracking force to stay in the groove and are less destructive to records, than cartridges with a center of gravity towards the tone arm cuff.

Overhang Adjustment

○ distance from tonearm cuff to stylus tip
○ 52mm: optimum sound quality on Technics 1200s
○ too far forward / long = skip on back cue
○ typical scratch settings: 50.5 - 52mm

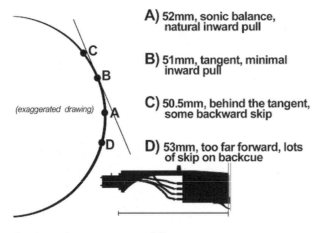

A) 52mm, sonic balance, natural inward pull

B) 51mm, tangent, minimal inward pull

C) 50.5mm, behind the tangent, some backward skip

D) 53mm, too far forward, lots of skip on backcue

(exaggerated drawing)

Overhang diagram courtesy of Shure.

As mentioned earlier, the amount of "overhang" determines the stylus' placement along the arc of the record. For Technics SL-1200s it's recommended that the stylus be positioned slightly after the apex in the record's curve. (That's a distance of 52 millimeters from the stylus to the tone arm cuff.)

Every turntable is different; turntables with straight tone arms should probably have the stylus perfectly tangent to the record's curve, at the apex. If the overhang is too great or too short, skipping may result.

Tone arm height also has a direct bearing on the position of the stylus; read on for more information.

Head Shell – The head shell is a mounting for the cartridge, which holds it onto the tone arm. There are two basic designs: Separable head shells, epitomized by the Technics head shell, and integrated designs, in which the cartridge and shell are combined in a single unit. The Stanton Trackmaster II SKs shown in the next spread are one such example.

The head shell routes the lead wires into the tone arm. To attach a head shell to a tone arm, hold the head shell in place next to the tone arm, gently slide it onto the end of the tone arm and twist the tone arm cuff until it is secure.

Contact Pins – Four electrical contact pins are visible at the rear end of any cartridge. These pins transmit electrical signals from the cartridge and are seated into four corresponding sockets located in the end of the tone arm. The pin-out is as follows:

- White = Left +
- Blue = Left –
- Red = Right +
- Green = Right –

Shure M44-7 cartridge in Technics head shell. Photo courtesy of Shure.

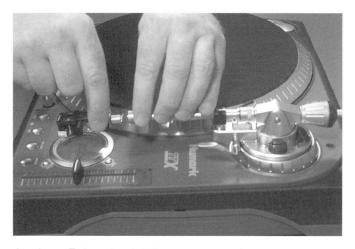

Attaching a Technics head shell to the tone arm. Photo: Linda Monson

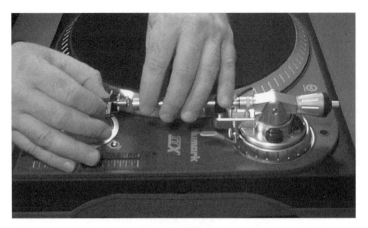

Mounting a Stanton Trackmaster II SK integrated cartridge on the tone arm—insert, then twist the locking cuff. Photo: Linda Monson

Tone Arm

The tone arm supports the head shell, cartridge and needle, positioning them over the record, and providing any needed counterbalancing. The tone arm also provides a routing channel for the cartridge's output wires.

There are two basic tone arm models, straight and S-shaped. S-shaped tone arms are generally best for simple mixing; straight tone arms are optimal for scratching, cutting, and aggressive mix techniques. S-shaped tone arms have a natural inward pull, which can be offset with anti-skate. Straight arms, on the other hand, have no inherent inward or outward force.

One of the unique features of the Numark TT-X1 is that it includes both straight and S-shaped tone arms, which are easily interchangeable.

Tone Arm Cuff – A locking sleeve that holds the head shell onto the tone arm. Once the head shell is in place, twist the cuff to secure it.

Height Adjustment – Height adjustment fine-tunes the alignment of the stylus in the record groove and compensates for slip mat thickness. Too little angle and the bottom of the cartridge may bang on the record. If the tone arm is too high, it changes the stylus' angle of contact with the vinyl groove.

The normal approach is to use a level tone arm, or have the arm angled slightly down. Some DJs like an extreme angle and crank up the tone arm height. This approach can change the way the stylus sits in the groove, twisting a spherical contact area into an elliptical shape, and increasing record wear.

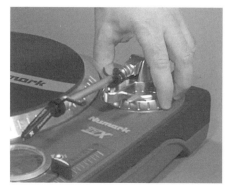

To adjust tone arm height, start with a perfectly level tone arm. Most pro turntables have a ring around the tone arm base; grab the ring and twist it to increase or decrease tone arm height. The TT-X1 has a height lock lever, which needs to be released before height can be adjusted.

Adjust tone arm height by twisting the ring at its base. Photo: Linda Monson

Counterweight – The counterweight balances the tone arm, controlling the amount of pressure that the stylus applies to the record. The needle may not stay in the groove if too little weight is used. Too much weight may cause unnecessary wear on the records and stylus. Rotate the counterweight to adjust it, moving it toward the stylus to increase weight, away from the stylus to decrease.

Adjusting the counterweight. Photo: Linda Monson

For maximum weight one can reverse the counterweight, removing it from the tone arm and replacing it with the number dial facing toward the stylus. That adds two grams to the tracking force range. Check your turntable's manual and note the recommended tracking force (or weight range) for your particular head shell and cartridge.

Anti-Skate Control – Anti-skate helps keep the needle in the groove, preventing skipping and skating as the stylus nears the center of the record. It offsets the natural inward pull that occurs with S-shaped tone arms and certain cartridges. Anti-skate gently pushes the tone arm outward, away from the center spindle.

Anti-skate controls typically add one to three grams of outward force. Start with the lowest anti-skate setting. If the tone arm pulls outward and skips toward the outside of the record, the turntable may be out of alignment and need calibration. If the tone arm pulls inward, and skips towards the center of the record, add anti-skate.

Increase the anti-skate value in small increments, testing as you go, until skipping abates. Anti-skate increases the wear along the outside wall of the groove and isn't usually recommended for DJs, as it can increase skipping on back cues.

Arm Clip – Holds the tone arm securely in place. Apply the arm clip before moving or transporting the turntable.

Cue Lever – The cue lever slowly lowers the tone arm, gently placing the stylus on the record. It can also smoothly lift the needle off the record. It's a vestige of the hi-fi era. You'll probably never use it.

Undercarriage and Rear Panel

Remove the record and slip mat, put the stylus protector over the needle, and secure the tone arm with the arm clip before picking up any turntable to examine the undercarriage.

Rubber Feet – Most turntables have rubber anti-skid feet to absorb vibrations and keep the base secure.

Base – Provides a housing for the motor, electronics, platter, and tone arm. Heavier bases offer greater stability.

Power Cable – Detachable power cables have become standard; most use the same type of standard power cable found on any computer or professional electronic device. Make sure the power cable is seated securely or it may work loose.

Outputs – All turntables have at least two phono outputs, which are usually RCA (stereo) jacks. Connect the outputs to the phono inputs on your mixer, using an RCA stereo cable. Outputs are usually color-coded: red for the right channel, white or black for the left channel.

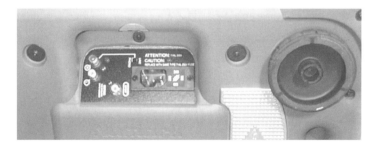

TT-X1 undercarriage; includes analog, line-level and digital outputs, plus switchable voltage selector. This model doesn't need a ground wire.
Photo: Linda Monson

Some turntables have additional line-level outputs, providing a pre-amplified signal. Line-level outputs produce high-voltage signals, which must always be connected to a line-level mixer input. Do not connect a line-level output to a phono input, or you could blow out the mixer channel!

Ground Wire – Many turntables include a ground wire, which should be connected to a ground screw on the mixer's rear panel. Attaching the ground wire prevents sixty-cycle hum, a low-pitched background noise caused by the 60Hz fluctuation of AC power.

Fuse and Voltage Selector – Some turntables include an electrical fuse, if there's a power surge the fuse will break to prevent damage to the turntable. Most modern fuses are reset with a push button.

As for voltage selection, it allows you to go worldwide. Although everyone uses alternating current, countries have adopted different, incompatible voltage standards. The United States is on 120 volt, alternating at 60Hz, or sixty cycles per second. European countries use 50Hz current at voltages ranging from 220 to 240V. Check the local power standard and get appropriate transformers and adaptors before traveling.

Digital Features

Although phonograph records are an analog playback medium, some modern turntables have added cutting-edge digital features. Here are the main ones, all of which are found on the Numark TT-X1 and other high-end turntables:

Digital Outputs – Digital outputs can be connected to a digital recorder, digital mixer, or the digital inputs on a computer sound card, providing a pristine, top-quality signal path. Digital audio is not susceptible to interference or degradation during transmission, unlike an analog signal. Digital gets you the cleanest possible signal path; if you're producing with a computer you'll definitely want to think about a turntable with digital outputs.

Digital outputs (and inputs) come in several different shapes. Digital DJ gear (including the TT-X1) typically has S/PDIF inputs/outputs, which use a coaxial cable – your basic RCA stereo cable. Another common flavor of digital I/O is AES/EBU, which uses a Canon connector – any mic or "XLR" cable. Optical, a.k.a. ADAT "Lightpipe," uses a thin fiber optic cable.

BPM Calculation – A BPM calculator, or beat meter, figures out the tempo of a song. There are two basic models: automatic sensing and tap tempo. Tap tempo requires the DJ to press a button in time with the beats. Obviously this introduces the possibility of human error.

Automatic sensing uses a digital signal processing technique called transient detection. Transient detection measures peaks in the audio signal, from which it figures out the tempo. Automatic BPM calculation usually works well with records that have an obvious pulse or beat. The Numark TT-X1 measures tempo automatically; pressing and holding the BPM button will cause it to recalculate.

Pitch/Time Shifting – One of the basic facts of the twentieth-century phonograph was the relationship between speed and pitch. As a record is slowed down the pitch or key of the music is lowered. When a record is sped up, the pitch goes higher.

Today, thanks to digital signal processing, pitch and speed can be de-linked, and adjusted independently. The Numark TT-X1 includes a pitch shifting function, called key lock, which can automatically correct the pitch or key of a record that has been sped up or slowed down. This allows you to change the speed of a record yet keep it in the original key.

This brings us to the end of our survey of turntable features. We expect that the analog and mechanical portions of turntables will remain much the same for the foreseeable future. And we expect that manufacturers will continue to add new digital features with each subsequent model year.

As great as all this stuff is, none of it makes any sound until it's plugged into something and used to play records. We'll talk about the other parts of the DJ signal chain in Chapter 5. And we'll survey the colorful, convoluted history of record spinning in Chapter 4. But before that, let's visit with one of the biggest names in scratch DJing.

Numark TT-X1 turntable. Photo courtesy of Numark

Interview:

DJ QBert

DJ QBert first came into the spotlight as a member of the Invisibl Skratch Piklz. A former DMC world champion, he's the preeminent scratch DJ of his generation.

You've been on the road a lot this year—What gear do you take on tour?

I just bring my needles, records and scratch pads—"Butter Rugs"—and they usually supply the turntables there. And turntables in the hotel room, where I practice, or backstage.

Do you specify your gear in your (contract) riders?

Yes. I ask for either two Technics 1200s or two Vestax PDX 2000s.

Do you have a home studio setup?

At my studio here (near San Francisco), The Lair of the Octagon, I have sixteen turntables. In Hawaii at the Temple Warplex we got the same thing, about sixteen turntables.

And I have a car called the Kutmobile. I have one Technics 1200 in there, and sometimes a Vestax PDX 2000 and an ISP 07 Pro mixer. In my car. So I'll drive to the beach and I'll scratch in the back.

That's so rude. What kind of car?

It's a Range Rover, 2003.

What kind of recording setup do you use?

When I made my first album I recorded onto Alesis ADAT. From there
I put it into Pro Tools. I have the Pro Tools 001 (audio interface) with a
laptop computer.

*What should people look for (or avoid) when putting together their
first DJ sound systems?*

I think the really rawest stuff that I'll be happy with if I had no equipment
in the world, and this was all I had, is exactly what I said. A Vestax Pro
mixer and two Technics or two Vestax PDXs.

To really, really break it down, it has to be two Technics and a Vestax Pro
mixer. That's all you need to make all the music in the world. As far as
being raw and sticking to the true culture of what a scratch DJ is about.
That's all you really need.

*How did you learn to be a scratch DJ, how would you suggest a
youngster approach it?*

Do it for fun. If it's not fun, don't do it. Don't do it for money or anything,
it's all about art. Do it out of love. Not to make some money, to get
this or that, I mean that's cool too, but always add in your own personal
touch.

Tell us about your practice, are there exercises or drills you use?

I start off with a little warm-up. Don't put your hands into cold water. Wash your hands in warm water. Make sure your body's warm, the room around you is warm. So you can start stretching. Stretch each muscle, all the muscles in your arms and through your back. And just hold each muscle there for a minute, because it really starts stretching after like thirty seconds. Breathe and shit. Your ribs, biceps, shoulders, and back. There's a good book on that stuff called *The Art of Practicing* (by Madeline Bruser) it'll show you a good stretching routine.

When I get on the tables I start off slow, getting all the techniques down really clean, real slow. Then gradually build up speed. And I practice for at least two hours a day.

QBert in the Kutmobile. Photo courtesy of ThudRumble.

We read that you were studying with a grandmaster, can you tell us about that experience?

In Hawaii there's this guy that's been DJing for ten years longer than I have. He's showing me things about making your sound more natural. He taught me that scratching, or playing any other musical instrument, is not about competing, or trying to outdo your opponent. I mean that's the hip-hop aspect, so that's cool too, but then there's the other aspect. Playing an instrument is an offering, it's like a prayer. You're being one with God and the universe, and you're pouring out your love to him, through your musical instrument.

That's very spiritual.

It is, it's extremely spiritual. That has helped me a lot, trying to make my sound more natural. More rounded, rather than sharp and edgy. Like maybe if you listened to wind, it's not really sharp or anything, it's round, the sound at the edges. Rather than "dat-a-dat-a-dat-dat" it's more like "whew-whu-whu-whu-whew-whu," know what I mean? Kind of like rounded – I don't know how to explain it. (Laughs.)

Scene from Wave Twisters. Photo courtesy of ThudRumble.

I think that makes perfect sense. Bass players talk about making a round tone.

Yeah, yeah, yeah.

Can you say who your teacher is?

We have this video called *Turntable TV* which is coming out soon, and we're going to show him on one of the episodes. *Turntable TV* on DVD, the first episode's coming out real soon. And I'm filming myself practicing at all the beaches in Hawaii, in my car. It's pretty ridiculous.

Battling was a big part of how you came up. Can you tell us about how that helped build your career?

It was like a game to me. As well as being a release for myself, and my creative side. I did it for fun. In the beginning, before I was battling, I was learning new things. I was like "oh, that's cool, can you do this? Can you do that?" I'd meet all these people that were like "oh yeah, I scratch too, come over" and we'd show our stuff.

Each person I met I learned a little new technique from. Like they would beat me, know what I mean, I'd be like "oh, wow, I can't do that yet." So I'd learn from them, and then I'd go to the next guy…I'd think I was cool, but I'd always get beat, and learn something from that.

So it was an educational process for you?

Exactly. Yeah. Total. Get my ass beat and learn the hard way.

Wave Twisters *is an amazing record. Did you have things all mapped out prior to recording?*

The whole idea was planned out before I made the album. After I made two or three songs, I noticed that every song was like a little story in itself. So I said, "why don't I just make a big album which is a story?" Then I started thinking about videos. So why don't we make an animated graffiti video, there's never been one of those, I've always wanted to see those graffiti characters get animated.

It's apparent that children's records were a major sound source for **Wave Twisters,** *but where else do you look for audio?*

Anything. Could be a séance to a god of mud. Any kind of weird record. Here's a tip: Go on eBay, type in "record" or "LP" and whatever weird thing, like "robot LP" or "masturbating LP" or "Strange LP."

There's a lot of sound-effect records that DJs make nowadays, obscure scratch records. With all these weird sounds. So listen to those, they kind of get logged into your mind. So then whenever you think of a song that you want to make, you'll hear that sound in your head, and then go back and look for that sound on those records. Or search for it. Like "maybe I can find it on one of these records." There's so many ways to find sound.

You work with found sound elements, pieces of other people's records. Is licensing problematic?

That's not really what I do nowadays. I mean that is one aspect, like the album *Wave Twisters* or whatever. But I make my own beats, and scratch my own sound effects. I like to make sound effects in samplers and stuff. I have an E-Mu SP-1200, an Ensoniq ASR-10, Ensoniq EPS, Ensoniq ASR-X, an Akai MPC-2000, a Korg Electribe, a Roland TR-808, and a Roland JP-8080 synthesizer.

Are you designing any gear?

We're making a new turntable and mixer with Vestax.

What's your goal with scratch DJing, what are you trying to achieve?

Aside from all the gear I just mentioned, I want to break it down to basics. Turntable and mixer, that's it. Make all the effects from that. I used to use wah-wah pedals, all kinds echoes and all that stuff. But I want to make all those with just the rawest elements, of turntable and mixer. Kind of like the jazz guys, they don't really use any outboard stuff, some do, but the raw pure guys like Coltrane, he just was straight up.

We've read that you're a jazz lover. What do you get out of jazz?

I don't know if it's true, but when I was growing up my mom always taught me that jazz was the highest level of music. I spent years and years studying these guys, getting videotapes and books and CDs, just learning what makes them so cool. Miles Davis and Thelonius Monk have that whole brazen thing. Coltrane. Pee Wee Russell, ever heard of him? Pee Wee Russell's timing is way off. And Benny Goodman is just so free. Especially Louis Armstrong, that's like my favorite. I love Louis Armstrong to death. Like his Hot Five and Hot Seven? I listen to it all the time.

What scratch DJs influenced you as an artist?

There's so many people. Mix Master Mike was one of my first influences. Mix Master Ice. Joe Cooley. Cash Money, definitely. Jazzy Jeff for sure. Mister Mix, DJ Mad, Bobcat, The Glove. A lot of new guys too, of course, all the X-ecutioners, the Beat Junkies, the Scratch Perverts.

I still love my whole jazz thing. I feel it's so much more advanced than scratching that I look to that, and try to emulate that style more.

Are there people who helped you build up your business?

The key guy that helped me developing my business is Yogafrog, my business partner. We work together, he lives in Hawaii as well. He just knows how to let people know about products and stuff. Before he came along it was pretty much just word of mouth. And he was like "we need to make the first DJ kind of Web site, use the Internet…"

There was never any kind of DJ album on CD. Everyone was thinking about mix tapes, no one was thinking about mix CDs. And so we did all that. We did a DVD, *Wave Twisters*. It doesn't sound so outstanding, but it is something.

A lot of people will be like "nah, we should just stick to the old ways." But he was the guy to say "no, let's do the new style, that no one's ever done before." It's kind of common sense to do these things, but no one's really trying to do it.

Before Yogafrog I relied a lot on my winnings in competitions. They would make their videos, the DMC/Technics World DJ Competitions and stuff, and I got a lot of press from that, because those videotapes would go around the world. We were there for three or four years doing that, competing, and being on all the videotapes. So that was a marketing thing in itself, before Yogafrog.

What was Scratchcon?

That's the first ever world scratch DJ convention. All of the best scratchers around the world at one convention. That was definitely Yogafrog's idea. We're working on Scratchcon 2005, it's gonna be in Japan, France, and U.S., I believe. That first Scratchcon is going to be on DVD soon.

Can you tell us about your signature moves?

I guess I was known most for the crab, the one where you use all your fingers. I saw this guy, DJ XL, using two fingers, kind of like tapping the fader. And he asked me "is that how you do the flare?" And I was like "Uh, no." But then I thought "hmm."

So when I went home, I used like all my fingers. Instead of tapping it I rubbed them across the fader. And that was like the crab scratch. Which is really pronounced "chraab" (exaggerated accent).

We were in Lebanon, me and Mix Master Mike, and we were ordering some crepes. I was like "yeah I'll have the strawberry crepes." (Imitating waiter) "Oh the strawberry 'chraap'" (exaggerated accent). I was like "ooh that's a nice name for a scratch."

And there's all kinds of things, different scratches.

You've done a landmark all-scratch concept album, the first all-scratch film, you've traveled the world, and appeared in major TV ad campaigns. What's been the most fun?

The most fun for me would be knowing that I kind of, like, gave the world something, you know? Just knowing that fact feels pretty good. Like, well, if one person appreciates it, hey man that's cool.

Scene from Wave Twisters. *Photo courtesy of ThudRumble.*

I guess an equal thing that's fun is just scratching. And being able to listen back to it, and being like "wow I think I made something new here." I think?! Until I embarrass myself. Like let someone else hear it and they're like "uh, that's wack." But at the time, when I think it's good, that makes me happy (Laughs).

When are you gonna drop the next solo album?

As soon as I get inspired. I really want to go back to my roots and just train really hard. And make the next album sound totally different.

Any plans for an Invisibl Skratch Piklz reunion?

That's up to them. I'm always down for that. Maybe one day.

DJ QBert. Photo courtesy of ThudRumble.

Chapter 4

Occupation:
DJ

It's a dirty job, but someone's got to do it. From the very inception, DJs have been beset by record labels, songwriters, the government, and organized crime. Practically every stage of the DJ's development was accompanied by attempts to restrain the DJ, and to separate him or her from the cash.

This chapter traces the evolution of DJing: how the role and techniques of the disk jockey grew, how DJs affected the world around them, and how their environment and working conditions changed, forcing adaptations and creating opportunities. DJs have a few natural allies, namely club kids, technicians, and musicians. DJs also face numerous predators, including club owners, the music industry, lawyers, the government, self-appointed guardians of public decency, shady business partners, and of course, other DJs. We'll meet them all in this chapter, along with some of the DJs who paved the way.

Fessenden: The Primordial DJ

As mentioned in Chapter 2, the first DJ was Canadian-born scientist Reginald A. Fessenden. Fessenden was also the first to send audio—speech and music—over the radio airwaves, in 1906.[1] Up to that point, "wireless" just transmitted Morse code, and was only used by telegraph operators.

A Thomas Edison fan, young "Fezzie" Fessenden left a teaching position in Bermuda and traveled to New York, determined to meet his hero. He hung around an Edison factory and eventually talked his way into a job as a tester. This was the era when wealthy people had their own generators; one day Fessenden went on a service call at industrialist J. P. Morgan's mansion. As he troubleshot Morgan's frayed wiring, Fessenden realized that encasing wires in rubber, then surrounding them with a galvanized metal tube, would protect the wires (and the homeowner).

Edison heard about this and assigned Fessenden to develop better insulation, eventually promoting him to chief chemist in 1890. After a lay-off at Edison, George Westinghouse hired Fessenden, setting him to work on generators and improvements to the electric light bulb. But Fessenden's main interest was radio; he took a couple of teaching positions and a Westinghouse-sponsored sabbatical so he could continue his research.

A stint with the U.S. Weather Bureau came to an end when the government demanded a share of Fessenden's patents. He then hooked up with two millionaire investors and started the National Electric Signaling Company (NESCO). One of their biggest clients was the United Fruit Company; Fessenden set up wireless telegraph transmitters in

---

1 A Kentucky phone repairman named Nathan B. Stubblefield may have actually transmitted voice and music fourteen years earlier than Fessenden. Stubblefield invented a wireless telephone system that broadcast through the earth and water, instead of through the air, using the principle of induction. He was marketing wireless phone service by 1898, but got caught up in a fraudulent stock promotion scheme, which cost him his company and patents. Stubblefield was sued by his backers, his wife deserted him, his kids sold the family farm, and he became an eccentric hermit who died of starvation.

New Orleans and Guatemala, providing the company's headquarters, ships, and plantations with instant communication. NESCO were eventually sending and receiving wireless as far as Alexandria, Egypt, and preceded Marconi by demonstrating the first trans-Atlantic wireless communication.

Fessenden's big advance was amplitude modulation (AM), in which the waveforms of speech or music are superimposed onto a "carrier" wave. Although Fessenden first transmitted the human voice between two test stations in 1900, the event that goes in the history books was his legendary Christmas Eve broadcast of 1906.

After a Morse code signal alerting all operators within range, Fessenden got on the microphone, made a brief speech, then played a phonograph record of Handel's "Largo" performed by singer Clara Butt. Next, Fessenden picked up a violin and played and sang "O Holy Night." It's reported that Fessenden's assistant was urged to talk, but was struck by stage fright. Fessenden repeated the show several days later, on New Year's Eve.

The holiday broadcasts surprised wireless operators on United Fruit Company ships in the Atlantic. Imagine the shock, bewilderment, and delight of those lonely seafaring telegraph operators as voices and music emitted from NESCO radios that previously just received Morse code.

Unfortunately Fessenden's investors didn't care about voice communications or entertainment and tried to seize his patents. Fessenden sued, finally winning a $500,000 out-of-court settlement in 1928. In the course of his career he also invented sonar, beeper/pagers, the voice-scrambler, tracer bullets, and even the automatic garage-door opener.

The Promoter: Lee de Forest

Interest in radio grew following Fessenden's experimental broadcasts. While shipping was still the primary commercial application, more and more land-based amateur radio operators began to appear. At this point radio was usually considered a "wireless telephone" used for point-to-point communication, but there were exceptions.

Charles "Doc" Herrold started giving crystal sets to his San Jose, California neighbors in 1909, so they could hear the music and interviews he broadcast. In 1911, New Yorkers Dr. Elman Meyers and his wife, Sybil True, began daily 18-hour programs that were predominantly records; it is believed that True was the first woman DJ.

Lee de Forest, Yale graduate and inventor of the triode vacuum tube, became one of the most prominent radio advocates and bragged (somewhat inaccurately) that he was the first disk jockey. De Forest grabbed European headlines in 1908 with a PR stunt, a broadcast from the Eiffel Tower in which he played Gramophone records for a group of distant listeners.

By 1909 de Forest was building wireless telephones for the U.S. Navy, testing each set by playing phonograph music. In 1910 de Forest perfected his "audion" tube, sold it to AT&T for a reported $50,000, and began producing live broadcasts from the Metropolitan Opera for a small number of New York listeners.

It's said that de Forest didn't actually understand how his vacuum tubes worked, and was equally naïve about business. He bungled his way through twenty separate bankruptcies. In the course of promoting one wireless telephone business, de Forest found himself indicted for stock fraud. His backers went to prison in 1913, but de Forest was acquitted.

In 1916 de Forest was doing a phonograph concert show three times a week from an experimental station in the Columbia laboratories, using a transmitter based on his audion tube. Columbia also provided the records and received on-air promotional announcements, becoming one of the first radio sponsors.

Civilian radio was suspended with the onset of World War I in 1917. The U.S. government took over all land-based radio stations in the country the following year. Combatants pressed the wireless telegraph into service signaling enemy positions from the front lines and the skies. Radio brought music and morale to troops on both sides of the trenches. As mentioned in Chapter 2, Marconi later sued the U.S. government over its use of radio in WWI, resulting in the eventual denial of his U.S. patent.

Lee de Forest was able to resume his DJing in late 1919, when the wartime ban was finally suspended. The following year, de Forest's station in the Columbia labs on New York's West 38th Street was shut down by a federal radio inspector. The government agent who revoked his broadcasting license told de Forest "there was no room in the ether for entertainment." It was a taste of things to come.

The Commercializer: Frank Conrad

A Westinghouse engineer named Dr. Frank Conrad picked up on the DJ idea and took things a step further. Reportedly bored by the endless tech-talk chatter of amateur radio nerds, Conrad set up a phonograph next to his mic and started playing records. Pittsburgh radio enthusiasts went wild for the broadcasts, so Conrad established a programming schedule, spinning records for two hours every Wednesday and Saturday night. A local music store got involved, supplying Conrad with records in exchange for advertising.

Conrad's bosses at Westinghouse recognized the opportunity and began marketing wireless receivers specifically for consumer listening. Free music was the key selling point. Before long Conrad had named his station KDKA Radio and was broadcasting from the roof of a Westinghouse building in East Pittsburgh. KDKA's November 2, 1920 broadcast is considered a milestone in commercial radio; Conrad's colleagues announced presidential election results, relayed by phone from the *Pittsburgh Post*. This was a big advance in news reporting, but it was DJ shows that built the audience for KDKA.

Commercial radio was off and running, disk jockeying became a programming staple, and hundreds of other stations would soon crop up around the world offering their own variations on the KDKA format. AT&T began linking groups of stations by phone line, to create the first large-scale radio networks. By 1926 RCA had set up the National Broadcasting Company (NBC), the first permanent nation-wide radio network. Radio became a fixture in most American homes during the 1920s, and the lure of free music from the airwaves drove the adoption. Bandleaders and on-air personalities became celebrities, some crossing over to film careers.

From the DJ perspective, the 1920s were a boom time. There was just one hitch: Playing records over the air was prohibited.

The Music Industry versus the DJ

Most of the world's governments recognized the propaganda value of radio, nationalized the airwaves, and established state-run broadcasting services that provided officially sanctioned culture and information.

America had the notion of "the public airwaves," meaning any American with a transmitter and the license fee might be granted a chunk of frequency spectrum and be allowed to broadcast. Instead of monopolizing radio, the U.S. government wanted to license, regulate, and tax the new industry.

Able to deliver and influence mass audiences, American broadcasting quickly became a serious business driven by advertising revenue, much like the newspapers. Compelled to increase their audiences, broadcasters gravitated toward popular culture; vaudeville comedians became a fixture on radio, as did the DJ.

When broadcasters began raking in ad dollars, they became a target for the record labels, music publishers, and musicians. The music industry old guard claimed radio was stealing their work, and demanded a piece of the action.

Record labels were fully aware of radio's promotional power; airplay could send people running to the record store, clamoring for the latest hit. Yet they also feared losing sales, concerned that consumers might curtail record buying in favor of free listening. Radio and DJs threatened to tip over the apple cart for the whole record business. They were influential new participants, who the labels could not directly control. And they were playing records, whether labels and artists liked it or not.

The U.S. government set the stage for the series of confrontations and shakedowns that followed. The agencies that licensed and regulated radio gave preferential treatment to broadcasters who didn't play records. The Federal Radio Commission (forerunner of today's FCC) reemphasized the point in 1927, declaring phonograph shows were "unnecessary."

Licensing and Performing Rights

The concept of licensing was at the core of the battle over radio, and has a similar bearing on today's battle over music on the Internet. A song, meaning the musical composition consisting of words and notes, is an "intellectual property." A song is an idea, an intangible thing. It can be represented by marks on a page, or by a sound recording, but those are simply embodiments. The song itself is ephemeral.

Songwriters, and their partners/exploiters the music publishers, make money by licensing or "renting out" the songs they own. This type of intellectual property ownership is called a copyright. Copyright stems from sheet music publishing; it's the notion that a song's owner has the exclusive right to make (or sell) a copy of the song. Anyone can perform or record anybody else's song, but they have to pay a license fee to the copyright owner for the "performing rights," and they can't substantially alter or make unauthorized changes to the composition.

When a company issues a record containing a songwriter's work, the label is supposed to pay a "mechanical license" fee to the composer and music publisher. It's called a "mechanical" because phonograph records are literally mechanical copies of the work. To minimize squabbles, the industry adopted a "compulsory royalty" arrangement for mechanical licenses, currently set at $0.08 per song for recordings up to five minutes (although frequently negotiated lower).

Live performances need to be licensed as well; bands routinely play other songwriters' works. This can be a goldmine, but songwriters can't possibly negotiate separate contracts with every bar, club, and restaurant. So publishers and songwriters got together and essentially set up their own protection racket, called a performing rights organization.

ASCAP, the American Society of Composers and Publishers, was the first American performing rights organization. Founded in 1914, ASCAP representatives went around to nightclubs and concert halls armed with the Copyright law, and offered venue owners three choices: pay a blanket annual license fee, clearing use of all the songs in the ASCAP catalog. Or stop playing all ASCAP compositions, or we'll sue you.

It was a persuasive pitch, and most businesses that used music went along with it. When radio cropped up, ASCAP jumped in immediately and began signing up, or intimidating, radio stations as early as 1922. (ASCAP didn't care whether a broadcaster was using records or live performers; they represent composers and publishers, not record labels.)

Partly in response to ASCAP, a radio trade group was formed in 1923, called the National Association of Broadcasters (NAB). Sore from the hefty licensing fees, and determined to break ASCAP's grip on their businesses, the NAB set up their own performing rights organization in 1940, Broadcast Music Incorporated (BMI). Most established pop composers were already ASCAP members. So BMI opened its doors to African-American songwriters, who had been barred from ASCAP, as well as country, folk, and jazz artists of every stripe.

In 1941 ASCAP demanded a big increase in their annual radio license fees.[2] Broadcasters resisted, and ASCAP called a strike that lasted nearly a year. Although ASCAP eventually won a smaller rate hike, only BMI music was aired during the strike, exposing many listeners to jazz, blues, bluegrass, and other "outsider" genres for the first time.

---

2 Sources disagree about the exact amount of ASCAP's 1941 demand. In *Last Night a DJ Saved My Life* Brewster and Broughton say ASCAP wanted a "nearly seventy percent" increase. BMI's online *50th Anniversary History Book* says ASCAP's "proposed contract called for a 100 percent increase" in rates over the previous year.

The Broadcast Prohibition

During the 1920s it was common for musicians to play live in the radio studio; live shows from dance halls and concert auditoriums were also routine. But by the time the Depression hit in 1929, economics had forced most broadcasters to forego live music and play records instead. Record labels had already drawn a line in the sand, stamping "Not Licensed For Broadcast" on the label of every disc they issued. The warnings were generally ignored.

Bandleader and blender promoter Fred Waring knew how much money there was in radio. A popular Victor artist in the 1920s, Waring had curtailed recording by 1932, concerned that DJ airplay was competing with his lucrative radio gig. He did a show for Ford, which reportedly paid Waring and his band the Pennsylvanians $12,500 per program.

Although he hadn't recorded in years, Waring was still under contract to Victor. When a sound engineer cut a "transcription" disc from a Waring broadcast, then sold the disc to a radio station, Waring won an injunction against the bootlegger. The following day he sued WDAS of Philadelphia for playing the record and eventually won the case.

Flush with success, Waring went after a bigger prize. He set out to stop (or tax) the unauthorized playing of all records. Although songwriters were being compensated through ASCAP, the record labels and musicians got no payments for airplay.

Waring and the record industry tried to establish a performance right for sound recordings, (the embodiments of songs), so they could negotiate fees for the use of those works. The State Supreme Court of Pennsylvania agreed in 1937 that "Not Licensed For Broadcast" labels were binding, and record purchasers must comply with such terms. But that decision was overturned, and the U.S. Supreme Court refused to hear an appeal.

Other recording artists, including Walter O'Keefe, Donald Voorhees, and Lawrence Tibbett, were also suing broadcasters. So was bandleader Paul Whiteman, one of the biggest acts of the 1920s, and the man who discovered Bing Crosby.

The U. S. Supreme Court eventually stepped in, taking on the case of *RCA v. Whiteman*, which arose from a dispute about radio airplay on New York station WNEW. In his 1940 decision, Judge Learned Hand rejected record labels' attempts to expand copyright and limit use of their records. Merely stamping "Not Licensed For Radio Broadcast" on a record didn't make it so. Hand wrote that the record label "had no power to impose the pretended servitude upon the records; and (the broadcaster) is free to buy and use them in entire disregard of any attempt to do so."

Waring and Whiteman's defeats meant radio DJs could play any records they wanted, and didn't owe record labels or musicians anything. Only songwriters were owed a performance royalty.[3] A big cash cow was snatched away from the labels and musicians, as airplay became a promotional tool instead of a revenue stream. Faced with this set of rules, the labels switched tactics and began wooing radio programmers and DJs, seeking as much airplay as possible.

Founded in 1942, Capitol Records set the pace for this new approach. Capitol was the first label to routinely give free records to DJs. That policy reportedly made a big impression with the jocks and helped establish the label. Other record companies followed the pattern.

But it wasn't the end of the hassle over radio disk jockeys; next in line was the musicians' union.

---

3 Royalties for sound recording performances wouldn't exist in the U.S. until 2002, when the Copyright office's **CARP** negotiation set a rate for Internet streams.

The Musicians' Strike

James Caesar Petrillo, president of the American Federation of Musicians, once commissioned a study to ascertain whether records took away jobs from musicians. When his researcher found that record labels paid millions to musicians and suggested labor action might not be a good idea, Petrillo ignored his own report. He also ignored the then-recent Supreme Court decision in *RCA v. Whiteman*, and began demanding in 1941 that labels pay more money to musicians, or block records from radio and jukebox play.

The labels balked, so in August 1942 Petrillo actually ordered musicians to stop making records. Beset by World War II and the strike, the U.S. record business nearly ground to a halt. For more than a year the only recordings permitted by the union were "Victory Disks" made for the war effort.

It's reported that bandleaders opposed the strike, believing records were good for business. Vocalists weren't allowed in the musician's union, so singers made a cappella records while their bands were sidelined. Unable to monetize their airplay, and barred from recording, some musicians opted to enlist in the military.

Decca and Capitol finally gave in to Petrillo in the autumn of 1943; RCA and Columbia held out until November 1944.[4]

---

4 Four years later, in 1948, Petrillo was at it again, calling a second musicians' strike as television was getting under way.

Wartime DJs

World War II began impacting the record business as early as 1940, when the Japanese invasion of Southeast Asia caused a worldwide shortage of shellac. Labels scrambled to reformulate their disks, eventually arriving at vinyl, a type of plastic. But with the ensuing musicans' strike, the ASCAP strike, and wartime production priorities, vinyl didn't amount to much until the introduction of the "microgroove" LP and 45 at the end of the decade.

It was also in the early 1940s that the terms "disk jockey" and DJ came into use. Martin Block's *Make Believe Ballroom* was a popular show on WNEW in New York City. Block pretended artists were in the studio with him as he spun their records. It's said that Block inspired newsman Walter Winchell to coin the term "disk jockey." Other sources point to Jack Kapp, a record exec who called DJs "record jockeys," perhaps because they "rode" the volume or gain controls on their mixing boards.

When the U.S. entered World War II, DJs went too. Armed with a turntable, a box of records, and a simple amplifier, mobile DJs would set up in mess halls, bringing big band sounds and patriotic music. Vans and trucks with small 50-watt radio transmitters and record libraries would broadcast music and information to soldiers on the front lines.

Some of the best-known wartime DJs were women. Jean Ruth had an early-morning show on a Denver station called *Reveille with Beverly*. Reading excerpts from soldiers' letters and playing their requests, "Beverly" quickly became a favorite with troops stationed at Fort Logan, Colorado. After a glowing profile in *Time* magazine, CBS brought Ruth and her show to Los Angeles. She catered to service people and their families and attracted huge loyal audiences.

In May 1942 the War Department formed the Armed Forces Radio Service. Although they were already syndicating the CBS *Beverly* show, they hired Ruth to do additional programs, such as *G.I. Jive*, especially for the military. Shows were recorded to transcription discs, and sent overseas for broadcast. Her popularity led to a *Reveille with Beverly* movie from Columbia Pictures, starring Ann Miller with Frank Sinatra and Duke Ellington.

Jean Ruth wasn't the only alluring female voice competing for the G.I.'s attention. Her most infamous counterpart was the notorious "Tokyo Rose," propaganda voice of the Japanese empire. More than a dozen different English-speaking women appeared on a Japanese radio show called *The Zero Hour*. Broadcasting morale-damaging messages to American troops in the Pacific theater, they told men that their sweethearts at home had forgotten them and urged them to give up the fight. The name "Tokyo Rose" was coined by allied soldiers, to describe the various, mostly indistinguishable, female announcers.

Although the Japanese government pressed many women into service behind the mic, the one that took the fall was Iva Toguri, an American UCLA graduate who spoke no Japanese. While caring for an ailing aunt in Tokyo, she became trapped behind enemy lines after Pearl Harbor. She was considered an enemy alien, but remained free to move about. Unable to leave, and forced to support herself, Toguri took a typist job at Radio Tokyo. A captured Australian named Charles Cousens, a former Radio Sydney celebrity, was conscripted into producing *The Zero Hour*. Toguri became his assistant and mouthpiece, broadcasting under the name "Orphan Ann."

Cousens' scripts were approved by his Japanese captors, but some believe he was sneaking in veiled messages for allied intelligence.[5] Toguri's sexy delivery was the real drawing card, signing on with "Hello boys, this is the

---

5 "Tokyo Rose" wouldn't be the only DJ passing secret messages. Jean *Reveille with Beverly* Ruth writes: "At times I would receive orders from 'on high' as to which records to play; they were handed to me personally, along with written introductions that I was required to read word for word. It was mystifying to me, but I never argued with the top brass."

voice you love to hate…This is your Number One Enemy, your favorite playmate, Orphan Ann on Radio Tokyo, the little sunbeam whose throat you'd like to cut! Get ready again for a vicious assault on your morale." It was almost a send-up, Cousens and Toguri were practically making a parody of propaganda.

After the war, not thinking she'd done anything wrong, believing she was a celebrity, Toguri admitted to being "Tokyo Rose," even signed autographs with the name. She was eventually arrested, and brought back to the U.S. for a highly publicized trial, which resulted in Toguri's conviction for treason. Toguri spent more than eight years behind bars, where she played cards with another convict/DJ: Mildred Gillars, imprisoned for her "Axis Sally" propaganda broadcasts.

Gillars, an American, worked at Radio Berlin as an announcer and actress. Her show, called *Home Sweet Home* was heard throughout Europe, North Africa, and the U.S., from 1941 to 1945. "Hi fellows," she purred. "I'm afraid you're yearning plenty for someone else. But I just wonder if she isn't running around with the 4-Fs way back home."

Gillars obtained the names, serial numbers, and hometowns of captured and wounded soldiers, and made comments about the men, calculated to demoralize their comrades and families. Gillars even impersonated a Red Cross worker, so she could obtain interviews with POWs and injured G.I.s. She tape-recorded messages from the soldiers to their loved ones, and used the tapes as raw material for psychological warfare.

Gillars was simply a Nazi. The prosecutor at her trial pointed to the fact that she'd signed an oath of allegiance to the Third Reich when she took her job at Radio Berlin. "She thought she was on the winning side, and all she cared about was her own selfish fame," he said in closing arguments. "Axis Sally" spent more than twelve years in prison.

For some of the WWII allies, radio was much different from the American model. The Soviet Union and China chose to forego broadcasting over the airwaves, and instead installed wired radio. They found it cheaper to string wires than to ensure broadcast coverage in remote locations and the receivers were less expensive to build. Wired radio only transmitted one channel until the 1960s, and it wasn't until the 1970s that broadcast radio began to replace it in the USSR. China stuck with wired radio until the 1980s. Loudspeakers installed in villages, market squares, and work-places would constantly shout messages to the citizens.

Armstrong, Sarnoff, and FM Radio

Teenage wireless enthusiast Edwin Armstrong was a student at Columbia University when he invented the regenerative receiver circuit, which increased the volume and improved the sound quality of radio receiv-ers. He secured a patent on the invention in 1914, but Lee de Forest and AT&T disputed it. It came out in court that de Forest had no idea how his own vacuum tubes worked. But Armstrong understood them and went on to design many innovative circuits using tubes.

When World War I broke out, Armstrong became an officer in the Army Signal Corps. Assigned to detect faint signals from enemy shortwave, Armstrong invented the superheterodyne circuit, which dramatically improved receiver sensitivity, and is used in radios, TVs, and cell phones to this day. He withstood a challenge to that patent application, securing the patent in 1920.

Armstrong sold the rights to the superheterodyne circuit to Westinghouse and sold an improved "super-regenerative" circuit to RCA; the transactions made him a fortune. In the course of the deals he became acquainted with Marconi's former errand boy, David Sarnoff.

Young David Sarnoff had worked his way up from messenger to telegraph operator, and was on duty at Marconi the night the Titanic sank.
Newspaper coverage of the tragedy made Sarnoff world-famous at
age twenty-one. He was promoted to Chief Inspector and charged
with acquiring new technologies for Marconi. It was while working for
Marconi that Sarnoff first encountered Edwin Armstrong. But before they
could do a deal, Marconi's American operation collapsed.

Congress, at the behest of certain investors, passed a measure requiring
American-made radios on all American ships. The law killed Marconi's
business in the United States. Those same investors snapped up
Marconi's factories and U.S. patents at fire sale prices and founded a
company called the Radio Corporation of America, or RCA. Thanks in
part to his residual celebrity from the Titanic disaster, Sarnoff was hired
by RCA in 1919 as New Development Manager, and eventually became
president of the firm.

One of the people Sarnoff brought to RCA was Edwin Armstrong. The
two men had become friends, Armstrong even wound up marrying
Sarnoff's secretary. One day Sarnoff complained about the static that was
inherent in radio broadcasts of the time. Already aware of the problem,
Armstrong set out to create static-free radio. He found that by modulating the frequency of the carrier wave instead of the amplitude, one
could transmits signals free from electrical and atmospheric interference.
Signals could get around physical objects like buildings more easily and
a wider audio frequency range could be transmitted. Armstrong called it
FM radio and applied for four patents related to FM in 1933. Sarnoff gave
Armstrong offices in the Empire State Building and let him use the tower
to experiment with FM broadcasting.

In 1934 Armstrong lost his two-decade-long patent battle with AT&T and de Forest; the Supreme Court didn't understand the technical aspects of the case and stripped Armstrong of his regenerative circuit. Meanwhile David Sarnoff was growing concerned about the costs of upgrading the NBC radio network for FM, and became enamored with another invention called television. Sarnoff put the brakes on FM and evicted Armstrong from the Empire State Building to make way for TV research.

Armstrong was both passionate and wealthy, so he set out to build FM broadcasting on his own, not realizing what he was up against. He petitioned the FCC for some FM spectrum and the right to build a test transmitter in New Jersey. After years of stalling they finally allowed it and Armstrong began broadcasting in 1939. GE took interest in the format and started manufacturing FM receivers. Armstrong also found support from John Shephard, whose Yankee Network included about a dozen stations throughout New England. As FM began to gather steam, Sarnoff offered Armstrong one million dollars for a non-exclusive license to the FM patents; Armstrong refused, holding out for a royalty like he received from other radio manufacturers.

Sarnoff wanted FM to go away, fearing it would distract consumers from television. Sarnoff had tremendous influence with the FCC and had lobbied the agency to delay, hinder, and foil Armstrong's efforts at every turn since 1936. The capper was two decisions by the FCC in 1945 that changed the frequency range and signal strength for FM. The rulings forced all existing FM stations off the air (around fifty at the time), obsoleted about a half million pre-war FM receivers, and drastically reduced the broadcast range of FM stations. FM literally went back to the drawing board, as every receiver and transmitter needed redesign. Meanwhile, RCA had patented a rival FM system they claimed was different from Armstrong's, and licensed it to various firms.

Armstrong fought back. In 1948 he sued RCA and NBC for patent infringement. The corporation's main strategy was delay; pre-trial proceedings dragged on for five years. The predicament eventually took a toll on Armstrong's marriage; his wife walked out on Thanksgiving night of 1953 after a quarrel. Despondent, physically ill, facing more years of litigation, and nearly drained of resources, Armstrong committed suicide in January 1954, jumping from the window of his tenth-floor apartment.

Armstrong had filed twenty-one patent infringement lawsuits a month before his death. His widow carried those suits forward, won two, and settled the others. The Armstrong estate collected more than ten million dollars, including a million dollar settlement from RCA. By the mid-1960s Armstrong was vindicated; FM radio was universally regarded as superior to AM, most radios included an FM tuner, and all microwave relay links and space communications used FM. As for Sarnoff, his TV initiative worked out spectacularly. He remained president of RCA until 1965, when he installed his son into the office and ascended to chairman of the board.

Avant-Garde Turntablists

Disk jockeys found themselves somewhat legitimized during the post-war era. No longer viewed as living off the backs of musicians and labels, the DJ was another part of the showbiz machine. The DJ's job was laid-out, and well-understood by this point: pick the records, juxtapose them, set a mood, make announcements, and keep the party rolling. The DJ's job duties were essentially frozen at this selector/announcer level for the next 25 years, until hip-hop provided a whole new way of handling records.

But the hip-hop godfathers weren't the first to treat records as sound objects. The avant-garde art music scene had already been there. While serious classical or experimental music never sells like the pop acts, it's a field with a rich tradition that attracts some very smart composers and players.

One of the smartest was John Cage. As a Los Angeles teenager, John Cage had his own radio show where he played the piano. He was valedictorian of his high school class, but dropped out of college to pursue composing.

Cage saw the potential of using phonographs as samplers long before digital samplers came into use. In 1937 Cage wrote that with a "phonograph it is now possible to control any one of these sounds and give to it rhythms within or beyond the reach of imagination. Given four phonographs we can compose and perform a quartet for explosive motor, wind, heartbeat, and landslide."

Cage's 1939 composition "Imaginary Landscape No. 1" had variable-speed phonographs playing test-tone recordings alongside a piano and cymbal. "Imaginary Landscape No. 2" (1941) included a giant metal coil amplified by a phonograph cartridge. 1942's "Williams Mix" was a collage of more than 500 sound clips spliced together on tape.

"Imaginary Landscape No. 5," from 1952, used sounds culled from 42 LPs, re-edited on tape. The same year also saw the premiere of Cage's most notorious work, "4'33" (a.k.a. "Silence") in which a pianist sits at the keyboard and plays nothing.

Cage's most audacious move was "Cartridge Music" in 1960. Cage attached contact mics and phonograph cartridges to household objects, including furniture, ladders and wastebaskets. Cartridge needles were replaced with wires, springs, matches, pipe cleaners and feathers. The performers would handle these implements, creating an improvised noisescape.

Pierre Schaeffer, a French avant-garde composer, had similar ideas and lots of gear. Armed with a disc cutting lathe, four turntables, a four-channel mixer, filters and an echo unit, Schaeffer would cue sounds on vinyl, then alter the sounds by changing speed, direction, and volume. Schaeffer worked with loops, cutting his own records with "locked grooves" that played repeatedly. The term "musique concrete" came to describe such experiments.

While Cage and Schaeffer had distinguished careers, they couldn't sell a lot of records or concert tickets, and they didn't have much immediate impact outside the rarefied world of art music. They were precursors to the turntablists, but they didn't stick with it. Like most of their con-temporaries, Schaeffer and Cage got involved with tape editing and left vinyl manipulation behind. Nonetheless, their phonograph strategies were significant forerunners of hip-hop DJing techniques.

Alan Freed, Rock 'n Roll, and Payola

Post-war America was a racially segregated society. Racial discrimination was institutionalized, legitimate, and pervasive. Music provided a meeting ground; DJs wound up in the vanguard and hot seat of racial integration, midwifes for an emergent black culture.

The introduction of African-American music onto radio was followed by an explosive period of growth in both the record industry and the craft of popular music. The ascendance of black artists into the mainstream music business helped set the stage for the civil rights movement.

Many parts of the United States have enormous black populations, and those communities were not being served by radio in the late 1940s. A little Memphis station called WDIA was hitting hard times. They'd tried playing country, classical, and pop, but they just couldn't compete. In desperation, they asked Nat D. Williams, an African-American writer, to host a black music show. It was the first time it had ever been tried in Memphis.

Nat D.'s *Tan Town Jamboree* premiered October 25, 1948, and although it drew bomb threats, the show was an immediate hit. WDIA adopted an all-black music format, hired African-American staff members including DJs B. B. King and Rufus Thomas, and soon became the top station in Memphis.

Other stations took notice of WDIA's success and copied their format; before long blues, gospel, and the new "rhythm and blues" (R&B) sounds were being heard in every major radio market. In 1954 WDIA upgraded from a 250-watt transmitter to 50,000 watts, beaming their signal from Missouri to the Gulf Coast. This vast footprint allowed WDIA to reach as much as ten percent of America's black population.

Black DJs immediately broke with the bland, restrained, network announcing style of their white colleagues. They brought in personas and deliveries that were far more entertaining and much more real to black audiences. Daddy-O Daylie, a "rhyming bartender," went on the air in Chicago in the late 1940s, with a prototype freestyle rap act. Another freestyler was Levada Durst, a rhyming sports announcer in Austin, Texas. Durst played R&B on an AM station owned by one John Connally, who was later Governor of Texas. Durst and Daylie's "rhyming and signifying" styles were widely imitated on black radio.

Black DJs weren't the only ones being influenced. Some white disk jockeys, such as Poppa Stoppa in New Orleans, adopted faux-negro personas.[6] Legions of white musicians began emulating black musical styles, emphasizing the beat. African-American slang began entering the white vernacular. White teenagers became some of the most avid consumers of black musical culture. One man, more than any other, was at the forefront of this confluence of trends. His name was Alan Freed.

A jazz and pop DJ in Cleveland, Ohio, Alan Freed had been urged by a local record storeowner to do an R&B program. He adopted the name "Moondog" and hit the Cleveland airwaves in the summer of 1951 with a stack of hard-driving records. Freed's show struck a nerve, and he tried to capitalize on it by getting into the concert promotion business. His "Moondog Coronation Ball" held in 1952 at the Cleveland Arena is considered the first "rock" concert, and the first rock fiasco. An estimated 20,000 fans (mostly black teenagers) showed up at the 10,000-capacity hall and crashed the gates, forcing cancellation.

---

6 Wolfman Jack (Bob Smith) became the most well-known blackface DJ. Broadcasting from the 250,000 watt XERB in Tijuana, Mexico, his signal covered most of North America during the 1960s. After playing himself in the blockbuster film *American Graffiti*, the Wolfman became a television celebrity.

Freed was sincerely enthusiastic about the music, beating his hand on a phone book to accentuate the backbeat of his favorite records. Freed had a rapid, raspy delivery, dropping lines like "anyone who says rock 'n roll is a passing fad...has rocks in his head, dad!" Over time Freed's broadcasts began to reach a white audience.

WINS radio brought Freed's *Moondog Show* to New York in 1954, eliciting a lawsuit from local street musician and composer, Louis "Moondog" Hardin. Freed scrambled to find another name for his show, and went with *Alan Freed's Rock and Roll Show.* He'd been using the term "rock 'n roll" to describe the tough, uptempo R&B dance records he played. The record industry quickly adopted the phrase, which facilitated racially segregated marketing: R&B for black people, rock 'n roll for white people.

Freed's manager and business partner was a legendary figure named Morris Levy. Levy owned a number of New York nightclubs including Birdland and the Blue Note, as well as independent record labels and music publishing businesses. Respected, even revered by many in the record industry, Levy was also a front man for the mob. Although he worked with many different racketeers, Levy was closest to the Genovese crime family. Levy was a boyhood friend of future Genovese don Vincent "The Chin" Gigante and a business partner to many Genovese soldiers.

Levy wasn't eligible for the Italian mafia because he was Jewish. But as an ostensibly legitimate businessman with diverse interests in the entertainment field, Levy could provide cover, laundering, no-show jobs for parolees, fresh shakedown targets, and return-on-investment for his partners. Levy assembled a sizeable empire, and was the icon and role model for every corrupt music executive that followed. Tommy James, an artist on Levy's Roulette label, called him "the Al Capone of the record business."

Levy understood the value of music publishing and had his name attached as a "co-writer" to many compositions, including the hits of Frankie Lymon, Lightnin' Hopkins and Lee Dorsey. Alan Freed got in on the scam; Freed's name was added to seminal Chuck Berry records including "Maybelline" and "Nadine."[7] Levy was also an experienced promoter; with Freed he staged a series of landmark rock 'n roll concerts, initially at the St. Nicholas Arena, then the Brooklyn Paramount. After breaking attendance records at those halls, they took their Rock 'n Roll Show on the road.

Freed appeared in some movies, including *Rock, Rock, Rock!* (1956), and *Go, Johnny Go!* (1958). Freed also hosted a nationally televised rock 'n roll series on ABC television in 1957. Frankie Lymon danced with a white girl on one episode, prompting the show's cancellation.

At one point Levy tried to trademark the phrase "rock 'n roll," hoping to control and license its use. When Levy formed Roulette records he gave Freed twenty-five percent of the firm's stock. Freed turned around and sold his shares, "to some wiseguys from around town," according to Levy.[8] Levy demanded his stock back and terminated their management contract, but their live concert business and personal relationship continued.

Violence occurred outside a Boston Arena show in 1958, and Freed was indicted for inciting a riot. The charges were dropped, but WINS fired Freed and he moved to WABC radio.

Disk jockeys had been receiving direct cash gifts and loads of other favors from record labels since 1947. "Payola" was a regular part of the music business, tracing back to Gilbert and Sullivan in Victorian England.

---

7 Freed's heirs later sued ARC Music, Chuck Berry's publisher, for unpaid royalties on seven Freed/Berry "collaborations." Morris Levy bankrolled the suit, covering the Freed family's legal fees!
8 Interviewed by Fredric Dannen in *Hit Men*, Vintage Books, 1990.

It was utterly normal and okay to pay DJs for putting records on the air. Like waiters, DJs were paid very little, and were expected to receive tips. A payola scandal arose in 1959; what may have been an attempt at cleaning up rock 'n roll turned into a Congressional witch hunt against DJs. And Allen Freed was target number one.

Target number two was Dick Clark, host of ABC's *American Bandstand* since 1956. Like Freed, Clark had accepted many gifts from record labels and had built a cluster of businesses that profited from his TV show. Clark owned pieces of labels, publishers, pressing plants, and an artist management firm. Like Freed, Clark had been assigned copyrights on a number of rock classics, including "Sixteen Candles." Clark eventually divested some of his companies and walked away from the scandal relatively unscathed.

Although payola wasn't illegal until 1960, commercial bribery was against the law in New York. Freed admitted taking money from United Artists, Roulette, and Atlantic Records, as well as two distributors, receiving about $50,000 between 1957 and '59. He claimed these were "consulting" fees, and he wasn't playing-for-pay.

Freed was immediately fired from WABC; he eventually plead guilty to commercial bribery, a misdemeanor, and was fined $300 in 1962. Morris Levy of Roulette Records wasn't called to testify before Congress. Investigators tried to get Levy to admit giving payola, but he refused.

Freed failed to get his career restarted, with abortive stints at KDAY in Los Angeles and WQAM, Miami. When the federal government couldn't nail him on payola, the IRS went after him for tax evasion. A broken man, he drank himself to death by 1965.

Bribing DJs became illegal, so payola moved upstairs; program directors were greased instead of jocks. Over time the labels built a firewall between themselves and payola, hiring independent promotion firms that distributed bribes and favors. To add deniability, indie promoters are purportedly contracted by artists, not labels, and paid (at least in part) from the artist's advance.

Today payola is bigger than ever, costing artists and labels an estimated $150 million per year. Radio DJs, servants to their playlists, are out of the equation.

One of the ways promoters circumvent payola law is funding station promotion budgets. Another indie promotion tactic is paying broadcasters for the right to "represent" their stations as a liaison to the record labels. The labels, in turn, pay the promoter each time a new record is added by the station.

Clear Channel, the largest U.S. radio network, eventually barred its employees from freelancing as consultants for promotion firms, which had become another standard practice. Clear Channel's moonlighting ban appeared to be more of a cash grab than an ethical consideration. "The industry spends a tremendous amount of money promoting records to our radio stations," said then-CEO Randy Michaels. "What we have here is an opportunity to take some of that money in right through the front door and put it on our books."

Clear Channel now sells "research," derived from polling its program directors, to the tune of $20,000 per song. Most recently, in April of 2003, Clear Channel announced they were severing relationships with independent promoters, and would henceforth work directly with labels on "contesting, promotions, and marketing opportunities." By cutting out the middlemen, Clear Channel aims to book one hundred percent of every payola dollar.

Freeform FM

By 1965 the AM band had become very crowded, and many FM stations were simply "simulcasts" of AM stations, offering the exact same programming with better fidelity. During this year the FCC issued the FM Nonduplication Rule, which limited the simulcast practice. Hundreds of commercial FM stations scrambled to find a new format before January 1, 1967, when the rule took full effect. Some of them opted for no format whatsoever, a style of radio called "freeform."

Freeform simply means letting the DJ pick the music. No playlist, no rotation schedules, and no stylistic boundaries. The first freeform radio programs appeared on non-commercial community FM stations owned by the Pacifica Foundation: John Leonard's *Nightsounds* on KPFA in Berkeley, and Chris Albertson's *Inside* on WBAI in New York.

KPFA was the first "community" radio station in the United States. Pacifica founder Lewis Hill envisioned stations dedicated to free expression, offering access to the airwaves for radical cultural and political ideas. DJ John Leonard began producing collages of music, poetry, and satire for his *Nightsounds* program soon after KPFA signed on in 1949. Leonard influenced Albertson, who in turn inspired WBAI's Bob Fass and WFMU's Vin Scelsa.

Seattle's KRAB-FM, founded by former KPFA staffer Lorenzo Milam in 1962, helped spread the freeform concept. Milam went on to found a series of freeform-oriented community stations.

When the FM Nonduplication Rule came down, freeform radio's youth-market appeal had already been proven by college and community stations. It was natural that some commercial broadcasters would latch onto the format and try to win youth market share. Also known as "progressive" or "underground" radio, commercial freeform stations such as WPLJ and WNEW in New York, WXRT Chicago, WABX Detroit, and WHFS in Baltimore, all flourished for a few years, but their management gradually reinstated playlists, or put other controls on the DJ's.

Although soul, jazz, blues, international music, and spoken word recordings were often broadcast, rock music and the hippie counter-culture dominated freeform radio. The practice of playing non-hit cuts off albums, as opposed to hit singles, led to the idea of album-oriented radio, which eventually petrified into the "Album-Oriented Rock" (AOR) and "Classic Rock" formats.

The most legendary commercial freeform stations were KMPX and KSAN in San Francisco. The owners of KMPX, a Spanish-language station, had been approached by a music biz macher with a wild scheme.

Tom "Big Daddy" Donahue came to San Francisco in 1961, and took top forty station KYA-AM to the top of the ratings. He began each show by saying he was "here to blow your mind and clean up your face." Donahue's DJing provided a platform from which he built a concert promotion business, a nightclub, a music-publishing firm and a record label. Donahue left KYA in 1965 to focus on these other businesses; Donahue produced shows in San Francisco's Cow Palace, and presented the final Beatles performance at Candlestick Park in 1966. Among his colleagues was a black DJ and record producer named Sylvester Stewart; Stewart eventually found fame as a recording artist, under the name Sly Stone.

Donahue saw the untapped demand for less-commercial music from more album-oriented artists. The "San Francisco Sound" was beginning to catch fire, adventurous New York and LA bands were coming to the fore, and a second wave of British Invasion groups were appearing, all getting little or no play on AM radio.

KMPX already had a late-night DJ that played whatever he wanted, who was finding some listeners among the Haight-Asbury crowd. Donahue convinced the owners of KMPX to go completely in that direction and play nothing but album-oriented rock, with no playlists, around the clock. Donahue and his posse of longhairs took to the airwaves in April 1967.

"The disk jockeys have become robots," Donahue wrote in a 1967 *Rolling Stone* article titled "AM Radio Is Dead and Its Rotting Corpse Is Stinking Up the Airwaves." DJs are "performing their inanities at the direction of programmers who have succeeded in totally squeezing the human element out of their sound. They have succeeded in making everyone on the station staff sound the same—asinine."

KMPX was a fabulous success, broadcasting the music of the day to a city bursting with blissful hippies, throughout the "summer of love." In the spring of 1968 KMPX management tried to restrict the DJs, so Donahue and his staff went on strike, eventually moving en masse to KSAN.

KSAN flew the freeform freak flag for about a decade; in 1972 Donahue was named station general manager. The most bizarre incident occurred on April 3, 1974, when a terrorist group called the Symbionese Liberation Army shoved a tape recording of hostage Patricia Hearst through the KSAN mail slot. On that tape Hearst chided her parents, accused the FBI of trying to assassinate her, and announced that she was joining her captors, under the nom de guerre of Tania.

Instead of calling the police, Donahue instructed a DJ to copy the cassette to a reel-to-reel, so it would look more dramatic. Then Donahue called the local TV stations; before long the KSAN control room was crowded with cameras, filming the tape as it played over the air. Today such a stunt would probably cause a public outcry and cost the station its license. In 1974 it was just another gesture of counter-culture solidarity.

Donahue died of a heart attack in 1975, and KSAN ratings began declining. By 1978 the jocks had latched on to punk and new wave, but ratings continued shrinking, forcing the abandonment of freeform. Playlists were established, personnel turnover accelerated, and in 1980 KSAN went country.

Commercial freeform was over, a temporary breach in the ongoing monopolization of radio. Among the last holdouts are KPIG-FM (Freedom, CA), which continues to let DJs make all the decisions, and which became the first radio station to stream over the Internet. Aside from KPIG, freeform programming today is usually heard on the types of community and college stations that spawned the style in the first place.

Proto-Disco

Dancing to records is inexpensive working-class entertainment found almost everywhere in the world. It's impossible to pinpoint with certainty the true origins of mobile and nightclub DJing. The jukebox paved the way, bringing records and dancing into bars and burger joints. The high school sock hop has been part of American public education since the 1930s. Authors Brewster and Broughton point to legendary British DJ Jimmy Savile as the first true club DJ; Savile began playing records in dance halls as early as 1943.[9]

Savile assembled his own sound system and took it around to ballrooms throughout England. Savile's big innovation was using two phonographs. He wanted to reduce the silent moments between records and to segue between songs. Savile had a custom-built two-turntable mobile system in 1946, and established live, in-person DJing as an entertainment format in the U.K.

---

9 Brewster and Broughton, *Last Night a DJ Saved My Life: The History of the Disk Jockey*, Grove Press, 1999. Although shamelessly Anglo-centric, and occasionally inaccurate, it's a fantastic book, and provided some of the background for this section.

Discotheque is a French word, literally "record library." It's said that sailors would store their record collections in the stockrooms of cafes and return to play them during shore leaves. The first club to use the term was La Discotheque, a bar in wartime Paris that spun jazz as a sonic tonic against the Nazi occupation. After the war a number of discotheques opened in Paris, the Whiskey-A-Go-Go leading the pack in 1947. It took until 1960 for the idea to be exported to America, when a French immigrant opened Le Club, a chichi society hangout in New York City.

French émigrés also brought the discotheque to England. The mods, a British youth subculture of the 1960s, liked African-American and Jamaican music. The BBC was very restrictive at that time, so going to clubs was the only way to hear hot dance records. Mods would pack into discotheques, take amphetamines, and dance all night.

The Twist became a worldwide dance craze during the early 1960s. The Twist caused outrage among authority figures and guardians of propriety; the pelvic movements seemed more sexual than previous dances, and one could dance alone or in groups. It was a racy dance for the time, and it drove people into discotheques.

In 1965 the top discotheque in New York was an upper-crust watering hole called Arthur. Owned by an ex-wife of actor Richard Burton, Arthur's DJ was a former professional twister named Terry Noel. Noel wanted to do more than just spin records. He took over control of the lights. He installed a rudimentary surround-sound speaker system, allowing him to pan a track to any point in the room. And he began mixing records in a way that had never really been done before.

Noel would go for wild segues, layering bits of one record over another. He is believed to be the first nightclub DJ to use records as sound collage, and the first DJ to make a real performance out of playing records. Noel eventually left Arthur, winding up at a club called Salvation, followed by Salvation Too.

Francis Grasso's Mix Revolution

Legend has it that one night in 1968 Terry Noel decided to drop acid before going to work at Salvation Too. When he finally showed up, many hours later, a club kid named Francis Grasso had taken over his job, and Noel was fired. Another former go-go boy, Grasso was a natural, and he went on to define the art of the nightclub DJ.

"Nobody had really just kept the beat going," he recalled in a 1999 interview with Brewster and Broughton. Grasso was the first DJ to present an uninterrupted flow of music, where the dancing never had to stop. To make this happen, Grasso used two copies of a record, one on each turntable. Grasso applied the technique of "slip-cueing" to stitch it together: using a felt slip mat, he softly held the disc stationary while the turntable rotated below. Listening on headphones, he would find the "one" beat, then turn up the turntable's main volume and release the record precisely on the beat.

Grasso learned slip-cueing from radio DJs who used it to create tight segues. Grasso took the technique into the clubs and put it to an entirely different use: extending the length of songs, what would become known as "cutting." He would rebuild two-part singles, fading from the end of side A into the beginning of side B so accurately that the audience couldn't notice the transition.

Grasso used the live and studio versions of "Soul Sacrifice" by Santana, alternating between the records, or layering them to produce echo and phase effects. Another trademark was layering Chicago Transit Authority's "I'm a Man" with the moaning from "Whole Lotta Love" by Led Zeppelin. Disco music didn't exist per se, circa 1969-70; Grasso built his grooves from rock, funk, R&B, Latin, and African records.

When variable-speed turntables became available, Grasso began using the pitch control to adjust the speed of records, widening the possibilities for tempo matching and mixing. Like Noel, Grasso used segues and layering to build a performance. But Grasso respected and cultivated the dance floor in a way that was entirely new. He used his skills as a selector and mixer to keep the dancers excited, to reflect and control the energy in the room.

When Salvation Too closed, Grasso moved on to a club called Sanctuary. Housed in a former church, Sanctuary's turntables were set up on the altar. Initially a straight club, it eventually became (in the words of writer Albert Goldman) "the first totally uninhibited gay discotheque in America."

There had always been gay bars in New York. Until the Stonewall rebellion in June 1969 they had to operate on the fringe, and there was a very real sense of danger. Cops could bust them any time, and the patrons would be beaten, arrested, and smeared in the newspapers. When police raided the Stonewall Inn on the night of Judy Garland's funeral, drag queens pulled off their wigs, went after the cops, and kick-started the gay liberation movement. Before long, gay nightclubs were operating in the open and Sanctuary was in the vanguard. Sanctuary became a wild scene, a lot of sex and drugs, and DJ Francis Grasso was one of the only straight people in the place. Grasso and his style of mixing had found their first real audience.

Grasso got out of the business in 1981, after being beaten and disfigured by a club owner's enforcers. Grasso had tried to quit a residency to launch his own club and wound up in the hospital for three months, during which his records were stolen.

Mainstream Disco

Francis Grasso's mixing techniques and the proliferation of gay nightlife had created a burgeoning dance scene. Discos were everywhere; in New York alone there were hundreds. The best were patterned on the Loft, which had started the trend towards more extensive, high-end sound systems. Improvements in speaker and amplifier design allowed DJs to really make use of volume, so patrons could have the physical experience of music pulsating through their bodies.

Both the sound and scene were labeled "disco," and they were successfully marketed to mainstream (straight, white) audiences from roughly 1976 to 1979. For a while disco records sold in huge numbers, discotheques popped up in shopping malls across America, and grannies were learning the Hustle. The *Saturday Night Fever* film and soundtrack album were the high water marks of the trend. The mass marketing of disco's crassest elements, the excessive lifestyle it advertised and a spate of cheesy third-rate records led to a consumer backlash and sales meltdown. Fueled by homophobia, racism, and envy, public protests against disco were organized, and rock DJs led the way.

Two Chicago radio jocks, Steve Dahl and Garry Meier, came up with Disco Demolition Night in 1979. Listeners who brought unwanted disco records to Comiskey Park received discounted admission to a baseball double-header. The idea was to destroy the records between games, but things got out of hand. Fires were started, fans began brawling, records sailed through the air, people were injured, arrests were made, and the game was finally cancelled, White Sox forfeiting. The media portrayed the fracas as signifying the end of the "disco era."

When the mainstream marketing of disco scaled down, the dance music audience essentially reverted to its original core: people who wanted to go out dancing, many of them black, Hispanic, or gay. It remained a lively, mostly underground scene until the emergence of rave in the late 1980s. Today the style of mixing Francis Grasso pioneered, now known as disco or club mixing, is the dominant model for nightclub DJs and is also heard frequently on radio.

Grasso's influence, and the rise of disco, also precipitated changes in how dance records are marketed. The twelve-inch 45 is the most tangible embodiment of that change; with the twelve-inch came extended versions of songs, remixes, instrumentals, and other variants, all geared for dance floor use.

During the first seventy years of the record business, artists only released one version of a song. Today any dance recording is merely a "mix," one of an infinite number of possible versions, all of them intended as raw fuel for DJs. We'll talk more about the origins of the twelve-inch single later in this chapter.

Disco marketers didn't originate the idea of having different versions. That came straight from Jamaica, along with a whole new approach to record making, and a new style of announcing.

Jamaican Sound Systems

Far from hotspots of New York, London, and Paris, a parallel DJ evolution was taking place in Jamaica. Many Jamaicans were too poor to afford radios or phonographs, so in the 1950s Jamaican entrepreneurs began setting up mobile DJ sound systems, and running open-air dances. In Jamaica the person who plays records is called a "selector"; the "deejay" is the guy on the mic, what Americans call an MC or rapper.

With the help of talented local musicians, a new musical genre called reggae sprung up around the sound systems. Initially labeled as Jamaican R&B, ska, or rocksteady, the style eventually intersected with the Rastafarian religion, and the turmoil of Jamaican politics, to create a powerful cultural force that radiated far beyond the island's shores.

Tom the Great Sebastian had the top Jamaican sound system in the early 1950s, but was displaced in the second half of the decade by the "Big Three": Sir Coxsone Dodd's Downbeat, Duke Reid's Trojan, and King Edward's Giant. These systems initially played American R&B, jump blues, and calypso records.

Sound systems would battle for supremacy, as occurred later in hip-hop, sometimes setting up directly across from each other and playing head-to-head. Louder systems and better tunes were two ways to compete, and there were others…Selectors began scratching the labels off their records, or pasting on blank white labels to disguise their finds from competitors; that's now a common DJ practice. Competition didn't end there; legend has it that Duke Reid's crew once shot a rival sound system to pieces because it had better records.

Count Machuki (Winston Cooper) spun records for Tom the Great Sebastian, then moved over to Sir Coxsone Dodd's team. Influenced by the jive-talk of rhyming radio DJs, Machuki got on the microphone while playing records at an Easter dance in 1956. "I started dropping my wise-cracks…everybody fell for it," he recalled. Machuki proceeded to cook up his own rhymes and also added percussive vocal sounds. Called "peps," they pepped up the record and were precursors to the "human beatbox." Other Jamaican deejays followed and created the role of toaster or MC, which led eventually to rapping.

Continually trying to top their rivals, by the end of the 1950s sound system operators were going into local studios and recording their own instrumental tracks for their deejays to rhyme over. Rather than pressing vinyl, they would just make a few acetate copies; these became known as "dub plates." Coxsone Dodd, Duke Reid, and Prince Buster led the way; by 1959 they were releasing the tracks commercially on 45s. Dodd opened his own studio in 1963, the first black-owned recording facility in Jamaica.

Cecil Bustamente Campbell, better known as Prince Buster, got his start in the business doing security for Coxsone Dodd. In 1959 he set out on his own, opening Buster's Record Shack, and the Voice of the People sound system. The following year he began producing, and immediately hit on a new, syncopated beat – ska was born. That ska rhythm, emphasiz-ing the upbeat, would evolve over the next decade into reggae. Buster became an incredibly prolific producer and a performer as well.

Jamaican producers seized upon multi-track recording when the first four-track tape decks appeared in the mid-1960s. From this technological advance came "versions," what we now think of as "remixes." Years before white dance music picked up on the idea, Jamaican producers were reusing drum and bass tracks, again and again, layered with new melodies and lyrics. Economic necessity was a factor; by recycling bass and drum parts, they drastically reduced recording costs and time-to-market. They also maximized the return on hit tracks, putting out any number of variations on a proven groove.

Having stripped the music down to isolated bass and drum tracks, an electrical whiz named Osbourne Ruddock, a.k.a. King Tubby, took things a step further. A former radio repairman, Tubby found a lot of work fixing sabotaged sound system equipment; rivals would often wreck each other's speakers. In 1968 he set up his own mobile system, Tubby's Home Town Hi Fi, and soon began working with Duke Reid at Treasure Isle studio. Although hired as a disc cutter, Tubby turned his attention to remixing, and by 1970 had developed a radical approach. Tubby muted long passages, dropped out parts, put the spotlight on other parts, and bathed it all in a thick smokescreen of echo, reverb, and other effects. This stripped-down, refried production style became known as "dub."

Lee "Scratch" Perry, a producer who got his start with Sir Coxsone Dodd, had already made a name for himself with a 1968 single called "Pretty Funny Boy," the first record that emphasized the lazy, looping reggae bassline. Perry jumped on the dub sound and experimented wildly with the format. Dub's deep front-and-center bass sound, tight snare drums, long linear arrangements, and lavish use of studio effects, established the sonic profile and structural principles for most dance music that followed.

Perry went on to produce many noteworthy artists including Bob Marley and the Clash, but lost his Black Ark studio in a fire and subsequently moved to Switzerland where he continues to record today. King Tubby worked with great Jamaican vocalists including U-Roy and Big Youth, had a prodigious producing career, and owned a studio plus several labels.

Tubby was shot outside his house in 1989, and his studio was looted afterwards. Many of the tapes stolen that night have since found their way into release on various anthologies and collections, while Tubby's murder remains unsolved.

Although a few American DJs had moved on to recording careers, notably, BB King and Rufus Thomas, Jamaican selectors were the first DJs to directly parlay dance floor expertise into careers as producers and remixers. They were the first DJs to get their arms around the entire music recording process, and in doing so they revolutionized studio production techniques. And it was in the open-air dancehalls of Jamaica where deejays morphed into rappers, an idea that exploded when it hit the streets of New York.

Kool DJ Herc, Hip-Hop, and the Breakbeat

Jamaican Clive Campbell grew up near a Trenchtown dancehall. Relocated to the Bronx at age twelve, Campbell eventually set up his own sound system and took on the name Kool DJ Herc. While he wasn't the first mobile DJ in the area, Herc brought in some distinctive Jamaican elements, reinvented for the American ghetto.

Herc had MCs who talked and rhymed over the records. He used volume and bass to an extent that rivals couldn't match. He added heavy echo and reverb. And most importantly, Herc handled records as dance floor machinery, to be stripped, chopped, and reassembled.

Herc was a dancer himself, and a graffiti artist; he began throwing parties in 1971. Kool DJ Herc spun rare funk and Latin records at public playgrounds, rec centers, block parties, and nightclubs, attracting young people from the Bronx and Harlem. As we mentioned in Chapter 2, a form of competitive dancing had evolved largely from the gang milieu. Kids would face-off and prove who had the best moves.

Kool DJ Herc knew how the dancers reacted to certain drum breaks, in records such as "Apache," "Bongo Rock," and "The Mexican," as well as cuts by Mandrill, James Brown, and the Jimmy Castor Bunch. Dancers would hold back until the drum breakdown, cutting loose when the music finally dropped out. Herc called those drum passages "breakbeats." Since it's the best part of the song, Herc cut straight to the breakbeat. Then repeated it, to extend the dancing further. Herc would go from one breakbeat into another, a mix he called the "merry-go-round." He coined the term "b-boy" to describe the dancers, eventually called "breakdancers" by the media.

Although other DJs such as Francis Grasso and Pete DJ Jones (a prominent African-American disco DJ) segued between two copies of records to keep the beat going, they would play most, or all, of the recording. Herc introduced a new analysis, reducing records down to their single most essential component: the beat.

Choosing to focus on DJing, Herc relinquished the mic and brought on MCs Coke La Rock and Clark Kent. His wild all-night parties, at places such as the Twilight Zone and the Hevalo, became legendary. Kool DJ Herc's sound inspired many other DJs and MCs, and was one of the original wellsprings of hip-hop and rap. Herc retired before hip-hop became commercialized, after getting stabbed at a party. Kool DJ Herc didn't have a recording career like those who came after him. Fortunately he is now back on the scene, DJing in New York and internationally.

Conflict is an ever-present element in any life, including that of DJs, and it's expressed in the hop-hop practices of battling. Sound systems compete on the basis of volume and selection, just like the Jamaican ancestors. DJs compete through musical knowledge, turntable and mixer skills, showmanship, and crowd-pleasing. MCs rank each other on lyrical ability, flow, attitude, looks, stage moves, and audience response. MC battling has special roots in the African-American oral tradition of competitive insults, known as "the dozens." Battling is an outlet for competitiveness, a venue for skill building, and establishes a peer-status hierarchy within the scene. Battling inspires technique advancement and innovation, and is part of the engine that keeps both hip-hop and turntablism exciting.

Kool DJ Herc battled his way to the top of the original school scene and inspired a number of successors, including two who would reinvent the turntable as a musical instrument. We'll meet them next.

Grandmaster Flash and the Quick Mix Theory

Joseph Saddler was studying electronics at Samuel Gompers vocational high when he encountered Kool DJ Herc. While Herc was the first to demonstrate the power of the breakbeat, his mixing gear was primitive and his technique was not seamless. Saddler had also been exposed to Pete DJ Jones, who was doing slick, Grasso-style, continuous-beat mixes. Saddler eventually fused the Jones and Herc approaches, and adopted the name Flash from the comic book character.

Flash had to overcome some obstacles in order to perfect and elevate breakbeat cutting. The first problem was gear; Flash needed to listen to the record being cued without the audience hearing it. Although radio mixing consoles and some high-end club systems had cue channels, Flash was a do-it-yourselfer. He assembled what he required from off-the-shelf parts, combining a simple microphone mixer with two small preamplifiers, joined by a switch glued to the top of the mixer. Flash called it the peek-a-boo system; it allowed the audience to hear one record while he cued up another, listening through headphones.

Next, Flash set out to perfect the physical technique of cueing and switching between records fast and seamlessly. It required immense dexterity, intimate knowledge of his records and turntables, and sheer determination to practice the moves until he could keep the beat going as perfect loop. The scientific Saddler called his technique the "Quick Mix Theory."

Along the way Flash developed the "Clock Theory," a way of locating breaks. He looked at the record like a clock face, and placed a mark on the record label indicating where the passage began. Today nearly all hip-hop DJs utilize this technique; artist's tape is typically used, and can be placed directly on the vinyl or label. Once he'd found the beginning of the break, Flash counted the number of revolutions; then he could easily spin the record back to the start of the passage.

Like avant-garde precursors Cage and Schaeffer, Flash used the turntable as an analog sampler, playing tiny excerpts of records. But unlike them, he had made himself into a human looping system. It's a classic tranformation story: the smart, motivated kid who locked himself in his bedroom, practiced and studied intensely, then emerged with amazing powers. Able to perform cuts that seemed impossible at the time (and are still difficult today) Flash took on the title of Grandmaster, derived from the martial arts bad-asses in kung fu movies, as well as Grandmaster Flowers, a local disco DJ.

Flash said in an interview "when I first created the style, I played in a few parks in the area but nobody really quite understood what I was doing. A lot of people ridiculed it. They didn't like the idea of it. I was so excited, but...nobody would get it for quite some time."[10]

Unbeknownst to Flash, a white disco DJ named Walter Gibbons had been doing something very similar at the Galaxy 21 discotheque in Manhattan. Gibbons acquired a sizeable downtown following, but left New York in 1976 and converted to Christianity. Because he opted out, Gibbons' influence was limited, while Flash kept at it and eventually carried breakbeat cutting into the pop mainstream.

10 Brewster and Broughton, p. 217

Flash was no MC, so he began working with rappers, initially Cowboy (Keith Wiggins) and Kid Creole (Nathaniel Glover). Creole's brother Melvin Glover joined in, known henceforth as Melle Mel. Instead of just relying on catch phrases and shout-outs, they began writing rhymes and telling stories with their lyrics. And they took it further still, perfecting back-and-forth, call-and-response styles, where each would take a phrase or a word.

Eventually joined by Mr. Ness, (Eddie Morris, also known as Scorpio) and Rahiem (Guy Williams), the crew became Grandmaster Flash and the Furious Five. The intensity, flow, and excitement of these MCs, combined with Flash's turntable gymnastics, took the nascent hip-hop scene by storm.

Flash's innovations weren't limited to the turntable. He acquired an early Vox drum machine, and was the first to use the "beatbox" in hip-hop, or in any DJ context. The drum machine had no sequencer, it could not store and play back patterns. So Flash cloistered himself again and learned how to "drum" by pressing the machine's buttons. It became a highlight of their performances; Flash would stop the turntables and keep the rhythms going, playing the beatbox by hand. Later DJs would bring in more sophisticated, programmable drum machines, layering and augmenting the beats on records.

GrandWizzard Theodore: Scratching

The record buying public first heard the sound of scratching—moving the rrecord back and forth beneath the needle, in a rhythmic fashion—on "The Adventures of Grandmaster Flash on the Wheels of Steel". A phenomenal integrator, Flash had already fused breakbeats with seamless mixing; adding scratching to the mix was like icing on the cake. Flash got the scratch idea from his one-time protégé, teenager Theodore Livingston, a.k.a. GrandWizzard Theodore.

Before the Furious Five, Flash was partnered with DJ/sound system operator "Mean" Gene Livingston. Mean Gene's younger brother Theodore displayed an early aptitude for the turntables; Flash encouraged the boy and tutored him.

Theodore was the first DJ to do "needle drops," looping breakbeats by lifting the tone arm, then re-placing the stylus at the start of the groove. Theodore could do this in time with the beat and without headphone cueing, thanks to his sharp eyes, dexterity, and intimate knowledge of his records. At the age of thirteen he would stand on milk crates so he could reach the decks, and Quick Mix by eye, without back spinning.

GrandWizzard Theodore discovered scratching by accident. "I was in my room playing music too loud. My mother...was pointing her finger at me, telling me to turn the music down. While she was screaming at me, I had one record playing, and was moving the other record back and forth. In a rhythmic motion. Once I realized what I was doing, I experimented with different records. It became the scratch and the rest is history."[11]

Flash's Quick Mix Theory used the turntable as a rhythm instrument to provide an ongoing backing of looped beats. Theodore's scratching made the turntable into a lead or solo instrument, producing percussive accents, melodic signatures, or forays into sheer noise. Flash picked

---

11 Our exclusive interview with GrandWizzard Theodore follows Chapter 2.

up on Theodore's invention, and eventually showcased scratching on "The Adventures of Grandmaster Flash on the Wheels of Steel" single. Practically every hip-hop DJ that followed has made use of scratching; it's part of the language and practice of hip-hop.

When Flash and Mean Gene parted company, Livingston siblings Gene, Theodore, and Cordie-O formed a crew called the L Brothers. In 1980 Theodore left that group and hooked up with some MCs, to become GrandWizzard Theodore and the Fantastic 5. The Fantastic 5 became one of the most popular groups in the New York hip-hop scene and engaged in an ongoing rivalry with the Cold Crush Brothers. Fantastic 5's first recording, "Rappin' Fresh Out the Pack" failed to capture the group's essence, featuring studio musicians instead of Theodore's turntable pyrotechnics.

"We refused to perform that song at our shows" said Fantastic 5 MC Whipper Whip.[12] "We didn't want a record deal. Everybody's puttin' out your stuff, then you get nothing from it. So we didn't want to do records." Their refusal may have been shortsighted; while the Fantastic 5 were highly regarded by the hip-hop in-crowd, that respect didn't translate into mainstream success.

Today GrandWizzard Theodore is still active as a performer, producer, and educator. He is acknowledged by his fellow DJs as the inventor of scratching and needle dropping, and as one of the instigators of turntablism.

12 Interviewed in Fricke and Ahearn, *Yes Yes Ya'll: The Experience Music Project Oral History of Hip-Hop's First Decade*, Da Capo Books, 2002.

Rap on Vinyl: Sugarhill Records

In spite of their popularity and influence, Grandmaster Flash and the Furious Five didn't make the first rap records. The performers themselves underestimated the commercial potential of this underground party scene. "I was asked before anybody" recalled Flash, "and I was like, who would want to hear a record which I was spinning, rerecorded with MCing over it?"

While there were many antecedents to rap, including the dub forefathers, and the records of Gil Scott Heron, Barry White, and Isaac Hayes, hip-hop style rapping didn't appear on a record until 1979, with the release of "King Tim III (Personality Jock)" a funk B-side by Brooklyn's Fatback band featuring an unknown MC. The breakout rap record came from a studio concoction called the Sugar Hill Gang, a group thrown together by indie label Sugarhill Records to cash in on the emergent hip-hop scene.[13]

Their groundbreaking, nearly fifteen-minute-long "Rapper's Delight" was essentially an imitation of hip-hop. It featured a band of studio musicians re-creating the groove from Chic's "Good Times," emulating the turntable looping style of Grandmaster Flash. Some of the lyrics were flagrantly purloined from other well-known rappers, Grandmaster Caz (Casanova Fly), and Rahiem from the Furious 5. Although it was kind of wack, the single caused a sensation.

Sugarhill was founded in 1979 with financial backing from Morris Levy, who we met earlier in this chapter, when he was managing Alan Freed. Co-owner Sylvia Robinson had been in the singing duo Mickey and Sylvia; her hit "Love Is Strange" was memorably featured on the *Deep Throat* soundtrack. Husband and business partner Joe Robinson was a large, imposing man, rumored to have been involved in the Harlem numbers racket (which he denied). Together they had run a series of funk and soul

---

13 Sugarhill: one word or two? The original pressing of Rapper's Delight had "Sugarhill" as one word when referring to both the label and the group. On later pressings they spelled the label name as two words. The group name has appeared both ways over the years. We use one word for the Sugarhill label and two words for the Sugar Hill Gang for ease of reading.

labels under Levy's wing. A previous imprint, All-Platinum records, went bankrupt in the mid-1970s amid a grand jury payola investigation. That inquiry led to a conviction on tax evasion for Joe Robinson.

"Rapper's Delight" was a smash, initiating a series of hits for the Sugarhill label, inaugurating the recorded era of hip-hop, and setting the stage for hip-hop's commercial exploitation. Grandmaster Flash and the Furious Five recorded "Superappin'" for the Enjoy label before signing to Sugarhill.[14] Their initial singles "Freedom" (1980) and "Birthday Party" (1981) were both R&B hits, but 1981's "The Adventures of Grandmaster Flash on the Wheels of Steel" was a towering achievement, arguably the first real display of modern DJ skills on vinyl.

Flash cut together segments from Chic, Blondie, and a handful of other records into a dazzling sound collage. There had never been a pop record quite like it before, built from an assortment of re-purposed recordings. A revolutionary, post-modern statement, "The Adventures..." may have been the first time real DJ-based hip-hop had been captured on record; prior recordings relied on musicians for the backing tracks and left the DJ sidelined. "The Adventures..." put the DJ in the spotlight, as a performer and soloist, on a par with any other musician.

Grandmaster Flash and the Furious Five's next hit, 1982's "The Message" was their biggest success, and marked a departure from the usual boasting into socially conscious lyrics. Co-written with Duke Bootee (Ed Fletcher) and Sylvia Robinson, Melle Mel's wide-ranging, Dylanesque panorama of urban life struck a nerve with black and white listeners alike. It was hailed by critics, and set the stage for every relevant, socially aware, or controversial rapper to follow, from Run-DMC to Eminem.

---

14 There was also an earlier Furious Five single on the Brazilia label, "We Rap More Mellow," released under the name the Younger Generation.

The Furious Five scored again with their 1983 cocaine anthem "White Lines," but the situation with Sugarhill led to a split-up. Flash ended up suing Sugarhill for unpaid royalties, and signing with Elektra. Melle Mel took on the title "Grandmaster" and stayed at Sugarhill. Although Sugarhill made a lot of money from rap, they appear to have played by Morris Levy rules; other Sugarhill artists alleged they were cheated as well.

Reggie Reg, MC for the Crash Crew, recalled Sugarhill telling his group that somebody had counterfeited a lot of their records. "So we checked that out, and come to find out that it was them! They bootlegged their own record."[15] It was a classic Levy tactic.

Sugarhill bought the Checker/Chess catalog, a treasure chest of seminal blues and rock recordings, in another Levy-financed transaction. Sugarhill and Levy wound up in a tangle with MCA over a shady distribution deal, and a "cutout" (discontinued) records transaction that went sour and turned violent. By the end of the debacle, Levy was convicted of extortion in the cutout scheme, and Sugarhill was bankrupt. Levy died soon after his conviction, having never spent more than a night in jail. The defunct Sugarhill's assets were eventually acquired by SHR, Inc., a company owned by Joe Robinson, and are currently in the hands of Rhino Records.

15 Interviewed in Fricke and Ahearn, *Yes Yes Ya'll*.

Afrika Bambaataa: The Electro-Funk Sound

Afrika Bambaataa was a contemporary of Herc and Flash, and another key influence in the development of hip-hop DJing. Bambaataa, a former gang member, was one of the founders of the Zulu Nation, an organization with an Afro-centric, community-minded agenda of hip-hop brotherhood.

Bambaataa threw jams at school gyms and housing project community centers, and in doing so built his rep as a DJ and crew leader. Bambaataa's musical tastes were wide-ranging, encompassing not only funk, rock, and Latin, but also reggae, calypso, new wave, and European electronic sounds. His large, diverse record collection was accompanied by a vast, authoritative musical knowledge; as Bambaataa's parties gathered steam he adopted a second name: Master of Records.

Afrika Bambaataa's big vinyl discovery was Kraftwerk, the pioneering German synthesizer group. While fairly well-known in Europe, and appreciated by a small hard-core of progressive/electronic music heads in the U.S., Kraftwerk were almost entirely unknown among Bambaataa's black urban audience. Bambaataa happened across a Kraftwerk album one day; intrigued by the cover he bought it on impulse.

"When I heard that group," Bambaataa recalled, "I said 'what is this?' This is so funky…these are some bad-ass white boys!"[16] Inspired by the funky Germans, Bambaataa set out to form an electronic group.

Kraftwerk's "Trans-Europe Express" provided the inspiration for his breakthrough hit, 1982's "Planet Rock" by Afrika Bambaataa and the Soulsonic Force. It was probably the first time drum machines appeared on a hip-hop record; most prior recordings were in the Sugarhill mode, utilizing live musicians. "When we got into the Electro-Funk style of hip-hop, we was really trying to reach the black, Latino, and the punk rock whites."

---

16 Bambaataa quotes are also from Fricke and Ahearn's *Yes Yes Ya'll*.

The record, released on the Tommy Boy label, reached number 4 on the R&B charts and became the Rosetta stone of dance music, providing the sonic template for Chicago house music, Detroit techno, Miami bass, and other electronic dance styles that followed.

Bambaataa continued the Electro-Funk sound on his next single, "Looking for the Perfect Beat." He went on to collaborate with artists including funk godfather James Brown, downtown producer/bassist Bill Laswell, and John Lydon (Johnny Rotten of the Sex Pistols). The Zulu Nation gave rise to De La Soul, Queen Latifah, A Tribe Called Quest, the Jungle Brothers, and many others. Bambaataa continues to DJ, lecture, and produce to this day.

Dance Evolves in the Post-Disco Era

The death of disco was soon overshadowed by the real tragedy of HIV/AIDS. Although millions of people around the world would eventually contract it, the disease was first noticed among American gay men. Many early victims were club goers, some were DJs. AIDS wiped out big sections of the gay community in a few short years. Nightclub strips like San Francisco's Folsom Street were shuttered, right along with the bathhouses, leaving just a handful of places scraping by on the straight crowd. The AIDS epidemic essentially pushed the dance scene underground again. Yet some folks kept right on dancing in the face of tragedy, and the music never stopped completely.

The advent of cheap drum machines, synthesizers, and multi-track record-ers was making it possible for kids with a few hundred bucks worth of gear to make their own recordings. As we saw in Jamaica, certain DJs seized on the technology, brought their dance floor analysis to bear, and spawned new musical styles. DJs jumped on advances such as MIDI sequencing and com-puter-based recording, which allowed almost anyone to produce recordings of competitive commercial quality. The increased accessibility of such tech-nologies brought new people into the picture, cooking up hit dance tracks in bedrooms and basements.

DJs in Chicago favored a heavily synthesized sound, with a big synth bass and lots of air in the mix. As the supply of disco records ran out, a handful of home studio enthusiasts began making tapes for local DJs, which soon escalated into a burgeoning local record scene. The Chicago "house" sound got its name from the Warehouse, a Chicago club where expatriate New York DJ Frankie Knuckles held forth. A tweaked-out variant on house arose, called "acid house." From Detroit came an even more aggressive, mechanized sound called "techno."

These electronic dance styles from the U.S. struck a nerve with clubgoers in the U.K. and Europe, and fit nicely with the emerging ecstasy-fueled rave scene. While electronic dance music was, and mostly continues to be, an underground sound in the U.S., it found a big mainstream audience overseas.

The larger forces in the music industry noticed the growing success of dance music in Europe, as well as its widespread use in advertising and films, and horned in on the business. As rave became established, nightclub DJing evolved into a big time gig. Superstar DJs now command princely fees, live like rock stars, and don't have to drag a band along. From seminal venues such as the Hacienda in Manchester, to every open-air rave, to the VIP lounges of Ibiza, at each turn the DJ is the person setting the scene and driving the dancing.

Record label niche-marketing wizards witnessed the success of house, acid house, and techno. With help from the music press, they proceeded to balkanize dance music, splitting it into an array of ill-defined sub-genres and styles. Flavors of the month have included drum and bass, garage, speed garage, jungle, and many other variations.

As production methods and business conditions changed, the role of the DJ continued to expand. More and more DJs began transitioning to production careers, some even became recording artists.

Fatboy Slim (Norman Cook) is one of the most famous examples. A former bass player, he began spinning records in nightclubs and proceeded to use an Atari home computer to cook up his own quirky beats. Chart success ensued, driven by a series of goofy, good-natured videos. The Chemical Brothers and the Prodigy are further cases of British DJ/artist/producers who succeeded at selling sample-based house music variants back to the United States,

Named "World's Biggest DJ" by the *Guinness Book of World Records*, Paul Oakenfold practically embodies the DJ/remixer/producer/artist curve. Oakenfold helped break house music in the U.K., and then ushered in rock/dance crossover. DJing since the late 1970s, Oakenfold was exposed to Larry Levan's legendary sets at the Paradise Garage while working for Arista in New York. Upon returning to England, Oakenfold worked as a promoter, and did things for the Beastie Boys and Run-DMC.

Oakenfold DJ'd at a club called Project in 1985 and '86, one of the first U.K. venues for house music. In 1987 he started playing in Ibiza, an island off the coast of Spain. Here he combined house with a blend of styles dubbed the Balearic sound, after the island chain. Blessed with a great ear, extreme dance floor savvy, career longevity, and an appealing, low-key public persona, Oakenfold is practically the quintessential dance DJ. Oakenfold has worked on tracks by U2, Snoop Dogg, Madonna, and many others, toured with U2, served as an A&R man, helped establish London's Ministry of Sound nightclub, and launched his own label.

As Armand Van Helden points out in his interview in this book, DJing today boils down to two approaches: If you're a nightclub disk jockey you spin records (or CDs) and maybe you mix or layer them. If you're a hip-hop disk jockey or turntablist, the sky is the limit; scratching and every other type of turntable and mixer technique are called for. Both disciplines have their adherents, and their skill sets can complement each other.

Hip-Hop Mainstreamed and Gangsterized

While nightclub DJs like Oakenfold were being elevated to celebrity status by the international dance scene, hip-hop DJs either turned into producers, or got pushed to the back of the bus, as the rap industry developed into a mature business. By the mid-1980s hip-hop began to assimilate into the mass culture, a trail blazed primarily by Run-DMC. Run-DMC's core element was a stark, drum machine-based sound, recorded with no reverb or echo. This "up-front" recording style was combined with a distinctive flow and inventive, literate lyrics.

Run-DMC gained market traction (in part) because of early appropriations from hard rock. Indeed they called themselves the "Kings of Rock," positioning themselves at the same level as Elvis. Hard rock guitar chords were layered over the beats on certain songs, including their first hit, "Rock Box" (1984). Like other hip-hop DJs, Run-DMC's Jam Master Jay (Jason Mizell) had cut the classic breakbeat from "Walk This Way" by Aerosmith; MCs Run and DMC would style their own rhymes over the simple kick and snare pattern. Inspired by this linkage, producer Rick Rubin talked the group into doing a straight-up cover version of the song using the Aerosmith lyrics.

"Walk This Way" (1986) was rather ridiculous, and it was also very effective. Rubin's rock/rap hybrid had little to do with hip-hop, but it provided a stepping-stone to the real thing for many listeners, and signaled the beginning of rap's mainstreaming. Until "Walk This Way," black faces were few and far between on MTV; Michael Jackson, Lionel Richie, and saccharine "VJ" J.J. Jackson were about it. Run-DMC, and Rubin's follow-up, the Beastie Boys, both proved that rap could succeed on MTV, and could sell to mainstream white audiences that would otherwise buy rock. They paved the way for a flood of black talent and ushered in the corporate exploitation of rap.

Into that breach stepped Public Enemy, the most prominent hip-hop group of its time, who fused a pro-black political agenda with intense, pointillist sound collages. Public Enemy built on the huge beats and crossover vision of Run-DMC, and forged a type of protest rap with roots in Bob Dylan, the Black Panthers, Melle Mel and Boogie Down Productions. The "punk rock whites" ate it up.

Onstage, DJ Terminator X (Norman Rogers) provided the menacing, impassive anchor for MC Chuck D (Carlton Ridenhour), hype man Flavor Flav (William Drayton), and a whole parade of posse members. In the studio the spotlight was on PE's production team, the Bomb Squad (Hank Shocklee, with Carl Ryder, Eric "Vietnam" Sadler, Keith Shocklee, and others).

Hank Shocklee started out as a party DJ, and also hosted mix shows at a college radio station. His Public Enemy recordings drew immediate attention, because the dense, layered productions were so unique. Their crowded, surging mixes were the sonic equivalent of a riot. Shocklee went on to produce Ice Cube, LL Cool J, Bel Biv Devoe, and many others. But PE's highly referenced production style became cost-prohibitive with the Biz Markie decision (which we'll cover next.) And their political rapping was commercially overshadowed by the gangster style.

At the center of gangster rap is Dr. Dre (Andre Young). A devoted bedroom DJ with some performing experience under his belt, Dre hooked up with lyrical genius Ice Cube (O'Shea Jackson), and rapper/entrepreneur Easy-E (Eric Wright), to form NWA (Niggas With Attitude) together with DJ Yella and MC Ren.

Although they had precursors such as Ice-T, BDP, and Schooly D, it was NWA that established gangster rap as the dominant hip-hop sound. Their sophomore album, 1988's *Straight Outta Compton* was the most hardcore rap record ever heard to that point. Defiant, shocking, and funny, it was like ghetto punk rock, and upped the danger and aggression level for the whole rap market. Dre was much more than a DJ, he masterminded NWA's sound just as any record producer would, using the total recording studio.

After the NWA records Dr. Dre became a top-selling artist in his own right, reinventing George Clinton's Parliament/Funkadelic grooves as G-funk, a more chilled-out, doped-up gangster sound. Dre partnered with a felon named Marion "Suge" Knight, a former Mob Piru Blood and LA Rams football player; together they founded label called Death Row. While wildly successful at first thanks to multi-platinum albums by Dr. Dre, Tupac Shakur, and Snoop Dogg, Death Row courted trouble.

Knight not only sold gangster rap, he strove to embody it. Knight's tactics, which included intimidation, violence, and some believe murder, may be highly effective in the arms trafficking business (to which he pleaded no contest in 1995.) But such measures attract a lot of attention when applied in the music industry.

In September 1996 security cameras in a Las Vegas casino recorded Knight beating a man; a few hours later Death Row's best-selling artist, Tupac, was fatally shot while riding in a car with Knight. The beating was a parole violation, it won Knight a five-year stretch in prison. Death Row downsized; they lost their distribution deal with Interscope in 1997. Dre eventually terminated his contract with Knight, went on to further solo successes and produced many others, including Eminem and 50 Cent.

As for Knight, he did his time and got back into the business. He renamed his label "Tha Row" and secured distribution with Koch, the most prominent independent distributor. At the time of this writing Knight has a new stable of artists, continues to issue posthumous Tupac Shakur albums, is engaged in a media feud with Snoop Dogg, and may be facing additional jail time. Knight took the Morris Levy model to new extremes, and made himself a celebrity anti-hero in the process. Like Levy, Knight has been embraced by the record industry again and again.

The Battle Over Digital Sampling

In the 1970s and '80s, hip-hop DJs were redefining the turntable as a musical instrument. During this same period digital samplers began to appear in music production studios. Sampling keyboards and computer recording software make looping very fast and easy. One need not perform loops by hand, just hold down a key on the keyboard, or do a copy-paste operation onscreen.

These advances in recording technology accelerated the ongoing trend of remixing, which provides a point of entry into record production for many DJs. The ease and prevalence of sampling, and shifting musical tastes, also led the DJ into another war zone over intellectual property.

Sample-based production came into general practice in the late 1980s and continues to flourish today. The idea of making a record from somebody else's records has its roots in Jamaican music, and arrived on the popular mainstage with "The Adventures of Grandmaster Flash on the Wheels of Steel." Since that landmark recording, "derivative compositions" and sample-based production have become the pop status quo. DJ-turned-producer Marley Marl, who worked with Big Daddy Kane, Roxanne Shante, Biz Markie, and later L.L. Cool J and TLC, was a sampling pioneer. Biting loops off records allowed him to get away from the sterile drum-machine sound. Marl's production style was widely copied, and he's now credited with starting the James Brown sampling trend.

Predictably, the people whose records are sampled want a piece of the action. "Rappers Delight" elicited a claim from the guys in Chic, whose "Good Times" was copied by the Sugarhill studio band. As digital sampling became prevalent, the record industry scrambled to find a way to exploit it. For a while most labels ignored sampling, not pursing copyright infringements because their own artists were also biting. But that didn't last, and lawsuits began to arise.

The Turtles sued De La Soul, and settled out of court. James Brown went after a number of people, winning a string of settlements. Vanilla Ice was sued by Queen and David Bowie over "Ice, Ice Baby;" he settled with them, then was allegedly shaken down by Marion "Suge" Knight over the same song.

Hip-hop entrepreneur Luther Campbell and his Miami bass act 2 Live Crew were in court a lot, initially over obscenity, but when they got sued by music publisher Acuff-Rose, they took it all the way to the U.S. Supreme Court. Campbell tried arguing that all digital sampling should be fair use, but the Justices wouldn't buy that. The Court did uphold the fair use provision for parody, agreeing that Campbell's version of "Pretty Woman" was a send-up of the Roy Orbison original, therefore a protected form of free speech.

Unfortunately, even a plausible parody defense may not help a DJ or artist when the lawyer letters start flying. Sound collage pranksters Negativland wound up in a beef with the rock band U2 and *American Top 40* DJ Casey Kasem over a derivative composition in a confusing record sleeve. Kasem's off-color remarks, sampled from a radio blooper tape, were the highlight of the recording. Kasem got lawyers involved and forced the recall and destruction of all copies of the record.

Sadly the "cool" indie label SST didn't stand behind Negativland, but initiated their own lawsuit against the group. Negativland's record was surely parody, they might have withstood the heat had they been able to afford attorneys, but they were just cash-strapped musicians and had to accept it. Surprisingly, it didn't derail the crew; they did many more releases and chronicled the whole U2 episode in funny, thought-provoking book.[17]

Entertainment attorney Alan Korn writes: "Most legal experts believe the issue of digital sampling was resolved in 1991, when a Federal District Court ruled that Biz Markie's use of Gilbert O'Sullivan hit song "Alone Again, Naturally" amounted to copyright infringement. In addition to citing the Ten Commandments ("Thou shalt not steal,") the judge barred any further sale of Biz Markie's album and referred the matter to the U.S. Attorney for possible criminal prosecution. Another court later ruled that sampling phrases like "ooh," "move," and "free your body," may also be enough to find copyright infringement."[18]

Publishers and record labels used the Biz Markie ruling to set up the fences for a new revenue stream called sample clearance. In order to sample legally, producers now must get permission from the owner of the sound recording (the record label) and the owner of the composition (the music publisher.) Permissions must also be obtained when sampling from TV and movies.

Attorney Korn suggests: "Artists should obtain permission from all copyright owners before any song containing a sample is distributed publicly. Waiting until after your record is distributed can result in lost income, expensive legal fees and the removal of your record from the market. Releasing your record before obtaining clearances also reduces your bargaining power if you later attempt to negotiate a sample license."

---

17 *Fair Use: The Story of the Letter U and the Numeral 2* by Negativland, book and CD, self-published on their Seeland imprint.
18 http://www.alankorn.com/articles/sampling.html

Producers usually rely on sample clearance agencies to locate and negotiate with the copyright owners. This can be expensive, but self-reliant
producers can clear samples on their own. Letters must be sent to the
record company and music publisher of the sampled song; ASCAP and
BMI are a good source of publisher addresses. Identify the song being
sampled, and length of the sample, and ask for a quote on the clearance
fee. Include a tape of the new song that uses the sample, plus the original
song.

Alan Korn writes: "A record company may seek a flat-fee of anywhere
from $100 to $5,000, or possibly more. Record companies may seek a
royalty (from $.01 to $.07 per record sold) as well as an advance. Music
publishers may also ask for a flat fee or a percentage of copyright ownership in the new composition."

"Because copyright owners are not obligated to grant clearances, you may
have no choice but to comply with the owner's asking price, or remove
the sample," continues Korn. "A copyright owner may also deny permission to use a sample. Price may vary depending on how much of the
sample is used, how many other samples are used, whether your song has
already been released, and the type of rights a record company is willing
to grant."

Sample clearance can be an expensive, painful process, and we have
Gilbert O'Sullivan to thank for it. Had case law evolved differently, perhaps sampling might be recognized as a type of news reporting, art criti-
cism, and social comment, one that is particularly important to the most
disenfranchised segments of society, namely youth and people of color.
But musicians and DJs are traditionally marginalized classes, working in a
field that is highly commercialized, competitive, and litigious. So music producers are not accorded the same freedoms of reportage and reuse that
are granted other types of teachers, reporters, scientists, or comedians.

The DJ's predicament over the commercialization of sampling is shared by society as a whole. We are promised free expression, but we have to pay for it, and copyright owners have veto power. The immediate cultural impact of the Biz Markie ruling was that dense, anything-goes sound collages became too expensive to license, and Public Enemy-style hijacked soundscapes began to thin out. Like any prohibition, sample clearance pushed unauthorized users underground, institutionalized hypocrisy, and fostered a spirit of resistance in some quarters.

Some producers clear the major recognizable samples and let slide any samples that are too small or altered to recognize. DJ/remixer Armand Van Helden articulates a pragmatic approach to sample clearance: "The way we've been clearing depends on how big the record is, that saves everybody a lot of time, effort, and money. The dance music thing is so underground nobody cares about it. It costs more to hire a lawyer to come after 2500 copies of a record; nobody would sue for that. But if your record's on radio, and it starts rotating, you better clear it."

Unlicensed sampling also continues to flourish, somewhat under the industry radar, in the realm of mix tapes. Since the popularization of the cassette recorder in the early 1970s, DJs have circulated mix tapes as resume pieces, and as parties-to-go. Passed along by hand, sold from under the counter in specialty shops, distributed through the Internet, or hawked on sidewalks, next to bootleg videos and fake Rolexes, mix tapes provide career exposure and rep-building for countless DJs.

Today a mix "tape" is usually a CD-R, but the purpose is the same. Such mixes cannot be reproduced at professional CD factories unless the cuts have been licensed, cementing the mix tape's samizdat status. Since they can only be made at home, or in pirate factories, the mix tape is always a form of contraband, evidence of an underground culture's struggle for survival.

Current hip-hop mix tapes are usually a combination of current hits and previews of unreleased tracks, with freestyling by any number of MCs. Because they involve artistry in mixing, selection, and rapping, and because they're identified with a DJ instead of a musician or band, mix tapes have become a recording genre unto themselves. A genre that's only slightly more legitimate than counterfeit CDs and bootlegs.

The music industry has mostly turned a blind eye from mix tapes over the last quarter century. While some executives may recognize that mix tapes provide exposure for artists, and a farm league for upcoming producers, the high cost and low yield of prosecuting unauthorized mixes is a more salient factor. Such laissez-faire arrangements are usually pretty tenuous in the entertainment business, and whether this one will persist is uncertain.

As dance marketing evolved came the need for "authorized" DJ mixes. Coinciding with the ascendance of the superstar DJ, licensed mix albums began to appear from all the likely suspects, including Oakenfold, Sasha, Fatboy Slim, and even celebrity party crashers like Boy George. The concept is not much different from the garden variety K-Tel compilation album, except the songs are run together and purportedly mixed by the DJ in question.

College Radio and Low Power FM

As commercial radio ossified from tightly programmed formats, DJs who wanted to choose the music migrated to community stations and campus radio. Many of these stations were established to teach the skills of broadcasting. As commercial radio became a monolith, college stations provided safe harbor for DJs who select what they play, becoming the last bastions of the "freeform" ideal.

The first wave of punk rock didn't get much airplay in the U.S.[19] But as punk evolved into the more permanent "alternative" scene, certain college DJs (and likeminded counterparts at non-commercial community stations) seized on this underserved niche market, devoting blocks of airtime to such artists. Although college stations have limited range, nearly every large community has one. They provided a platform for artists like Black Flag, DOA, X, the Replacements, Hüsker Dü, Red Hot Chili Peppers, Soundgarden, the Pixies, Jane's Addiction, REM, U2 and many others, allowing them to tour and sell records on a national basis.

Stations such as KUSF from the University of San Francisco, and U.C. Berkeley's KALX, nurtured and advocated alternative artists. DJs pushed the records and brought the artists into the studio, in a down-home way that recalled the early days of country radio.

As we saw in the freeform FM era, commercial radio began copying college playlists. Steve Masters at "Live 105" KITS in San Francisco picked up on the college sound and successfully packaged it as the Modern Rock format. Labels set up special divisions to push artists and promotional dollars into the college radio farm league. Such efforts bore fruit with Nirvana, and the legion of grunge and alternative acts that followed Nirvana into the rock mainstream. That influx of energy from the post-punk scene, fed and watered by college radio DJs over the course of a decade, partially revitalized rock from its hair-metal hangover of the early 1990s.

19 Club owner/DJ Rodney Bingenheimer was an important exception, regularly spinning punk records on Los Angeles' KROQ, and basically championing the punk rock sound and attitude.

Thanks to its successes, college radio became part of the establishment, complete with its own hierarchies and a major label marketing apparatus that services and exploits it. For some enterprising DJs that signaled the time to pull up stakes and move on, in this case to pirate radio. More correctly known as low power FM (LPFM) radio, pirate stations are a throwback to radio's earliest days, in which small groups of dedicated enthusiasts put together the transmitter, studio, and playlist, broadcasting for the edification of their neighbors.

It's called low power because the transmission signals are weak, no more than 100 watts. A ten-watt station will reach a 1-2 mile radius; a 100 watt station can cover a radius of at least 3.5 miles. By comparison, full power FM stations usually have between 6,000 to 100,000 watts of power, and broadcast over an 18-60 mile radius.

Low power FM advocates realized there are unused parts of the FM spectrum, and demanded the right to broadcast on them. The FCC fought LPFM for years, most famously against microradio pioneers Mbanna Kantako (Human Rights Radio, in Springfield, Illinois) and Stephen Dunifer (Free Radio Berkeley). The FCC simply didn't want to license and regulate thousands of tiny broadcasters, among whose number included community activists, political dissidents, religious zealots, and crackpots of every stripe.

Part of the FCC's resistance was due to pressure from corporate broadcasters, represented by the NAB and National Public Radio, who lobbied the FCC and Congress against LPFM. Big broadcasters simply didn't want the competition from do-it-yourselfers, and pushed the (baseless) arguments that LPFM would interfere with commercial broadcasts and air traffic control.

But micropower enthusiasts didn't give up, and wouldn't get off the air. The situation became ungovernable, and the FCC had to maintain some semblance of the American ideal of "the public airwaves." So in January 2000, the FCC established a LPFM licensing process. But in December 2000 Congress passed legislation (hidden in an appropriations bill) to slash the number of low power radio licenses the FCC could issue, eliminating about half of the frequencies allocated under the FCC's plan. They also introduced a measure preventing any previously unlicensed broadcasters from getting a license, blocking all the pirates who got the ball rolling from going legit. The US Court of Appeals later overturned that provision.

As things now stand, LPFM is allowed in rural areas, but licenses are denied to urban broadcasters. LPFM is non-commercial; individuals can't get licenses, they are only granted to non-profit groups. About half the current LPFM licensees are churches. Unlicensed broadcasters are subject to equipment seizure and federal charges, which is exactly what happened to Mbanna Kantako.

Kantako, who is blind, began broadcasting in 1987 from a one-watt transmitter in a housing project, reaching a radius of about eight blocks. When the feds paid a visit in 1990 Kantako responded by stepping up operations, going to round-the-clock programming. Kantako didn't qualify for a LPFM license because he had been making unlicensed broadcasts. In 2000 federal agents seized his equipment, and won an injunction barring him from the airwaves. Within a month Kantako's Human Rights Radio was back on the air with donated gear. Weeks later the feds returned, and again impounded his gear. In the spring of 2001 he returned to the air once more, and he remains defiant to this day.

Internet Streams

Full-quality audio files (such as CD tracks) are too large to transmit easily over the Internet; a three-minute song might take twenty minutes or more to download over a 56k modem. Fortunately, a technology called audio compression allows one to reduce the size of an audio file to one-tenth or one-twentieth the original size, with only a small loss in sound quality. A number of compressed audio formats came into widespread use on the Internet during the late 1990s, primarily RealAudio, MP3, and Windows Media. Able to pack a music clip down into a very small file size, they made it feasible to transmit music over the Internet.

In order to hear a song on the Internet, an audio file has to be sent from a computer somewhere (called a server) to your computer. Once the data is at your computer, it can be converted from numbers into an electrical signal and heard over speakers or headphones.

There are two main types of Internet audio: downloads and streams. A download is when a copy of the audio file is made on your computer. That downloaded copy can be retained and played at any time, even when disconnected from the Internet. Streaming does not make a new copy of the file; bits are transmitted from the server, and played on the listener's computer, one bit at a time. Once played, the streamed information is then discarded. This adds a degree of security for content owners and reduces the need for large amounts of storage space on the listener's end.

Streaming was pioneered by a company now called Real Networks; their RealAudio format was the first practical example of streaming, and continues to be widely used by businesses. Downloading audio files became prevalent thanks to the MP3 file format. MP3 is an abbreviation for MPEG-1, Level 3, part of a larger digital audio/video specification, created by an industry consortium called the Moving Picture Experts Group.

When the first portable MP3 players came onto the market, the Recording Industry Association of America (RIAA) tried to block their sale in the U.S. The RIAA, a trade group that represents record labels, filed a lawsuit against the device's manufacturer, claiming they were music copying devices. The U.S. Ninth Circuit Court of Appeals disagreed with the record industry, ruling in *RIAA v. Diamond Multimedia Systems, Inc.* that the Rio player in question was a computer peripheral, not a digital audio recorder. The decision opened the floodgates for portable music players.

MP3 became a household word thanks to two online music services, MP3.com and Napster. MP3.com was a self-publishing site where any band or musician could hang a Web page, posting their music for all to hear. Listeners could become "DJs," compiling and posting playlists of their favorite MP3.com artists. MP3.com became the de facto record label and online showcase for thousands of independent bands. They had a wildly successful Initial Public Offering, in which their stock shot up more than 270 percent in the first day of trading. But MP3.com got into trouble by launching an album listening service that featured major label releases. The ensuing lawsuit crushed the company's stock to a fraction of its IPO price, and MP3.com was acquired and slowly bastardized by litigant Vivendi/Universal.

As MP3.com was hitting the rocks, along came Napster. While peer-to-peer file sharing has been around since computer networking began and is built into the Mac and Windows operating systems, it never made headlines until Napster. Napster made it easy for millions of music lovers to share their MP3 files and find new music. Free, fun, and full of great music, Napster became the fastest-adopted product of all time. Unfortunately it was also considered illegal, and the RIAA won an injunction in the Ninth Circuit Court that resulted in Napster shutting down their service.

By this time the RIAA was fighting to control sound recordings on several Internet fronts. In addition to all of the downloading, unauthorized streaming began cropping up everywhere. Free software, such as the Nullsoft Shoutcast plug-in for Winamp, makes it possible for anybody to set up an Internet radio station on one's own computer in minutes. Online services such as Live365 allow DJs to upload audio files and playlists to a server, so that the stream can originate from a reliable, high-bandwidth computer (as opposed to your home PC). By the end of the 1990s hundreds of businesses, and thousands of individuals, were broadcasting music over the Internet.

For DJs, the advantages of Webcasting are manifold. After the computer and Internet hookup, the start-up costs are practically nil. One can play anything, with no club owner, music director, or FCC to interfere. Playlists, including prerecorded announcements and mixes, can be programmed in advance and run continuously, unassisted. And Webcasting can reach listeners anywhere in the world.

One of the biggest Webcasters was Mark Cuban. Cuban set up a streaming service called Broadcast.com, which attracted a number of commercial Webcasters, including some "terrestrial" broadcast radio stations. Although it never turned a profit, Cuban sold Broadcast.com to search portal Yahoo in 1999 for more than five billion dollars (that's billion with a "B"). At the time, there was no royalty structure for Internet music. Record labels were demanding payments for music streams (and downloads), Webcasters were resistant, and the government hadn't sorted things out.

After its purchase of Broadcast.com (and video service Launch.com), Yahoo began negotiating with the RIAA to establish a license fee for the music played in their streams. Both parties knew the Copyright Office had been directed by Congress to set up a licensing structure based on "fair market value," and were conscious that their negotiation might establish the benchmark for license fees. Cuban later told reporters that Yahoo accepted an artificially high license fee for competitive reasons; they wanted to price smaller competitors out of the Webcasting business.

When the Copyright Office finally issued its royalty arbitration ruling in the summer of 2002, it used the Yahoo/RIAA deal as the criteria for fair market value. Yahoo's gambit had the desired effect. Faced with paying seven one-hundredths of a cent, per song, per listener, most Webcasters shut down immediately. In addition, most radio broadcasters, including the Clear Channel network, quickly unplugged their streams. Congress stepped in a few months later and ordered reduced rate schedules for educational, non-profit, and small commercial Webcasters. Small commercial Webcasters must pay ten percent of gross revenues, or seven percent of expenses, whichever is more.

As a result of all these negotiations and rulings, it's now finally legal to DJ on the Internet as long as you've remitted the license fees. While the RIAA was lobbying and negotiating over Webcasting, they also founded their own ASCAP-style performing rights organization, called SoundExchange. SoundExchange administers Webcasting royalties.

You gotta hand it to the RIAA, they established a performance right for sound recordings, which the record industry had failed to do fifty years earlier. They convinced the government to create the equivalent of a private Internet tax. And they got their subsidiary appointed as the exclusive tax collector and disburser. Top RIAA executives draw more than a million dollars per year in salary from this "non-profit" organization.

Occupation: Turntablist

GrandWizzard Theodore and Grandmaster Flash paved the way for turntablism, by proving the notion that you can do anything with a turntable. They showed that records do not always have to spin forward, or at the correct speed. Scratching and cutting were revolutionary inventions, which cemented the turntable's new role as a musical instrument.

The turntablist movement may represent the most evolved expression of DJing as an art form. Turntablism recontextualizes DJing into a concert performance, or performance art.

Over time the hip-hop spotlight moved away from DJs, and came to focus on MCs and producers. Naturally many of the top producers were former DJs themselves. But in the MTV-driven rap mainstream, hip-hop turntable techniques gave way to slick, R&B-flavored productions, karaoke-style pop retreads, and conspicuous displays of aggression, sexism and materialism.

Although the DJ continued to be an onstage centerpiece, the need for predictable, repeatable performances became an imperative as hip-hop commercialized. Many highly skilled DJs would simply play their studio recordings, then wave their hands in the air, limiting their real displays to occasional scratch solos. When digital audio tape (DAT) became available, it was no longer necessary to even play the record.

The turntable culture risks becoming codified and diluted, as it migrates from the hip-hop and dance music undergrounds into the pop mainstream. Jazz groups, funk bands, hard rock groups, and folk acts have all added DJs to their lineups. Today the turntable is, in many ways, just another instrument with its attendant groups of practitioners, prodigies, and enthusiasts. Its cross-genre use has become a cliché, as pedestrian bands try to acquire street credibility and post-modern appeal by importing some scratching. When turntable players start appearing in tuxedos with symphony orchestras, their underground roots are effectively severed.

Through it all a growing arsenal of new techniques evolved. Some came out of mainstream hip-hop; the transformer was popularized by DJ Jazzy Jeff, of Fresh Prince fame. Other moves, like the crab scratch, grew straight from this new "turntablist" scene. X-Men founder Steve Dee is believed to have invented beat juggling, manually alternating between individual kick and snare sounds to create original drum patterns.

The natural result of any scene's colonization and dilution is that certain cadres will go hardcore. This happened for the turntable in the early 1990s when groups of DJs began to form their own crews, sans MCs, such as the Invisibl Skratch Piklz, Bulletproof Scratch Hamsters, Beat Junkies, and the X-Men (later the X-Ecutioners). Although DJs had collaborated and battled on the same sound systems for years, the turntable crews took an expanded "band" approach, in which many sets of hands and turntables could build a mix.

DJ Apollo is credited with conceiving the DJ "band". Apollo and fellow Invisibl Skratch Picklz MixMaster Mike and QBert introduced the band style at the DMC/Technics World DJ Competition in 1992, and took top honors. The Skratch Picklz returned the next year, and won the DMC crown again. [20]

The Invisibl Skratch Picklz released a great, goofy series of mix tapes, and established a fun vibe that was an updated throwback to hip-hop's original party atmosphere. Mix Master Mike went on to DJ for the Beastie Boys (and others) while DJ QBert went solo and became a superstar.

---

20 **DMC stands for Disco Mix Club, the British concern that promoted the events; they got Technics onboard as sponsor.**

QBert released the first all-scratch concept album, a cartoony sci-fi opus called *Wave Twisters*. He followed with an even more ambitious move, producing an animated feature film to accompany the CD. The *Wave Twisters* movie visually reattaches hip-hop's graffiti practice to 21st century turntablism. A turntable *Fantasia*, it is the first film to put images to the service of scratching; animators created on-screen actions to represent every sound bite on the album. Although critically acclaimed, heralded as another *Yellow Submarine*, theatrical screenings were few. Fortunately this landmark work is available on DVD.

Faced with the problematic nature of licensing samples and seeking purer musical expression, QBert has moved to creating his own grooves and scratch sources. Using drum machines and synthesizers, he records his tracks to a record cutter, then uses them as turntable tools.

While other turntablists, and members of such crews as the X-Ecutioners, the Scratch Perverts, and the Beat Junkies, to name just a few, are argu-ably just as skilled, exciting, and noteworthy, QBert remains the leading exponent of turntabilism. The heat of QBert's celebrity, his credibility, and his youth appeal led to endorsements and national TV ads for the Gap and Apple Computers.

Cognizant of the business missteps of his precursors, QBert opted to stay independent instead of signing with a major label and management firm. With his business partner Yogafrog, QBert finances and releases his work on his own, retaining considerable artistic and fiscal control. He makes a good model for the self-reliant, independent, yet worldwide media entre-preneur, and may be the best template for the DJs of tomorrow.[21]

21 An exclusive interview with DJ QBert precedes this chapter.

Remixing, Producing, and Other Post-DJ Career Moves

When DJs release records under their own names, they become recording artists. When DJs make records for other people, they become producers. Remixing is a subset of production, the practice of remaking records into more dance-friendly versions.

As mentioned earlier in this chapter, the first DJs to segue into production and remixing were the Jamaican godfathers including Coxsone Dodd, Duke Reid, and Prince Buster. As disco became commercialized in the 1970s, record labels began placing more emphasis on getting club play, and started the trend of recrafting records with DJs in mind. To facilitate this, the logical people to hire are DJs, the experts on how things should sound in nightclubs.

Remixing encompasses a variety of studio practices. Some remixes are based entirely on the original multi-track recording; the remixer may simply adjust the volume levels and effects settings. Other remixes may eliminate instrumental or vocal parts, or add new parts. More aggressive remixes change the tempo of the song; that may require time-shifting trickery, or wholesale replacement of the original tracks with new performances. Expanding sections, changing the verse/chorus structure, adding new hooks, reducing the vocals to mere embellishments, all are tools of the remixer's trade.

Some remixes retain the general core and essence of the original recording. Others are almost completely unrelated to their sources and may contain only a fractional vocal line or tiny instrumental sound from the prior work. In any event, the practice of remixing is distinguished from garden variety record production and recording engineering only by the outside origins of the source material. The studio technologies and production techniques are mostly identical.

The person most associated with remixing is Tom Moulton. An accomplished mixer and mastering engineer, Moulton pioneered remixing, adding percussion breaks and instrument drop-outs to extend and reshape records. In 1974 Moulton remixed Gloria Gaynor's first album, *Never Can Say Goodbye*, extending all the songs and segueing the A-side together in a continuous mix.

Considered the top disco mixer circa 1974-77, and still active today, Moulton established the practice of doing long twelve-inch club mixes along with the shorter seven-inch radio versions. A former record promoter and male model, Moulton got exposed to the disco scene at Fire Island, a retreat for gay New Yorkers. Inspired by the milieu, and frustrated that the songs were so short, Moulton started to make mix tapes, initially for the Sandpiper club.

As he transitioned into producing for vinyl, Moulton stumbled across the twelve-inch format. Moulton went to mastering engineer José Rodriguez for some acetates (test pressings) but Rodriguez was out of seven-inch blanks. Undeterred, they opted to cut the song to a ten-inch acetate.

Moulton later recalled: "I said 'It looks so ridiculous, this little tiny band on this huge thing. What happens if we just…make it bigger?' (Rodriguez said) 'You mean, spread the grooves? Then I've got to raise the level.' So he cut it at +6dB. When I heard it I almost died. It was so much louder. For the next song we cut, we went for the twelve-inch format instead of the ten-inch, and the song was "So Much For Love" by Moment of Truth. That was the birth of the twelve-inch single."[22]

---

22 Interview with "Discoguy" at http://www.disco-disco.com/tributes/tom.html

"Because 45s were geared for radio," Moulton said in an interview with journalist Brian Chin, "they were all 'middle,' and you couldn't cut a lot of [bass] onto the record." The twelve-inch format made it possible to saturate the disc master with bass. Widely separated grooves could be cut deeper and transmit more bass and volume without inducing skipping, compared to microgroove LPs and seven-inch 45s.

Initially Moulton just handed out his twelve-inchers to favored DJs as a test-marketing tool. The first "official" promotional twelve-inch single was Southshore Commission's "Free Man." The first commercially-released twelve-inch was "Ten Percent" by Double Exposure. A prodigious worker, Moulton claims to have mixed more than four thousand songs during his career, and he hasn't stopped yet. "Disco Inferno" by the Trammps is one of his best-known efforts. Later remixers, including Francois Kevorkian, Larry Levan, and Armand Van Helden all followed in Moulton's footsteps.

Like remixing, the job classification of record production also encompasses a range of activities. Some producers just put their name on a record and cash the check. Others are glorified art directors, making high-level creative decisions while leaving the dirty work to subordinates. Some are wet-nurses to fussy recording artists, others are themselves the central artist on the project. Hands-on record producers have recording engineering skills, and can place mics, push buttons, and craft sounds with little or no outside assistance.

Just as cheap synthesizer and recording technologies made house music and the resultant electronic dance scenes possible, they also democratized record production in general, allowing a whole generation of prospective producers and artists to gain experience and express their ideas. Technology furthered the idea of record producer as auteur, something that originated with Phil Spector, but wasn't really feasible for most until the advent of digital recording.

Cheap digital recording resulted in a flowering of talent and a torrent of releases from across the musical spectrum. But it didn't change the fundamental nature of the mainstream record business, which continued its march towards consolidation and homogeneity. The action was, as usual, mostly on tiny independent record labels that cater to niche markets. As ever, indies serve as a testing ground for the major labels, which snap up and exploit any successes that may arise.

It's a very short stretch from remixer to record producer to recording artist; as mentioned earlier Fatboy Slim is one high profile example of that progression. DJ Shadow is another great example of the DJ as turntable auteur, crafting a moody, sophisticated brand of art music that owes as much to progressive rock, and symphonic recordings, as to the hip-hop old school. Shadow even tours with a "video jockey" who combines live camera shots with prerecorded video, providing a visual counterpoint to the turntable and sampler performance.

Mash-Ups

At the other end of the scale, far removed from the flash and commerce of superstar artist/DJs, are the sonic pirates of the mash-up underground. Mash-ups, also sometimes called cut-ups, bootlegs, or pirate remixes, are simply unauthorized remixes. A computer-bred corollary to DJ mix tapes, the mash-up has become practically a genre unto itself, characterized by radical juxtapositions of extremely dissimilar material. Mash-up producers are re-imagining popular music in surprising, ironic, and frequently comical ways.

Using audio software, particularly loop sequencers, one can easily combine snippets from practically any recording. Some of the best mash-ups present impossible yet compelling team-ups like Nine Inch Nails versus the Spice Girls ("Closer to Spice"), Destiny's Child versus Nirvana ("Smells Like Bootylicious"), or Christina Aguilera versus the Strokes ("A Stroke of Genie-us").

Eminem has found his way into a lot of recent mash-ups, as has Missy Elliot. Some of the most popular examples graft a hip-hop or dance vocal onto a hard rock riff, a strategy that touches back to the Rick Rubin/ Run-DMC formula. Mash-up methods include layering an a cappella vocal part over a different instrumental backing, as in "A Stroke of Genie-us," pumping up and augmenting a classic recording (see Elvis Presley vs. JXL, "A Little Less Conversation"), or simply cutting from one song to another, like on "Closer to Spice."

Although computers and samplers are the primary tools, mash-ups are clearly descended from DJ practices. Like all DJs, unauthorized remixers are part of an artistic and literary tradition of appropriation and juxta- position, whose exponents have included Marcel Duchamp, Andy Warhol, and William S. Burroughs.

One could argue that mash-ups are parody and critical comment or they should be permitted under the doctrine of Fair Use. But as we've found, music is a highly commercialized and litigious arena. Copyright owners can dun, or bar, any derivative work. Unlicensed remixes are considered a form of music piracy, or counterfeiting, and cannot be legitimately made available for sale. Like mix tapes, they cannot be pressed at com- mercial CD plants. Mash-ups are usually distributed as MP3 files over the Internet, or passed along hand-to-hand on home-burned CDs.

The mash-up trend was facilitated by Napster, and subsequent peer-to- peer (P2P) file sharing networks such as Kazaa. These massive file trading services attracting millions of simultaneous users, provide exactly the type of uncontrolled marketplace required for samizdat art forms like mash-ups and mix tapes.

Some pundits have suggested that mash-ups are the only new, exciting thing in an otherwise predictable, regressive music scene. They're made possible by cutting-edge technology. They're distinctly post-modern. The best mash-ups operate successfully on both sarcastic and sincere levels. Typically built from familiar hit songs, they're ultra-consumable. Evidence of a cultural crime, mash-ups have rebel appeal, a fresh sense of excitement and danger.

The most noteworthy mash-up artist is a British DJ called The Freelance Hellraiser. We have an exclusive interview with him later in this book. As he mentions, he wants to attract authorized, for-hire remix work. While he got worldwide notice for his Aguilera/Strokes remix, there was no money in it. For The Freelance Hellraiser, mash-ups are a stepping-stone for his club mixing and remixing careers.

That line of thinking probably traces the curve for the mash-up underground at large. Some, like elder statesmen John Oswald of "Plunderphonics" fame, or his associates in Negativland, will try to keep it real, staying semi-underground and pursuing sonic piracy for its own artistic rewards. Other mash-up hit-makers may quickly "graduate" to authorized remixing, trading cadre credibility for cold cash. For many entrants, mash-ups are a form of self-education, learning to mix and produce using the most readily available materials.

This concludes our look at Occupation DJ. We're not too far from where we began. The DJs who work at the cutting-edges of culture and technology typically do so without direct economic incentive, lack the sanction of the larger music industry, and take on a certain amount of personal risk. Eventually the legal, legislative, and business institutions will assimilate the Internet, mash-ups, mix tapes, and whatever comes next. Much as they caught up with records, radio, rock 'n roll, and hip-hop. It just takes a long time, and can be painful and costly for certain participants. In the meantime, these frontiers are to be explored and enjoyed.

Van Helden

Armand Van Helden started out as a DJ, became an in-demand remixer, and is now a critically acclaimed recording artist.

What kind of gear do you use?

On the DJ front I still like Technics, and I use a Pioneer mixer, and that's about it. I'm not really heavy on the CDs yet. I'm basically like the standard DJ, two 1200s and a mixer.

On the production side nowadays you don't need much. I have a Mac laptop and Pro Tools 001 audio interface. Plus a Mackie board and Genelec monitors. The rest is plug-ins and a turntable in the studio that I sample off. I have a lot of plug-ins, a whole bunch, some I use and some I don't. The Waves stuff is cool, and these little pedal things like Mooger Fooger. Amplitube is my favorite.

I really don't use sound libraries, I get my sounds mainly from vinyl. Although I have a Roland 5080 sound module and I use it for drums. I'll use it for hats and some percussion. That's about it.

Do you still use commercial recording studios, or is it all at home?

I do everything at home, everything from day one. I've never mixed in a pro studio. I just didn't understand why I had to. I've come to find out that nowadays barely anybody's doing their own stuff, everybody's got like this person behind them. Or they got engineers, or musicians, they're more like directors. I never knew that.

I come from the Todd Terry school, where it's like from dirt to record. That's all you, it's one person, nobody else. That's still how I am. From nothing to something, 'till it ends up on vinyl, that's all me, there's nobody else's hands in the mix. Sometimes I do collaborations, that's a different story, you're in the studio working with somebody else. But if it's like a regular thing that I'm doing, it's just me, the whole way.

What advice do you have for people who are coming up?

If you take a kid off the street and give him two turntables and a mixer, obviously he's going to have to do his homework for a long time. He's had to perfect his own skills. You have to sit at home and apply the effort to make your mixes tight. If you're a cut DJ you got to get your cut skills up. You got to do that on your own. If you can mix and you're pretty good, then it's a selection thing. Your material, what do you like to play? Do you like to play a strict style, one type of style all night, or do you like to mix it up, various stuff, all over the place? You have to define who you are.

My first gig was when I was 14, it was a high school dance. There was only one other DJ at the school, he was a senior. He was more in the rock vein. Which was cool, but he wasn't up on Prince and hip-hop and stuff like that. He wasn't picking up on Janet Jackson or whatever. He couldn't do that party, so they hired me. Word gets around in the neighborhood if you're a DJ (laughs).

My first gig I just showed 'em what I could do. I played more towards the break dancers and more towards the cultured crowd. I won 'em over more. The rock stuff was cool, but like, dancing to stuff like "Girls Just Wanna Have Fun"? It's cool but back in those days people wanted another sound.

I came with something different. My advice is: If you got competition, come with something different. Don't copy. Separate yourself from the competition. You're going to specialize your crowd and that way people will just come for you. In due time you'll eliminate your competition.

Who influenced you when you were coming up?

There was a time where I got into the whole cut and scratch competition thing. I was looking at Jazzy Jeff, he pretty much invented the transform. I was looking at Grandmaster Flash. DST is another one. When I was cutting and scratching, back in those days, that was big.

After that it would be Cash Money. This was like when the DMC started, the DJ competition. When I watched one of those shows once, in like '86 or '87 and I was like "oh man, I thought I could scratch." I was like the best in my area, but I saw the video of Jazzy Jeff and he was transforming, I lost my mind. I was like "oh my god" (laughs). Back in those days that was who I looked up to.

After that, when I started to get more into dance music, I was into Disciple, Louie Vega, Roger S., Kenny Dope, Todd Terry, pretty much like the early heads who were in New York. I wouldn't say I was trying to copy them or be like them. I was more into their music than into their DJ sets. I was definitely more into checking their production than going out to hear them spin.

You're talking to somebody who's been DJing since 1984, that's a long time ago. I've had times in my life where I was just into one particular type of music, but it was very short-lived. There was always like one or two types of music I'd be into. I was always into hip-hop. When I first got into house I became really into house. I still liked hip-hop but I just didn't keep up with the records. That was my only time I just played house. It was maybe a year.

But the rest of my life I been playing – I mean if I throw a party at my house – that's how I like to play (with variety). I play anything. And it ain't about mixing. 'Cause that's redundant. I don't care about mixing no more.

How did you acquire DJ skills, and how would you suggest a beginner approach it?

I taught myself, I didn't have anybody around to teach me. I would listen. I would get tapes from people like Mister Magic's radio show, Chuck Chillout, I'd listen to what they were doing. And then I would try it at home. You imitate, but you imitate in your basement. For you to come up you gotta start somewhere, so have to start with some type of imitation, you know what I mean?

You have to figure out what the formats are. If you're going to be a hip-hop DJ you have to learn how to scratch. More important for the hip-hop DJ is to know when to drop the next record. It's all about drops.

In house, it's all about selection. In house it's a given that you can mix. If you book (a job as) a dance DJ and you can't mix, you're definitely not going to get another job.

The hip-hop DJs, it's not that important about the mixing, but with dance music, hell yeah it is. Out the gate you just have to define what area you want to go in, be it hip-hop or dance. From there, well, dance you gotta mix, hip-hop you gotta know when to drop, when to do a little cut and scratch. You just gotta define those two, that's it.

How do you build a DJ career?

It's a simple process to get known as a DJ. There's only two ways:

Armand Van Helden. Photo by Julia Wollenhaupt.

The first way is to do the long way. The long way is to go out, start getting a local reputation amongst your peers, then your peers spread the word to their peers, and then it kind of spreads that way. It builds and years and years go by and you're still a DJ. Maybe you started doing house parties and then maybe you're even doing weddings and eventually maybe you end up in a club. Then it starts small there and you build it up in the club. Slowly through all this time you start building a following.

Then maybe you meet a good promoter and you become partners with him. Or maybe you become a promoter yourself, promote yourself as a DJ, and your night, and you pump it like that. Start throwing flyers out there and all. That type of build. And then eventually (laughs) it's a long process, but everything's a step.

After you start getting a name in New York, everybody's like "oh, you know DJ so-and-so in New York" you got this New York thing happening. And all of sudden you got New York locked. It's like New York is your town. Well guess what, then you gotta move forward from there, and you got to go international. It's a long process.

The way to shortcut all that is make music. Be a DJ, keep your DJ skills, but make music. You cut all of that out. You don't have to go local. You don't have to start from anywhere. Once you make a hot record, maybe it ends up number one in Germany or U.K. or somewhere overseas – not in America – because dance music records don't go number one in America. From there, once they find out you're a DJ, they're going to book you all over the world.

One of the main tips you gotta know is where to get exposed and what's the process. To me, through my research and history, you got nothing until you got a record in the U.K. That's for the world. That's in dance music, now in hip-hop it's a whole 'nother story. But in dance music you don't exist unless the U.K. is writing about you. It's like that right now, it could change. But that is the game, you have to play the game that the U.K. makes.

How did you get started as a remixer?

It came along with the production stuff. I had a manager back then, he had a remix service, and he was in touch with the major labels. When I got into remixing, remixing was hot. The majors would hire like Masters At Work or Todd Terry to do a remix, and Masters At Work wouldn't even take anything from the song. They'd just put their own track and it'd be out on Atlantic Records, or MCA. One of their tracks on a major label and all they might do is add like one word, like "huh," from the original record. It was a special time (laughs).

The labels didn't care, 'cause they just needed the spins. When they found out all the underground DJs would play Todd Terry or Masters At Work remixes, but it sounded nothing like the original record, they didn't care because they were getting their spins. It was counting in *Billboard*. And they were getting their chart position. That's all they wanted remixes for anyway.

That's when I came into the game. And I came in the same way. It didn't matter what the name was. They'd send me the parts, I'd grab like three little tiny one-second pieces off the vocal and make a track out of it. My own track.

Other people, like Frankie Knuckles, would complement the remix, try and work with it as much as possible. I was in the opposite vein; it was like a ghetto tactic. But it worked in the beginning for me, because I was giving the streets what the streets wanted. In other words everyone else was giving them the fluffy major label remix, I was giving 'em straight street records, on a major label. It was an aggressive tactic but it worked.

Are you still taking on remixes?

Yeah, here and there. I took two at the end of the year. Somebody on Fatboy Slim's label, the song is called "Crazy Talk," I don't remember the artist. The other track I think is called "Behind," somebody out of France. I can't remember (laughs). Once the record's out I'll remember.

Do you get credit as a songwriter and royalties on these remixes?

No, flat rate. I like flat rate. I've done remixes that sold big-time, but I've always done flat rate. The way I look at it, if I do a remix and it blows up and I did it for whatever amount of money and it's flat, doesn't matter. I'm going to get plenty of work from that large mix after the fact. It more than makes up for the royalties I'm going to have to go out and collect on that record, know what I mean? It all works out at the end of the day.

You've found some amazing breaks; we particularly like the Gary Numan loop on "Kootchie." What attracts you to a track or loop, what do you seek when choosing sounds?

It's more felt than thought. I've been in studios and watched other producers get a track going. How I work is not how most people work. I just don't really think. I just do what I feel, if it sounds cool to me at that minute, then it sounds cool to me. It might not sound cool to me the next minute, but I usually don't change it. When I'm making something, whatever that first thing is that I'm kind of like "oh that's kind of cool, do that" I just follow through with it and finish that. If I don't like it later I won't put it out. But I usually don't go back and change.

You don't search out specific things, you more bump into sounds?

Yes I bump into sounds, that's exactly right. They're all accidental. The loop in "Kootchie," the Gary Numan, I have a huge vinyl collection. When I'm into the studio to maybe make some new songs I grab a new stack of vinyl. I go through and find little things and put them into the computer. They're all just thrown in. From there I figure out what I like and what I don't like.

Have you ever been sued over a recording, or had legal issues over a loop?

No, I've cleared all my samples that were right out there. Now I'm not going to say I haven't let some slip, but I haven't been caught. To me it's like you can sample a piece of a record and manipulate it so much that, like, why are you going to clear it? It doesn't even sound like it was. A lot of my heads are music collectors as well. If they don't know what it is, most average people don't know what it is, that's it.

In dance music it's not a big deal at all anyway, because most of it's underground. But if your record starts blowing up, and you have a pretty obvious loop in it or vocal, you better clear it. Chances are they will find you.

The way we've been clearing depends on how big the record is, that way saves everybody a lot of time, effort, and money. The dance music thing is so underground nobody cares about it. It costs them more to hire a lawyer, to come after 2500 copies of a record, it's a joke, nobody would sue for that. But if your record's on radio and it starts rotating, gets this hype, maybe a major label behind it in the U.K., you better clear it. Because you never know what's going to come around (laughs).

What's your goal with DJing, what are you trying to achieve?

Somebody just asked me that the other day. I haven't had a goal in a long, long time. I kind of enjoy what I do. I look at what I do like fishing. In the beginning I had a goal, my goal was to get like a rod and a boat. But after that, there's no more goals, you're just fishing. My goals was like way, way back. For me I just fish. Maybe I catch one, maybe I don't. That's how it is.

You've been called the father of speed garage. What is the meaning of speed garage?

I don't know, I didn't make the name. I can tell you what it's supposed to mean is basically drum and bass and house. Jungle and house. Whatever you want to call it. In any way, shape, or form. I'd been listening to drum and bass for a long time. Since pretty much the beginning. So the marriage to me was something that I did because I just didn't know how to get respect doing drum and bass.

I knew for a fact that no Americans were going to get any love doing drum and bass. This was 1994, '95. I'm not going to attempt it, I'm not even going to try and mess with them because they got their scene, it's locked, they don't like newcomers, especially Americans.

So I was just take their bass lines, take their sounds and put it over house beats, and that was it. It wasn't anything more than that. In terms of what happened after all that, the repercussions, it was the invention of speed garage, but don't ask me anything else about that. To me it was just an idea that got formulated because I really didn't have an option.

You've covered a lot of ground stylistically. Is there any relevance to sub-genre distinctions within dance music, aside from their marketing usefulness?

The only thing that's relevant is tempo. That's it. I don't like to split anything, to me dance music is dance music. When you're talking about 185 BPMs or you're talking about 125 BPMs, well yes there's a difference. It's not like you can mix those two. So that's about the only breakup, dance music's only broken up by tempo. Now when people go Progressive-this or Tribal-that or Deep-this or Vocal-this, I don't care about all that. That means nothing to me.

It's more like, okay, is it drum and bass or jungle? Then obviously it's going to be 165 BPM plus. Techno might go up to 145. Or you got like the old hardcore scene, whatever, faster than jungle. Chill out might be at a hundred BPMs. The breakups to me are in the tempo, that's it. It's all by tempo.

You've been outspoken against meaningless or superficial music. Do you think the industry finds it easier to sell faceless, shallow music?

(Laughs) Isn't that the music industry itself? That's everything, as a whole. I've never seen anything like the music industry as of late. And then again I haven't even lived much. I know, 'cause I'm a record collector, I know what the past was. All I have to do is look at the records, and look at the artists. And the pictures on the record to know that whatever was then is definitely not now.

Right now, on a large level, I don't even think I can find an artist over 35. Back in those days that was like one out of two people. People had age, they had a lot to say. They had a lot of experience in their lyrics that they could put into their music because they had the age and the wisdom to do it. That's why all of the stuff, regardless of dance music, right now is all disposable. The demographics and the way marketing departments work, when you come in to get a record deal and they go "you're forty years old."

And you go "yeah, well how's my music?"

They go "we don't care. You're forty years old." (Laughs) Know what I mean?

Do you think MTV caused that?

Absolutely. I'd say it is the number one culprit, and radio just follows along. To me it's just an age thing. It all has to do with age.

The only thing that is cool about dance music is it's ageless. Dance music you can be sixteen, you can be sixty-six. Obviously there's people that are real old in the game. And it's open, and it's welcome. That's one of the best plus sides about dance music.

But a lot of music in that scene isn't saying anything. There's no content, there's nothing classic about it. It's not Fleetwood Mac, it's not Led Zeppelin or the Beatles. There's nothing in it. It's not even close to anything, it's just faceless.

Chapter 5

DJ Mixers
and Effects

The turntable by itself doesn't make much sound. The electrical signals emitting from the phonograph cartridge are very weak. They must be amplified, and converted to sound waves, in order to be heard.

The simplest setup might be a turntable, an amplifier, and speakers. In order to mix or layer sounds from two separate turntables, a mixer is required. One may want to shape or change those sounds to various degrees, a practice known as signal processing or "effects." We'll investigate all of these areas in the course of this chapter.

Although there are many other texts about signal processing, amplifiers, and mixers, this is the first reference book to really document the DJ or "battle" mixer. This chapter provides information your mixer's owner's manual left out. Nonetheless, be sure to refer to any documentation that accompanied your mixer, because all mixers are slightly different.

Amplifiers and Speakers

An amplifier increases the amount of energy in an audio signal. Amplifiers once required vacuum tubes such as Lee de Forest's Audion, discussed in Chapter 4. Today many amplifiers use transistors instead of tubes, guitar amplifiers being a notable exception. There are two basic types of amplifiers, voltage amplifiers and power amplifiers. Voltage amplifiers increase the voltage of a signal; power amplifiers increase the wattage or amplitude of a signal.

DJs encounter a number of amplifier circuits, some of them hidden in other gear. Amplifiers called pre-amps are built into the mic and phono input stages of DJ mixers to boost the weak voltages produced by microphones and turntable cartridges. Voltage controlled amplifiers (VCAs) are another type of amplifier circuit, which are used to control volume levels within mixers. Larger power amps are used to drive speakers and house PA systems.

Speakers are transducers that convert voltage fluctuations into movement; in this case the movement of a magnet connected to a speaker cone. Headphones are similar in principle to speakers, they just sit closer to your ears. We discussed transducers back in Chapter 2.

DJs need to manage multiple input sources. Home hi-fi amplifiers have a switch that selects between phonograph, radio, cassette, and so forth. DJs also want to layer and combine sound sources, to hear two or more signals simultaneously. That requires a piece of equipment called a mixer.

The Mixer

The mixer combines the sounds from two or more sources into one audio signal. In addition to combining the signals, mixers can adjust the relative strength or volume level of each signal. Volume level is usually controlled with a slider, called a channel fader.

Audio engineers use the term "gain" when talking about the strength of an audio signal. Gain is measured in decibels (dB), the same scale used to measure loudness or sound pressure level.

There are many different types of mixers, from the most rudimentary, no-knob models to gigantic recording consoles. While DJs will surely encounter PA mixing boards and mixers in recording studios, for the sake of brevity we're going to focus on DJ mixers.[1] Sometimes called a "battle" mixer, the DJ mixer is essentially a two-channel mixer, which combines two stereo sound sources. The most characteristic feature of a DJ mixer is the crossfader, which adjusts the relative volume of both sources with a single touch.[2]

Professional DJ mixers all support stereo (two-channel) audio; each sound source actually consists of two separate signals, left and right. For convenience, each stereo pair is controlled by a single set of knobs and faders in a DJ mixer.

Most modern mixers include pre-amplifiers on each channel, which can boost the voltage level of weak input signals before they are mixed. As mentioned above, microphones and turntables put out low-voltage signals that require pre-amplification. Most DJ mixers also have line level inputs, which can accept higher-voltage signals from a CD player or tape deck.

1 The workings of club and pro studio mixers are thoroughly documented elsewhere. William Philbrick's *What's A Mixer* (2001, Hal Leonard) is a good starting point. We also recommend Duncan Fry's *Live Sound Mixing* (1997, Roztralia Productions) and *Practical Recording Techniques* by Bruce and Jenny Bartlett (1992, SAMS).
2 Although there are four-channel boards, and other configurations, the two-channel battle mixer is most common, and contains all the same concepts found in larger DJ mixers.

There is a vast range of prices and feature sets among DJ mixers. We've seen low-end models selling new for as little as $30; the most glorified DJ mixers may cost as much as $1500. To help document this chapter, manufacturers kindly sent over three excellent mixers:

- American Audio Q-D5, "DJ Skilz Signature Series," suggested retail price $369, street price around $300.
- Korg KM-2 Kaoss Mixer, suggested retail price $750, street price around $350.
- Stanton SA-8, "DJ Focus Signature Mixer," suggested retail price $799, street price around $500.

"Street" prices listed here are actually "Minimum Advertised Price." Retailers are free to discount much lower. Now let's talk about the characteristics that these devices all have in common; practically all DJ mixers include the following components:

Rear Panel

AC Power Input – All of the DJ mixers we looked at have a removable cord or power supply. The American Audio Q-D5 uses a standard interchangeable power cord; its transformer is inside the mixer. The Korg Kaoss Mixer and Stanton SA-8, on the other hand, use special external power supplies, placing the transformer outside the mixer chassis. These mixers have a five-pin AC input jack that looks very much like a MIDI socket. If you have this type of power supply, don't ever plug it into a MIDI jack, you could fry the MIDI gear.

Power Switch – Often, but not always, located on the rear panel of the mixer. It powers the mixer on and off.

Inputs and Outputs – The rear panel of a mixer can be confusing to anybody. All DJ mixers accept two or more sets of stereo input signals (from turntables, etc.) and have at least one set of "Master" or "Mix" stereo outputs.

Balanced vs. Unbalanced – Balanced audio lines have three wires, and permit longer cable runs with less risk of noise and interference. Unbalanced audio lines have two wires, are used for short cable runs, and are prone to picking up noise from nearby equipment. Balanced inputs and outputs are a standard in professional audio equipment, whereas unbalanced inputs/outputs are commonly found in semi-professional gear. Most DJ mixers provide only unbalanced inputs and outputs.

The Stanton SA-8 mixer. Photo: Linda Monson

Stanton SA-8 rear panel; note the quarter-inch tip-ring-sleeve (TRS) jacks, which are balanced connectors. Photo: Linda Monson

Balanced inputs and outputs usually accept an XLR (or "Canon") plug, which looks like a microphone cable, or tip-ring-sleeve (TRS) connectors that look like a stereo headphone jack. Unbalanced inputs and outputs typically use quarter-inch jacks (just like a guitar cable) or RCA connectors (typical stereo cables).

Besides the differences in connectors, balanced and unbalanced lines carry different voltage levels. Unbalanced, "semi-pro" gear works at a nominal signal level of −10 dBV, the typical consumer line level, whereas balanced lines carry a stronger signal, referenced to +4 dBu.[3] This is only a consideration if your gear supports both balanced and unbalanced; in such cases be sure to not mismatch such devices.

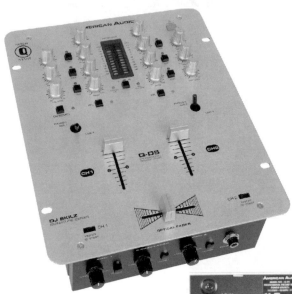

The American Audio Q-D5 mixer. Photo courtesy of American Audio.

American Audio Q-D5 rear panel; note the XLR balanced master outputs. Photo: Linda Monson

3 dBV and dBu are two different scales for measuring voltage levels; dBu ignores impedence. There is a long explanation for the existence of these two incompatible scales, which is beyond the scope of this text.

The American Audio Q-D5 has balanced (XLR) master outputs in addition to its unbalanced master outs. The Stanton SA-8 provides quarter-inch TRS balanced master outputs, and balanced direct channel outputs.

Analog vs. Digital – Like most turntables, most DJ mixers are analog audio devices. As explained in Chapter 2, analog means the audio is represented by fluctuations in a continuous electrical signal. More and more digital electronics are showing up in DJ gear with each new product generation. The Numark TT-X1 is one of several current turntables that have digital output. The Tascam X-9 four-channel mixer is one of the few current DJ mixers that can accept a digital input.

Although none of the DJ mixers we examined for this book have digital inputs or outputs, it's only a matter of time until digital I/O becomes a standard feature, at least in the higher-end models. While still a rarity on the DJ scene, digital mixers are now a common feature in recording studios, and most professional computer sound cards have digital inputs and outputs.

The big advantage to digital is that the audio signal is immune to interference or degradation. Nearby motors, TV screens, transformers, and other gear can't induce hum or noise in a digital signal, because it's a stream of numbers. Using an all-digital signal path helps maintain the highest possible audio quality when making a recording.

There are a variety of digital audio connectors, the most common being S/PDIF, which typically transmits over a coaxial cable, like any RCA cable. Optical, also known as ADAT "Lightpipe" is another common digital interface standard using a thin fiber optic cable.

Phono Inputs and Line Inputs – All DJ mixers have phono (phonograph) inputs, providing RCA stereo jacks that can accept signals from any turntable. As mentioned earlier, a phonograph cartridge produces a very weak, low-voltage signal. In order to be heard and mixed that signal must have its voltage increased, which is done by a pre-amplifier built into the mixer.

In addition to the phono inputs, nearly all DJ mixers accept line level inputs, providing RCA stereo jacks that can connect to any tape deck or CD player. Line level inputs work at a higher voltage than phono inputs; line level signals do not require any pre-amplification before mixing.

Be very careful about the inputs when setting up a mixer. A tape deck or CD player should never be plugged into a phono input; the higher voltage signal might blow out the pre-amp or mixer channel. Likewise a turntable should never be plugged into a line-level input; the result would be a weak, noisy signal.

Master Outputs – The master or "mix" output channels on a DJ mixer are usually connected to a power amplifier, which drives the house sound system or PA. DJ mixers usually include a master volume knob (somewhere on the top of the mixer) that controls the overall volume being fed to these outputs.

Channel Strip

Most mixers have a linear layout, in which the signals from each input channel are controlled and modified by a set of knobs called a channel strip. Once you understand the functions of a single channel strip you'll know them all. Pro DJ mixers follow this convention, offering two identical sets of controls, one for each channel. DJ mixers are typically placed between two turntables; the left side of the mixer manages the input from the left turntable and vice-versa on the right.

The knobs and switches in a DJ mixer channel strip may not be laid out in a straight line and may have slightly different orders or names, but they normally include the following elements:

Input Switch – The input selector switch is usually a toggle switch and is normally labeled "phono/line."

Practically all DJ mixers can accept low-voltage signals from phonographs, as well as higher-voltage (line level) signals from CD players and tape decks. The input switch selects the input source (phonograph or line) and sends its sound to the rest of the mixer. Although each channel can only transmit audio from one source at a time, two turntables plus two CD or tape decks, for a total of four sound sources, can all be controlled by a single, two-channel mixer.

The channel input switches on the Stanton SA-8 are optical switches, fast and light to the touch. Photo: Linda Monson

The input switch requires a very small range of motion and is always full volume or nothing. It's one of the most powerful volume controls on a DJ mixer, allowing you to gate a signal with just a flick of the wrist.

Gain – Also called "trim," the gain knob controls a preamplifier that cuts or boosts the amount of signal coming from the source (phonograph or CD player). Gain sets the maximum level for the channel; the volume slider can only attenuate that level. Adjust the gain to get a strong signal without overloading and distortion. Gain is adjusted when setting up the mixer; don't use it as a volume control during performance—that's what volume faders are for.

EQ – Otherwise known as equalization, EQ is tone control. Most DJ mixers have three EQ knobs for each channel, labeled "low", "mid", and "high" (or "bass", "mid", and "treble"). These knobs are not much differ-ent from the bass and treble controls found on any home stereo. Equalizers use a circuit called a filter, which reduces or increases the volume of a section of the audio spectrum while allowing the other parts to pass normally.

Korg KM2 Kaoss Mixer. White rectangle in center is the X-Y control surface. Photo: Linda Monson

While there are a number of different designs for equalizers, including graphic EQs with twenty separate filters or more, the EQs found on pro DJ mixers are gener-ally very basic, compa-rable to what you'd find on many PA mixers. They simply boost or cut the volume of a particular frequency range. Fancier parametric EQs found on pro-recording consoles allow the center frequency and frequency range to be adjusted, but DJ mixers succeed by keeping things simple.

The American Audio Q-D5 has cut buttons next to each channel EQ knob. Pressing a bass, mid, or treble cut button filters out 100 percent of the sig-nal in the respective range. Sometimes called "EQ kills," they drop out the frequency range with a single touch.

Volume Fader –
The volume fader
is a vertical (up
and down) slider
that determines
the amount of
signal to be mixed.
The volume fader
is located before
the crossfader;
each channel's
volume can be
adjusted inde-
pendently. Volume

Volume fader on the Stanton SA-8 mixer. Photo: Linda Monson

faders usually contain an electronic component called a variable resistor.
The resistor controls the level of an amplifier circuit, which determines
the amount of channel signal sent to the crossfader.

The volume fader is at its minimum setting (0 or off) when pulled
toward you to the bottom of its range. The maximum setting is when
it's pushed away from you to the top of the range. Two of the features
we really like about the Stanton SA-8 and the American Audio Q-D5 are
their adjustable fader curves, allowing you to set the effective throw or
range of the fader, and reverse fader switches, making the volume faders
be at max volume when at the bottom of their range.

Korg Kaoss Mixer rear panel. Photo: Linda Monson

Many mixers have the concept of pre-fader and post-fader. An aux or effects send/return, or a send to the cue stage can either occur before the volume fader (pre-fader) or after the volume fader (post-fader). Post-fader sends reflect the volume fader setting; pre-fader sends are at full volume and are not affected by the volume fader.

Cue Circuit

The cue or monitor circuit, sometimes called PFL (pre-fader listen), is a key component of all DJ mixers. It allows the DJ to listen to either of the sound sources while the audience continues to hear the main mix. By using the cue stage, the DJ can preview a selection on one channel without interrupting the music on the other channel. For example, the DJ can listen privately on the headphones to channel 1 and position the next record, while the record on channel 2 plays through the master outputs to be heard over the sound system.

DJ mixer cue circuits are very similar to the "peek-a-boo" mixing system that Grandmaster Flash put together in the 1970s. While some radio consoles and high-end club mixers had cue stages, they weren't a feature of low-priced mixers at the time. Today, even the most humble, inexpensive DJ mixer allows preview through headphones.

Cue circuits are usually pre-fader, meaning the signal is tapped before it is sent to the channel volume fader; pre-fader monitoring allows you to cue up selections without adjusting the channel volume. Some mixers, such as the Stanton SA-8, have selectable cue inputs allowing the cue stage to monitor pre-fader, post-fader (meaning after the channel volume fader), or even the master mix.

Cue Level – Since the cue stage usually monitors the sound pre-fader, DJ mixers provide a cue level volume control, which adjusts the cue volume level heard in the headphones. On the Korg Kaoss mixer this knob is labeled "monitor," it's the same thing.

Cue Channel Selection – The DJ needs to be able to select which channel to monitor and preview. DJ mixers handle this in different ways. The American Audio Q-D5 has two buttons labeled "PFL" (pre-fader level) that allow each channel to be inserted into the cue circuit. On the Korg Kaoss mixer these buttons are named "CH1" and "CH2." The Stanton SA-8 has a horizontal fader called "cue pan" that selects either channel or creates a blend of the two in the cue stage.

Crossfader

The crossfader (sometimes written as "x-fader") is the most characteristic part of a DJ mixer. The crossfader adjusts each channel's relative strength in the master mix. The crossfader is a horizontal fader, which goes from left to right (as opposed to the vertically-oriented channel volume faders). The crossfader controls the mix or blend of the input channels, adjusting the relative volume of both channels with a single motion.

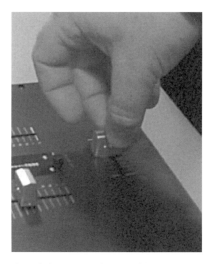

Crossfader on the Stanton SA-8 mixer. Photo: Linda Monson

When the crossfader is all the way to the left, only the signal from channel 1 is heard. When the crossfader is all the way to the right, only channel 2 is heard. When the crossfader is somewhere in the middle, a mixture of the two channels is heard.

A central characteristic of any crossfader is the "cut-on" point, the positions at which the sound from the opposite channel becomes audible. Cut-on points are usually located around the 25% and 75% marks of the crossfader's range. The location of the cut-on point determines the range of motion needed to add, or mute, the sound of the opposite turntable.

Most crossfaders are an electronic component called a variable resistor. They have a piece of resistive material, typically a graphite bar, with electrical contacts at either end. A third contact called a wiper slides along the bar as the crossfader knob is moved. The variable resistor is connected to small voltage-controlled amplifier (VCA) circuits, which determine the amount of each channel in the master mix.

Crossfade Shape – A crossfade is described according to the shape (or "curve," or "profile") of its fade. Shape means the amount of channel volume that is passed at each point along the crossfader's range. In theory any number of crossfade shapes might be possible. In practice, crossfade circuits are designed to give consistent signal strength, constant power, throughout their range. The rate of attenuation – meaning how quickly one channel gives way to the other – and the points at which each channel becomes audible, or muted, are the key variables.

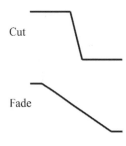

Examples of crossfade shapes. Cuts are abrupt; fades are gentle.

The Stanton SA-8 and the American Audio Q-D5 both have knobs that control crossfade shape permitting a range of settings from an abrupt cut to a slow fade. The Korg Kaoss Mixer has three x-fade shape choices, and allows the user to set the crossover point anywhere along the crossfader's range. For scratching try a short cut setting; long fade shapes may be more appropriate for mixing.

Optical Faders – Optical crossfaders have become a common feature of better DJ mixers. Instead of using variable resisters, optical faders use light; they contain a tiny light emitting diode (LED) pointed at an electric eye (called a photo-detector). A shutter slides between the LED and photo-detector, changing the amount of light reaching the photo-detector. The photo-detector's output signal controls the amplifier circuits that vary each channel's volume in the mix.

Because optical faders have no physical contact between the shutter and the optics, they have less friction than variable resistor crossfaders and offer a very light touch. Just a tap will send the fader to either side. The American Audio Q-D5 has an optical crossfader built-in. The Stanton SA-8 (DJ Focus signature model) includes an optical fader as a hardware option; it took about three minutes and one screwdriver to install their Focus fader.

Reverse Crossfader – The reverse crossfader option switches the poles of the crossfader, so that channel 1 is on the right and channel 2 on the left. It's also called a "hamster" switch, which derives from the hamster style of scratching, first practiced by the Bulletproof Scratch Hamsters/Space Travelers crew. The Stanton SA-8 and American Audio Q-D5 both have reverse crossfader buttons on their front panels.

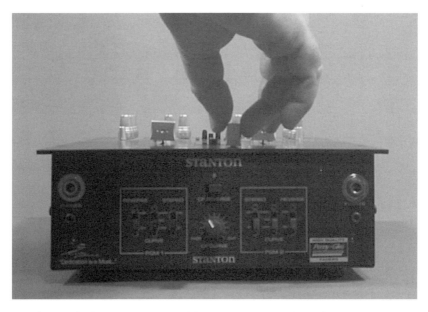

The Stanton SA-8 includes both variable resistor and optical crossfaders, which can be swapped out in minutes. Photo: Linda Monson

Master, Meters, and Ground

Master Volume – The master volume is the last stage of volume control in the DJ mixer. Located after the crossfader, it determines the amount of blended signal sent to the mixer's master outputs. Like the trim or gain controls, the master volume is another "set it and forget it" knob – set it to the maximum amount that your sound system can handle (without distorting). Master volume shouldn't be adjusted during performance; use the channel volume faders instead.

Meters – Meters are the lights on the mixer that indicate signal strength. Mechanical dials, called VU meters, used to be a familiar sight. Most modern mixers have LED "ladder" meters instead, also called peak program meters. They all use the familiar traffic-light color scheme:

- Green means the signal level is okay, or too low.
- Yellow is just about right, optimum signal strength.
- Red is too much signal, which may be causing distortion.

On most DJ mixers the meters display the pre-fader levels of channels 1 and 2 by default. The American Audio Q-D5 and the Korg Kaoss Mixer both have the option of showing the master level instead.

Meters are calibrated in terms of dBu's (decibels unterminated). As mentioned in Chapter 1, decibels are a logarithmic scale. When referring to sound in air, decibels represent sound pressure levels. When referring to an audio signal, as is the case here, decibels represent signal strength, specifically the peak voltage in the signal.

Meters all have an alignment point — the zero dB mark — with headroom above. Signal peaks are allowed into the first 8dB or so of this headroom; peaks above +10dB will cause overload, resulting in distortion.

Ground – DJ mixers have a ground terminal, usually labeled "GND" on their rear panels. Turntable ground wires should be connected to the ground screw. Improper grounding may cause a "ground loop," which produces a type of electrical noise called sixty-cycle hum. Any time a steady, low frequency hum is heard, check the grounding.

Mic Support and Other Mixer Features

The controls listed in the previous section are (for the most part) found universally on any DJ mixer. Naturally, many DJ mixers have enhanced features, which cater to different needs and help differentiate the products. Some of these may be core to your way of DJing, others might simply be nice bells and whistles, depending on your style.

Microphone Support – If you have the proverbial "two turntables and a microphone" you'll need a place to plug the mic. In a concert situation the vocalists are usually patched through the main "front of house" mixer, and additionally through an on-stage monitoring system. But in a club or party setting, the DJ mixer may be all that's available, so a "talkover" circuit can be very handy for announcements or rapping. The Korg Kaoss Mixer and the American Audio Q-D5 both have such microphone channels.

Mic Input – The microphone input may be located on the front panel of the mixer (as with the Kaoss mixer), or on the rear panel (as with the Q-D5). In both cases the input is a quarter-inch unbalanced jack. Most professional microphones have balanced outputs, utilizing a three-wire XLR ("Canon") plug. To plug an XLR mic cable into a balanced quarter-inch input requires an adaptor called a line transformer found at any Radio Shack or music store.

Mic Level – The microphone input is connected to a pre-amplifier within the mixer; this pre-amp's gain is controlled by the mic level knob (labeled "DJ Mic" on the Q-D5). Because most microphones have a very weak output signal, it needs to be boosted by the preamplifier before it can be mixed with line-level signals. The mic level knob determines the amount of gain added to the mic's signal. Like the channel gain (or trim) controls, the mic level should be set so that you get a strong signal, but with no distorting during loud parts.

Talkover – The talkover button, found on the front panel of the Kaoss mixer, and on the top of the Q-D5, inserts the mic signal into the master mix; pressing the button makes the mic "go live," allowing one to literally talk over the records.

One of the interesting wrinkles of the Kaoss Mixer is that the mic signal can be inserted into the master mix or made the source for channel 1. The latter arrangement lets one use the channel EQ or apply effects to the vocal, while leaving the music on channel 2 uneffected. Remember to click off the talkover button if using the channel 1 insert. The Q-D5 doesn't have that type of pre-fader mic insertion, but does provide separate treble and bass EQ knobs for the talkover, which can be used to shape the mic sound or eliminate feedback.

Choosing and Using Microphones – Microphones are a whole other topic unto themselves, far beyond the scope of this book to really cover. The two microphones Americans will encounter most often, staples of the live sound and recording professions, are the Shure SM-57 and SM-58.

The SM-58 is probably the most familiar vocal mic, it has a wire mesh ball at the business end and looks something like an ice cream cone. The SM-57 is more streamlined, with a black plastic end and is often used for instruments as well as vocals. Rugged, inexpensive, good sounding, and widely marketed, the SM-57 and 58 are essentially the standards. They don't require any power source and with the right connectors will plug into just about any mixer.

Professional studio microphones often require a power source, some-times called "phantom power," which can be supplied by batteries, an external power supply, or a power supply within the mixer. No DJ mix-ers we're aware of have built-in phantom power and that's no shortcom-ing. Fragile, expensive recording microphones would be out of place and at risk in any party or nightclub situation. If you have such a mic, keep it in the studio.

Booth Output – In addition to the master output channels, the Stanton SA-8 and the Korg Kaoss Mixer both have booth output chan-nels and booth volume knobs. This is just a duplicate copy of the master mix, allowing the volume level in the DJ booth to be controlled inde-pendently of the house volume. If the DJ must listen closely to a cue or talk to someone in the booth, the volume in the booth can be reduced without affecting the house volume.

Balance (or Pan) – As mentioned earlier in this chapter, all DJ mixers work with stereo signals, each of which are actually two signals, the left and right channels. For simplicity, DJ mixers combine the control over the left and right stereo signals into a single channel strip. The channel volume and EQ knobs control both left and right channel equally.

Simplicity is good, but sometimes complexity is required; the Stanton SA-8 is a case in point. The SA-8 has stereo balance faders for channels 1 and 2, and a balance fader for its Aux/FX channels. In this implementa-tion they're like little horizontal crossfaders, providing a good visual and tactile impression of the left channel/right channel stereo spread. On some mixers this control is called "pan," short for panorama and many mixers use knobs instead of faders, but the function is the same.

Remote Cueing – The American Audio Q-D5 and other mixers, allow compatible CD players to be cued by the mixer's crossfader. If using a pro CD deck, such as the machines covered in the next chapter, the player's cue input can be connected to the mixer's remote output.

Moving crossfader from left to right will cause the CD in deck 2 to play, and the CD in deck 1 to stop and return to its cue point. Moving the crossfader from right to left will naturally play CD deck 1, and cue CD deck 2. Some decks also allow samples or multiple cue points to be controlled by the crossfader. These are neat features, which really add new power to the crossfader, make some wild sounds, and are something that could never be done with vinyl. There's more on remote cueing in Chapter 6.

Auto Cue – Found on the Stanton SA-8, the auto cue feature allows the cue stage to be controlled by the crossfader position. When the crossfader is at the far left on channel 1, channel 2 is inserted into the cue circuit and heard through the headphones. Putting the crossfader to the far right on channel 2, places channel 1 into the cue stage. Like remote cueing (above) this eliminates some button pushing.

Auxiliary Send/Return – Auxiliary (or effects) send/return channels are a common feature on PA and studio mixers, but more of a specialized thing in the DJ mixer arena. Send/return channels allow the use of external signal processing devices, such as delay or reverb effects. When an effect device is connected to the mixer's send/return channels, signals can be sent out to the effect, then brought back into the mixer. In a DJ mixer these are always stereo channels, a left/right pair. Sometimes labeled aux, or FX, the purpose is always the same: Providing an effects loop so that one can color the sound.

On the Stanton SA-8, either channel can be sent to the Effects outputs by pressing the FX1 or FX2 buttons on the top panel. Set the channel input (PGM 1/2) switch to FX in order to hear the return signal from the effects loop. Effects can be inserted either pre-fader or post-fader on the SA-8, as determined by the FX select switch on the top panel. There is also an additional aux input, and either the aux or effects channels can be sent to the cue stage, or to a separate set of EQ, gain, and balance controls. It may be slightly complex for novices, but if you plan to use effects in your performances this type of flexibility really helps.

Tempo Detection – As digital bells and whistles go, this is one of the most useful. Tempo detection determines the beats per minute (BPM) of any song, so that one can more easily match tempos. There are two basic types of tempo detection, automatic and tap. The Korg Kaoss Mixer includes both; it can automatically sense tempos between 80 and 160 BPM, and does so quite well with records that have a steady, prominent beat. If it is having trouble getting a reading, press the tap button a few times in time with the music. The device will derive the tempo from the key presses.

Light Control – Certain types of lighting gear can be controlled by an audio signal so that they will change and react to the music. If a mixer has an extra output, such as a record or auxillary send channel, one can route an audio signal to the light controller. Some DJ mixers, notably the American Audio Q-D5, have a dedicated light control output. It serves the same purpose, providing a copy of the master mix to drive the light system.

Recording Outputs – Another extra set of outputs, offering a copy of the master mix for recording purposes, as seen on the American Audio Q-D5.

Sampling – Sampling means digital audio recording and playback. Although normally associated with sampling keyboards, samplers come in all shapes and sizes, including a variety of tabletop models that are essentially glorified drum machines.[4] Samplers can also be built into DJ mixers, as seen on the Korg Kaoss Mixer. The purpose of including sampling in a DJ mixer is clear: it allows one to record and continuously play back any segment of audio. Looping with a sampler is much faster to learn, far simpler to perform, and more generally accurate than back spinning or needle dropping.

Samples and effects on the Korg Kaoss Mixer are manipulated using the rectangular Kaoss Pad control surface. Photo: Linda Monson

Because an audio loop is a rhythmic building block, it can be a powerful tool for any DJ. In addition to loops, samplers can also play back non-repeated, one-shot sounds such as vocal bites, effects, or instrument hits.

Samplers for DJs typically have a series of buttons; a different recording can be assigned to each button. Every digital recording has a beginning and an end; if the recording is to be looped it will play from beginning to end repeatedly. The beginning of a loop is called the "in point," the end is called the "out point."

Although all samplers are different, most DJ samplers can record and play back loops "on the fly" in the course of a performance. The goal in loop recording is to set the in point and out point as precisely as possible at

4 Surveyed in this author's previous book, *Loops and Grooves: The Musician's Guide to Groove Machines and Loop Sequencers*, 2003, Hal Leonard Corporation.

the very beginning and ending of a measure or bar of the music. To do so, play the source music, start the recording on the first beat of the measure, and stop the recording after the last beat, on the next one. On the Korg Kaoss Mixer this is done with the rec/stop button. It helps to tap your foot and stay in tempo with the music when setting in and out points.

If you have a good loop you'll know it immediately; the loop will sound natural and seamless when played repeatedly. If you missed and the loop sounds strange, just back up the source music and try again.

Once a loop is defined it can usually be stored to the sampler's permanent memory so it will be retained even after the unit is powered off. That is certainly the case with the Kaoss Mixer; its write button will store up to four samples into long-term memory. Other (stand-alone) samplers have more storage, but they're not as nicely integrated with the mixer.

In addition to playing back a loop, a sampler can vary the speed of the loop (changing its pitch and tempo), and may also be able to adjust the in and out points. On the Kaoss Mixer these adjustments are made through the Kaoss Pad's X-Y control surface, which we'll talk about later in this chapter. Other samplers provide a keyboard, drum pad, or knobs to control these types of variables.

The Korg Kaoss Mixer's sampling features and their ease of use are among the best parts of that product. One could do an entire performance just with the sampler, or use the sampler as an adjunct "virtual turntable," providing grooves and drop-ins that bridge the other sound sources.

Obviously anyone can add a tabletop or keyboard sampler to a DJ setup, attached to one of the mixer's line or aux inputs. But by building a sampler right into the DJ mixer, Korg made it very easy to record from any of the mixer's sound sources and to manipulate the sample playback with the mixer's convenient controls.

Effects

By "effects" we mean signal processing, changing the sound of the audio in some way.

Some DJs are rather traditional and only use sounds that come naturally from the turntable, records, and mixer. Other DJs incorporate effects into their routines to various degrees; effects provide an expanded palette of sound and texture, and can be part of a DJ's distinctive style.

Almost all DJ mixers have built-in equalizers, which are filters that boost or cut certain ranges of the audio frequency spectrum. The EQ is a simple and very useful type of effect.

There are many, many other kinds of effects. In the pro recording world, effect processors are usually hardware devices, which often contain essentially one process in a rack-mounted box. Over time manufacturers began making multi-effect processors, which combine a number of effects in a single unit. Responding to the demands of guitarists and keyboardists, effect makers have lines of pedals or "stomp boxes" that can be controlled with one's foot. And with the advent of computer recording, effects have migrated into software, appearing as "plug-ins" that can be added to any audio recording/editing program.

External effects devices need to receive an audio signal from the mixer and to return the processed (wet) signal to the mixer so that it can be added to the mix. This is ideally accomplished by using a send/return loop; audio from one of the mixer channels is routed through the mixer's send outputs to the external effect unit, then back to the mixer's return inputs. The return signal is then added to one of the channels; this insert may be pre-fader or post-fader, depending on the mixer. The balance between the dry un-effected signal and the wet effected signal is determined by a return gain volume control. The Stanton SA-8 is an example of a DJ mixer with the send/return architecture necessary to make the best use of external effects.

Since it's a natural way of distinguishing a mixer, building-in effects has become a trend. Indeed, the DJ manufacturer Numark recently acquired Alesis, a well-known maker of audio electronics and promptly began including an Alesis multi-effect processor in their PDM01 mixer. The Korg Kaoss Mixer is another example of a DJ mixer with built-in effects.

The most distinctive part of the Korg mixer is the Kaoss pad, a touch-sensitive surface that allows control over two (or more) effect parameters with a single touch. The Kaoss pad is simply an X-Y grid, scaled from one to nine. Certain effect settings are mapped to the grid, and can be adjusted by tapping or swiping a finger across the pad. It's a dynamic, real-time way of tweaking effects that is a little more natural, and musical, than using knobs or sliders. [5]

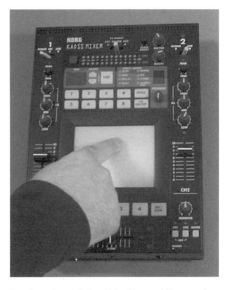

Another view of the Korg Kaoss Mixer and its Kaoss pad X-Y control surface (the white rectangle). Effects are accessed through the buttons above the Kaoss pad; samples are recorded and stored by the buttons below. Photo: Linda Monson

[5] This idea had been around a while, albeit in software circles. Arboretum Systems, for whom this author worked for several years, have an effects product called Hyperprism that features an onscreen X-Y control grid, first introduced in 1991. Korg's Kaoss line brought this type of "gesture" control into the hardware realm.

As for the effect processes themselves, Korg happens to break them up into eight banks generally arranged by process type. We're not going into the specifics of Korg's effect implementation. Instead, we want to make sure you understand the main categories of audio effects as found on any device and how they can change the sound. Effects have certain controls, called parameters, which can be adjusted to alter the processing characteristics. We'll discuss the most important parameters, the ones to grab first, as we describe the effects:

Filter – There are many types of filters; all of them block, or pass, certain ranges within the audio frequency spectrum. The low-pass filter, which removes frequencies above a certain cut-off point is the most familiar. The wah-wah pedal, a guitar effect, is a simple low-pass filter; low-pass filters are also found on many synthesizers. Sweeping the cut-off of a low-pass filter has become a sonic cliché within electronic dance music. There are also high-pass filters (which remove the lower parts of the sound) as well as band-pass and band-reject filters; all have their uses.

The cut-off frequency of a filter is the key parameter; audio above (or below) the cut-off is removed from the signal. Some filters have a parameter called resonance or "Q" (not to be confused with cue.) Such filters can resonate, creating a distinctive high-pitched feedback that is added to the sound.

Equalizer – As mentioned earlier in the chapter, equalizers are a variant on the filter. EQs reduce or increase the volume of certain frequency ranges. On DJ mixers these are usually simple low/mid/high knobs. Professional recording consoles usually have parametric EQs that allow a greater degree of selection over the frequency ranges to be processed. One often sees graphic equalizers in home stereos and sound systems; these are simply banks of filters that cut or boost specific frequency bands.

In all cases, EQ implies a decision: cut or boost? While the temptation is to add more, often the most effective results come from cutting certain frequencies. When dialing in a sound try reducing different frequencies first; you may find that less can be more. If you want to boost a particular frequency remember that you're increasing the signal's volume level. Watch the headroom on the meters so that you don't start clipping and distorting.

Modulator – Modulation means to go back and forth, to reduce and increase. The idea of modulation is embodied by the sine wave, which fluctuates up and down within a certain range. In fact, slow low-frequency sine waves are often the control source for modulation effects.

One might use a slow-moving sine wave to adjust the cut-off frequency of a low-pass filter. This creates an effect much like a wah-wah pedal. A sine wave could modulate the volume of an amplifier, increasing and decreasing the volume; that effect is called tremolo. Modulating the pitch of a sound source, such as an oscillator or sampler voice, creates an effect called vibrato.

The most important parameters with any modulation effect are the speed and depth. Speed means the rate of vibration, the amount of time each back-and-forth cycle takes. Rates below 20 Hz (twenty cycles per second) are the most common; above twenty it just becomes a blur. Depth is the amount of the modulating signal that is applied to the effect, so as to create shallow or deep modulations.

The ring modulator is a special type of modulator effect derived from synthesizer techniques. Ring modulators modulate audio signals by other audio-frequency waves, creating frequencies called "sidebands" above and below the frequency of the original carrier signal. Ring modulators have a distinctive metallic or bell-like sound.

Delay – The delay is an "echo" effect allowing you to hear a copy of the sound, which follows the original. Early delay effects, such as the classic Echoplex device, made use of tape loops. Practically all delay effects used today are digital delays. Delays were among the first effects to go digital in the early 1970s.

The delay simply makes a copy of the audio signal and reinserts that copy into the line at some later point, creating the echo. Delay length is the critical parameter, that's the amount of time between the original audio and the delayed version. Regeneration, meaning how often the delay is repeated, is another important setting. Depth is the other main variable, determining the volume of the signal copies.

Better delay effects will automatically lock the delay length to the song tempo. Delay length can also be set by hand to match the beat of the music.

Chorus/Flanger/Phaser – Chorus, flange and phase effects are all variants on the delay. They use relatively short delay times and typically apply a modulator to the delay length parameter. Chorus effects provide a pleasant doubling effect and usually use a delay length of around twenty-five milliseconds. For flanging or phasing try even shorter times, around ten or fifteen milliseconds, which can provide cool, metallic effects. Experimenting with the delay time, the modulation rate and depth, and the amount of regeneration can produce a great variety of textures.

Reverb – Unlike flanging or phasing, which impart a distinctly artificial sound, reverb attempts to reproduce a very natural effect: the reflections of sound within physical spaces. In a large space, like a canyon, one might hear an echo, which is easily emulated by a delay effect. In smaller, architectural spaces, like rooms, churches, or stadiums, sound reflections disburse in complicated ways creating a wash of short echoes. Reverb effects imitate this phenomenon.

Early reverb units used metal plates, springs, or specially built rooms. Today reverbs are digital devices. There are any number of ways to model the reflectance of various spaces and surfaces. One recent innovation is the use of sonic profiles, in which an audio "snapshot" is taken of the reverb characteristics within a room or hall and applied to any sound.

Although it goes by various names, room size is the key parameter in any reverb effect. The length or "decay" time of the reverb, and the mix between dry and wet signals are also important variables. Some reverbs have additional controls over properties such as early reflections, or may include an equalizer or filter stage. In general the reverb is meant to create a realistic impression of space. It can sound great on drums and vocals, but it can also muddy-up the mix.

Pitch and Time Shift – One of the central facts of the turntable is that when the record is slowed, the pitch (or key) goes down. When the record is sped up, the pitch gets higher. This phenomenon is useful in its own way. But there are times when one would want to change the pitch or key of a record and leave the tempo unchanged. By the same token, one might want to speed up or slow down the tempo of a recording, yet leave it in the same key.

Pitch shift effects change the pitch or key of a musical signal, without necessarily changing the speed or time frame of the music. Time shift effects can speed up or slow down a recording, without necessarily changing the pitch or key of the music. Although there were some analog pitch shifters, these processes really came into service in the digital era. They've been used for years by remixers, and with the advent of digitally enhanced turntables they're now becoming available for club mixing and battling.

Manufacturers have devised a number of pitch/time shifting schemes; many approaches use a "granular" technique, in which the sound is split up into tiny slices. The slices can be repeated, omitted, or played back at different speeds to create the required effect.

The key variable in any pitch shift effect is the range, the amount of shift, usually measured in Hz, notes, or cents. Time is the main parameter in any time shift effect, which may be measured in seconds or expressed as beats per minute. As these are often granular effects, the size of the grain (also called the window or slice size) is an important consideration. The effectiveness and realism of any shift depends largely upon the grain size and the amount of shift (shifts over small ranges work best).

Antares Auto-Tune, a software and hardware product used to correct the pitch of vocalists and instrumentalists, is an advanced pitch shifter able to "intelligently" change pitches so that a performance is always on key.

Loop sequencers, such as Sonic Foundry Acid and Ableton Live, and loop slicing samplers such as the Boss SP-5 and Yamaha SU200, have come into widespread use in recent years. All of these products provide time-shifting capabilities, using a technique called loop slicing. Loop slicing is a variant on the granular idea; it uses a large grain in which each beat or note is a single slice. Permitting the easy mixing and matching of music clips at any tempo, loop slicing has become a powerful production method for DJs, remixers and producers.[6]

Dynamics Effects – Dynamics processors control the volume levels within an audio signal. Any sound recording, speech or music, contains many volume fluctuations. Very rarely does any recording sustain a constant volume level; there are normally lots of peaks and valleys. Dynamics processors control the range of these peaks and valleys.

6 For the complete story on loop slicing, we again refer you to this author's own *Loops and Grooves: The Musician's Guide to Groove Machines and Loop Sequencers*, 2003, Hal Leonard Corporation.

There are two main types of dynamics processors, compressors and limiters. They frequently are combined in a single unit, called a compressor/limiter. Compressor/limiters are used to control the volume of a recording so that there are no unwanted spikes or peaks and a strong signal is maintained throughout. When used correctly, a compressor/limiter is transparent to the listener; things may sound a little fuller, soft passages may have a little more presence. When used incorrectly, you'll hear a giant sucking sound.

Threshold is a key variable, it's a "trigger" setting. When the signal volume exceeds (or drops below) the threshold, gain is applied to the signal. The amount of gain is another important parameter. There are many designs for compressors and limiters and they're the type of effects that require a degree of skill and finesse to use properly. Compressor/limiters are common in recording studios, less so in DJ situations.

Distortion – Distortion effects add noise to a signal; depending on how it's done this can be a very pleasing or grating effect. When a tube amplifier is over-driven, it can add a very rich set of harmonics to the audio signal creating a lot of beef and texture. An over-driven amplifier is said to be "clipping," because the top of each waveform is literally clipped off by the headroom of the amp. It is this clipping, changing the shapes of the wave peaks, that adds the additional harmonics to the sound, distorting the original tone.

Electric guitarists brought distortion into common use. Although there were precedents in the Hawaiian and blues genres, Dave Davies of the Kinks basically introduced guitar distortion to pop music on "You Really Got Me." Distortion (or fuzz) effects add a whole new character to the guitar and can be equally effective on bass, keyboard, or even vocal parts.

Most distortion effects have a volume control, sometimes labeled "level" or "gain," and a distortion amount knob, which determines the severity of the clipping.

Exciter and Bass Maximizer – Exciters and bass maximizers are relatives of the distortion effect. Like any fuzz box, they add new harmonics (overtones) to an audio signal. But they're more selective, the harmonics added are in the same series as the program material, so they enhance and reinforce the original signal instead of distorting it. By introducing musically related harmonics, these processors literally add sound to your audio.

Exciters are usually applied to the higher end frequencies, they can produce clarity and sparkle. Bass maximizers are a very similar process, but they only synthesize harmonics for the low-end frequencies of the recording, increasing the presence and apparent low-end power of the kick drum or bass. By adding harmonics to the bass, the maximizer tricks the ear into perceiving additional lower frequencies.

The key parameter on these devices is the harmonics or intensity value, which determines the number of overtones added to the signal. Frequency cut-off, sometimes called tune, is also critical; it determines how much of the audio signal's frequency range is processed by the effect. Timbre settings are available on some devices, determining the mix between odd-numbered and even-numbered harmonics so you can create hollow or rich sounding overtones.

Vocoder – Vocoders are derivatives of synthesizer technology, often a part of a larger keyboard synth. Vocoders modulate an audio signal with another audio signal, superimposing the characteristics of the first signal onto the second. The usual setup has someone singing into a mic, which modulates a synthesizer sound. It creates a really interesting robot voice effect.

Vocoding uses one signal to set a bank of filters, which are applied to a second signal. The signal from which the filters are set is called the modulator; the signal that gets filtered (and is heard) is called the carrier. In a simple vocoder the signal from the microphone (the modulator) is split into a number of bands by a set of band pass filters. The volume level in each frequency band is measured by a circuit called an envelope follower. Those volume levels are applied to another set of band pass filters, which process the carrier waveform (the synthesizer sound). As the vocalist speaks into the mic, the vocoder imposes the voice's energy patterns onto the synthesizer sound.

Modulation level, or amount is the key parameter on any vocoder. The pitch of the carrier signal is also important; many vocoders have keyboards attached to them so one can easily change the carrier pitch to fit the melody of the song. Some vocoders have no keyboard and will simply vocode any two audio signals.

Granular Effects – We mentioned granular processing earlier in the section on pitch/time shifting. Granular techniques involve slicing an audio signal into many tiny segments, or "grains," and can create a variety of interesting or adverse effects. One may vary the sequence, duration, volume, and other attributes of each slice. Some types of granular processing (like a time shift) may be completely invisible to the listener; heavier processing (like a blender effect) can rearrange the sound into something completely unrecognizable.

Granular processing techniques are so powerful that a whole new form of music synthesis, called granular synthesis, has arisen around them. There are a great variety of different granular processors, including the aforementioned pitch/time shifters. Grain size, the length of the slice window, is the central parameter in all of them.

Transform Effect – Found on several pro DJ CD players, transform effects try to emulate the sound of a transformer scratch, a la DJ Jazzy Jeff. Specifically, they imitate the effect one might get from moving a input switch or crossfader back and forth very quickly.

On the American Audio CD decks we examined for this book, the effect simply gates the signal at an adjustable rate and duration. The Denon DN-D9000 CD player can transform between the main CD channel and a sampled sound, creating alternating slices of each sound source.

We'll tell you all about the Denon DN-D9000, and other professional CD decks in Chapter 6. But first, check out our exclusive interview with Rob Swift!

Interview:

Rob Swift

Rob Swift is a member of the X-ecutioners and a solo recording artist.

Rob, what kind of gear do you use?

I have a studio in my apartment with a total of eight turntables set up. I have two Vestax PDX-2000 turntables. Those are the turntables I use to record. To practice with my group I use standard Technics 1200 turntables. Shure cartridges, Shure styluses…I think right now Shure is the most compatible cartridge and stylus company for DJs. I also have one of those Pioneer CDJ-1000 CD turntables

I use several mixers, I use the Vestax 05 Pro, I have a Vestax 07 and also an 06. The Vestax mixers are kinda like Technic turntables, in that they're really standard. No matter where you go, a club, or DJ battle, you're 95 percent likely to see one of those mixers.

I got the E-Mu SP-1200 (a vintage sampling drum machine). I have the E-Mu 6400 Ultra rackmount sampler, and I also have the Akai MPC-2000XL (tabletop sampler). To record I use the Roland VS-1680 and VS-2480 digital studios. I use Alesis monitors in the studio.

Are you all about the home studio or do you also work in commercial studios?

Honestly I'd rather work out of my house. I recently finished an album called *Sound Event* which was released last October (2002). Every song was recorded out of my house, with the exception of two songs. I also mixed the entire album out of my house. People didn't even know the difference.

I think the advantage to mixing and working out of your home is you can work at your leisure. You're not pressed for time. You don't have to worry about your car that's parked outside that you got to move by a certain time. You don't have to worry about a session that's booked after you. You don't have to get out of the studio just in time to make room for that session. You can wake up at five in the morning if you feel like it and work on some ideas.

Working out of the house, for me, is the best environment. You have all your records, all your resources are with you. You don't have to run home 'cause you forgot a record. You're right there.

Rob Swift. Photo courtesy of Rachel Mathews.

No engineers walking in on you, no strange people coming through the studio...

Exactly. I did an album before *Sound Event* called *The Ablist* which was my first solo release. That I recorded entirely in a studio. And when I compare the process, working out of my house was such an advantage for me, it definitely helped me create a better album.

Sound Event *has been out for a few months, how's it doing?*

Sound Event is doing good. Thank God the response to it has been really positive. I just feel that it is a better sounding album than my first solo album. Of all the stuff I've been part of musically, it's the most mature version of what I do. It features legendary artists like Bob James, I got Supernatural, one of the best freestyle MCs on it. Large Professor. I got DJs like D-Styles, Radar, Klever and Melo-d...DJ Quest. It's a well-rounded album. Definitely my best work to date.

Are you touring behind it?

I haven't gone on a full-fledged tour. But I have been doing a lot of shows, like on the weekends. I go out and I'm performing a lot. This past weekend I went to San Francisco, played at this club called Mission Rock. I went to Miami in the last couple weeks. Coming up I got to go to Massachusetts and Ohio. I'm looking forward to a short run of Japan that I'm going to do with Bob James, which is going to be in April (2003).

You'd been sampling from Bob James long before you hooked up, right?

Yeah, man, when I first started learning how to DJ. My older brother, the person that first taught me how to DJ, had an extensive collection of Bob James records. To hip-hop DJs back then, artists like Bob James were real popular because of the beats they had in their music.

So I grew up cutting records like "Take Me to The Mardi Gras," "Nautilus;" I remember looking at the album covers, seeing his picture on the back. Now fifteen years later I'm here working with the man I used to, you know, learn how to scratch on his record. It's like a really great feeling.

And I feel really lucky. Fortunate to meet him and work with him and stuff. I've been able to also work with people like Herbie Hancock, so I've been blessed, definitely.

Well, to expand the awareness of the young crowd about a guy like Bob James...

I hope that my album will help educate a lot of the younger music-slash-DJ lovers out there. So many people have heard his music and a lot of them may not know who he is.

Like "Mardis Gras," what a classic break.

Exactly, what a classic break, how people like Run-DMC would sample him, and Missy Elliot and Puff Daddy. You have all these people who may be fans of all this new rap music and may not know that a lot of this music comes from Bob James.

With songs like "Salsa Scratch," the song Bob James is featured on, on *Sound Event*, hopefully people will hear it and understand who he is, and how important he is to the music. And how cool it was for him to hook up with an artist like myself, a DJ. You know, it goes to show that he likes all kinds of music, and respects all kinds of creativity.

What should people look for (or avoid) when putting together their first DJ sound systems?

The best way I can answer that question: Roc Raida is one of the members of the X-ecutioners. When I first met him he had the worst equipment. He had the cheapest turntables, the cheapest mixer, his sound system wasn't necessarily that great. But he had such a strong passion for DJing and being creative, he made the most out of that equipment.

Starting out it's not really about having the best equipment. My father was a DJ, so I had access to the best equipment, Technics turntables and stuff like that. I was fortunate enough to practice on really good equipment. But Roc Raida had the worst equipment, but you would never know if you saw him DJ. Because he had such a passion for being creative on turntables.

Starting out it really doesn't matter what kind of equipment you have. What matters most is the energy you put into practicing. Naturally as you get better, as you grow, you want to build on your equipment. If you have the money to do so, you want to get yourself some good turntables, whether that's Vestax or Technics, a good mixer.

At what age did you start DJing?

When I was twelve years old.

How long have you been doing it professionally?

In 1991, I entered my first DJ battle. I battled from 1991 to 1992.

What role did battling play in developing your career?

Battling helped me make a name for myself. The battles gave me a forum to showcase who I am, and what my style was. And help me rank my skill amongst the world's top DJs. Battling was very important, it's something that I would advise any up-and-coming DJ to get involved with. You gain a lot of experience, you learn a lot about yourself and your world. And your ability to handle adversity and competition. It helps a lot.

How did the X-Men get together?

The X-Men came together in 1989, the original members were Steve D, Roc Raida, Shawn C and Johnny Cash. They came together to make a name for themselves. At the time there were other DJ groups that were out, that were well-respected and talked about. The X-Men just felt like "hey, we're just as good as anybody, why don't we make a name for ourselves and form a group?" That's how they came about.

When did you get involved with the X-Men?

It was about 1991, when I did my first DJ battle, the East Coast DMC battle. I met up with Steve D, who at the time was one of the DJs that I looked up to and stuff. We hit it off, we became friends. I actually placed third in that battle, he placed first. He won the battle, but I guess he and the rest of the crew saw something in me that would add to the group. At the time the group was maybe only three years old.

After getting really cool with Steve D and talking to him on the phone, sharing our theories on DJing, philosophies and stuff, he asked me if I wanted to be in the group. I jumped at the chance. To me that was better than winning, being affiliated with one of the DJs that you looked up to.

What other DJs or artists influenced you?

GrandWizzard Theodore, the person who invented the scratch. I remember my brother would play old, old tapes of the Fantastic 5 with GrandWizzard Theodore, I would listen to the tapes and try to learn what he was doing.

People like Grandmaster Flash. People like Grandmixer DST. Cash Money, Jazzy Jeff, DJ Aladdin, oh, so many DJs out there that I've learned from. I can honestly say that I've learned from pretty much every DJ that's been out, man. There's so many different ways to express yourself on the turntables.

Who do you listen to now?

I listen to all the new DJs, people like A-Trak, DJ Radar, DJ Clever, my crew, Roc Raida, Total Eclipse, I learned a lot from them. All the up-and-coming DJs, P-Trix, there's so many of them.

How did you acquire DJ skills?

I watched and studied DJs that I liked. I learned their routines, if they cut up a certain record a certain way, I'd buy the same two records and cut 'em the same exact way. Try to figure out what it was about their style that made them sound the way they did. And once I'd mastered what they did on a certain record, I'd sit down and say 'how can I take what I learned and re-invent it, add on to what I learned?'

I think that's a cool way of learning. There's nothing wrong with copying as long as the intention behind copying is to elevate what you learned. If you just copy for the sake of trying to get credit for what someone else did, you're going backwards. You're never going to really make a name for yourself that way.

Do you practice scratching and mixing today?

Definitely. Although I'm an established DJ and people know who I am and stuff, there's still more for me to learn. As a DJ that's known it's important for me to stay on my P's and Q's. So I still practice. It's harder to practice six, seven hours a day the way I used to when I was younger. I'm doing interviews on the phone, I gotta be doing studio work for albums or remix projects I get hired to do. Or I'm away touring. It's hard to really find the time to practice the way I used to. Now I make a strong effort to practice at the very least an hour a day. Just so I can stay loose and not lose what I learned.

Are there exercises or drills you use when practicing?

It's simple. I scratch to a real fast, up-tempo beat for a half hour, then I scratch to a down-tempo beat for another half hour. I just do that every day.

What type of career promotional things did you do when first starting out, to establish yourself as a DJ and build reputation?

In '92 when I won my first battle, the East Coast DMC battle, this guy Akinyele heard about me. He was a rapper that was signed to Interscope, and he asked me to become his DJ. I jumped at the chance. It was definitely a good decision on my part because I got to travel and tour and expose myself to people who didn't know about DJ competitions. It was a really good opportunity for me to get out and express my talent to the rest of the nation.

And then I learned a lot about working in the studio. A lot of these battle DJs are really good onstage, but if you get them to do scratches on someone's song, they're trying to compete on record. You gotta know when to compete onstage, and when to try to make music in the studio, and not to intertwine the two. That helped me kind of get more well-rounded and learn other aspects of how to incorporate the turntable with music. Not just trying to outdo someone or be better than someone.

Were there other people who assisted you in your career?

Oh, man I have a really great friend named Dr. Butcher, who played the most pivotal role in my life. I met him in 1990, before I even entered my first competition. He was the one that kind of, like, physically, always was there to mold me and help me find confidence in what I could do and what I could achieve as a DJ.

He's a real spiritual person. Practicing with him went beyond just physically learning how to do some scratches or learning how to do tricks. A lot of time we'd just sit and talk about having confidence and believing that you could accomplish more than what people you looked up to have.

And that's important in anything, whether you're a football player or a musician or whatever. If you look up to someone that you think is better than you, it's important to believe that at some point you could be better than that person. Or to believe that at some point you could bring something that (the other) person hasn't.

If there's kids out there that may say "oh, Rob Swift is the best DJ in the world, and I'll never be as good as him" you're already putting limits on yourself as to how much you're going to grow. If you're a fan of me, learn all that I've done and what I've achieved. But then at the same time understand that there's something inside you that may help you tap into an area of DJing that I haven't yet.

Where do you look for loops? What genres and artists are you taking sound from?

All kinds of genres, rock, jazz, R&B, I definitely don't discriminate when it comes to searching for music that I'm going to get ideas from. Anything really that sounds good, anything that has an energy that I'm looking for on a specific song. I'm gonna use or try to like, study. I'm a fan of Jimi Hendrix, Miles Davis, Bob James, Herbie Hancock, No Doubt, Red Hot Chili Peppers. Like I listen to all kind of music, you know?

Have you ever been sued over a recording, or had other legal issues with copyright owners?

Knock on wood, I haven't ever dealt with any lawsuits or anything like that. The essence of DJing is putting together a collage of music that indicates what kind of person you are. Or what kind of music you're a fan of. Now that I'm making music as a recording artist, that's all I'm trying to do. Kind of the same as taking a whole bunch of records and mixing them at a party. Naturally on an album there's money to be made and you just can't steal someone's music. We just really try to be creative with records because we don't know how to play trumpet or guitar or drum set. All we know are the turntables. Our tools are the vinyl that we find.

Tell us about the name change from the X-Men to the X-ecutioners.

It's not like the Marvel comic book people came to us, and said you guys gotta change your name. It was more our lawyers advising us that if we wanted to make records and be known publicly the name would have to change. Or we would run the risk of being hassled.

What's your goal with DJing, what are you trying to achieve?

All I'm really trying to achieve is for people to know that DJs like us exist. I've been on a quest to really just expose the art. I want people to know that I'm one of those DJs who's hopefully pioneering the whole movement.

When I perform I run into people who've never seen the kind of DJing that I do. There's so many people out there that still don't understand it, or don't even know it exists. Compared to the amount of people that know about DJs like the X-ecutioners, there are more people that don't know. There's still more to accomplish as far as getting awareness out there. That's really my biggest goal.

Do you consider yourself a DJ or a recording artist?

I would say that I'm a musician that uses a turntable as his microphone, as his tool to express himself. I'm a DJ, but I like to use the turntables the way Hendrix would have used the guitar. I don't wanna just DJ in the sense of just play music, I want to do something to the music that you're hearing, alter it in some way and be creative with it.

Chapter 6

DJ CD
Decks

As mentioned in Chapter 2, compact discs (CDs) were introduced to the U.S. market in 1983, and by the end of the decade had entirely replaced vinyl records as a consumer entertainment format. But early CD players were limited in their capabilities; there was no way to vary the speed of the disc, precise cueing was difficult, and scratching was out of the question.

Although some DJs immediately migrated to CDs (despite the initial limitations) and never looked back, others stuck with their turntables and vinyl. DJs with vinyl-specific skills like beat matching or scratching simply had no other choice. Over time CD technology progressed. Responding to demand from DJs, certain manufacturers developed advanced CD players suitable for professional DJ applications.

This chapter starts with a quick look at the compact disc itself, what it is, and how it works. The main part of this chapter is a survey of the features found on better CD players. We only discuss decks that have scratching, because those models do the most and represent the current stage of development in the field.

Pro DJ CD Decks are a relatively new product category, they're more complicated than turntables and they bear some explanation. This chapter emphasizes the features that are common among these devices and goes into some detail about the actual implementations. We'll point out the key features and make sure you know all the buttons and their functions.

The Compact Disc

Vinyl records contain a direct physical representation of sound waves etched in the undulating walls of a spiral groove. Compact discs contain an abstracted representation of sound waves, a series of numbers that represents the voltages in an audio signal.

Compact discs, meaning audio or music CDs, are just one of several digital disc formats that all have the same form factor. Readers are undoubtedly familiar with CD-ROMs, which contain computer data such as programs, text, or pictures. There are also CD-RW "rewriteable" discs for computer use, and "enhanced" CDs that contain both audio and computer files. All of these variants exist thanks to the success of the audio CD. The audio CD also paved the way for the DVD, which uses the same size disc, but holds lots more data.

Researchers at Philips and Sony did most of the heavy lifting to create the compact disc. They eventually issued a specification, called the *Red Book*, which defines the CD, what it is and how it operates.

Like all digital audio systems, compact discs are based on the idea of digital sampling. In its traditional, technical definition, sampling means making a measurement at regular intervals. Each measurement is a sample, and in this case we're taking measurements of signal strength. By putting the measurements together, one can reconstruct the path of the original signal.

The accuracy of sampling depends on the rate at which measurements are taken and the precision of each measurement. The *Red Book* audio specification requires that the signal be sampled 44,100 times per second, a rate also referred to as 44.1kHz. 44.1kHz sampling can measure and reproduce frequencies up to 22,050 Hz, the theoretical limit of human hearing.

The precision of each measurement depends on the size of the number used to record each voltage level; larger numbers allow more precise measurements. One digit (a single bit) can record two possible values—one or zero. A four bit (four digit) system can represent up to sixteen different levels of voltage variation. Eight bits can represent up to 256 different voltage levels. The *Red Book* (CD audio) specification requires sixteen-bit sampling, which allows up to 65,536 different levels of signal strength.

The number of bits used to represent an audio signal, or "bit-depth," determines the potential range of volume (dynamic range) within a recording. Sixteen-bit audio CDs can reproduce up to 96dB of volume change between silence and maximum.

This series of bits is saved on a compact disc as "pits," tiny capsule-shaped bumps on a mirrored surface. A raised bump indicates a one; a flat pit is a zero. A tiny spot of laser light is focused on this reflective layer and the presence or absence of a bump affects how the light is reflected back. The variations in the light reflection are detected to read the disc.

Because the CD is read using light, there is no contact or friction at the information layer; simply playing back a CD will not wear it out unlike a vinyl LP. The reflective information layer is sandwiched in a durable, clear plastic base material. The CD is read from the bottom; paint, ink, or stickers may be applied to the top without affecting the performance.

While vinyl record grooves spiral inward from the outer edge towards the label, CDs are read from the center to the outside. Look at the underside of any CD: in a good light at a certain angle you can see two bands. The inner band is data, and the outer band is empty space.

A tiny laser and a photo-sensor are carried along the CD's radius by a mechanism called a "sled." Little motors called servos are used to focus the laser, move the sled, spin the CD, and insert or eject the disc.

Once read by the laser head, the data goes through error correction, time base correction, and de-interleave processes. It is then sent to the digital-to-analog converters, which translate the data into electrical signals that can be amplified and heard.

Pioneer CDJ-1000 professional CD player. Photo courtesy of Pioneer.

About DJ CD Decks

While scratching CD decks have been around for a few years now, this is the first time they have been documented in a reference book. We couldn't have done it without the assistance of Pioneer, Denon and American Audio, who kindly provided these models for our research:

- American Audio Pro-Scratch 2; suggested retail price $600, street price around $400.
- American Audio Velocity; suggested retail price $1500, street price around $1000.
- Denon DN-D9000; suggested retail $1600, streets around $1300.
- Denon DN-S5000; suggested retail $1200, streets around $900.
- Pioneer CDJ-800; suggested retail $1000, streets around $800.
- Pioneer CDJ-1000; suggested retail $1300, streets around $1150.

Street prices quoted are actually minimum advertised price; dealers can discount even lower. As this book goes to press Pioneer has just released the CDJ-1000MK2, a minor upgrade, and slashed prices on the original CDJ-1000s to make way for the MK2. The Pioneer decks, the Denon DN-S5000 and the American Audio Pro-Scratch 2 are single-CD, tabletop models; they can integrate easily into any DJ setup. Denon's DN-D9000 and American Audio's Velocity are dual-CD players, with two drives and two sets of controls. These dual decks need to be rack-mounted, they don't lend themselves to tabletop use. In all cases, you'll need a mixer to control and layer the sound from the CD decks, plus headphones, amplifier, and speakers.

Consider the positioning of the decks. CD players do not have to lie flat, they can be installed at an angle. A gentle 10- or 15-degree forward tilt puts the deck on a different plane; you may find it more ergonomic.

Pro CD decks have certain characteristics that distinguish them from conventional consumer CD players. The key attributes include speed/pitch shift, cueing, scratching, looping, and a large dial called a jog wheel. We'll examine each of these features and learn how to use them in the course of this chapter.

While all of these decks have many features in common, they also contain some unique aspects that distinguish each model. Nonetheless, within each manufacturer's line we see great similarities in terms of feature sets and layouts – using the American Audio Velocity is not much different from the American Audio Pro-Scratch 2, for example.

The American Audio Pro-Scratch 1, released January 2001, was the first CD scratching deck. Pioneer followed with their CDJ-1000 that summer, and the competition was on. The 1000's less-expensive counterpart, the Pioneer CDJ-800, has fewer cueing and memory features but delivers the same experience and sound quality as its predecessor.

American Audio's Pro-Scratch 2 and Velocity respond to the Pioneer challenge by providing more memory and cueing features, sampling support, built-in effects and other enhancements, and carry a lower price tag than comparable Pioneer offerings. The trade-off is that they're slightly more complicated, with some buttons and knobs serving multiple functions.

We go up the complexity scale another degree when approaching the Denon CD players. The DN-S5000 and DN-D9000 both have a second audio channel called the alpha track, which can be mixed with the main CD playback. Denon also went the extra mile on cueing, sampling, memory, play modes and more exotic features. Unfortunately the alpha track's functions and its relation to the cueing/looping features, are not particularly intuitive – this chapter will help sort it out. Many buttons on the Denon decks serve two or more functions, accessed by long or short button presses. This type of modality makes a device more difficult to learn and more rigorous to operate than devices where each control serves just one purpose. The upside is they do more tricks.

Connections

AC Power Input – Connect to any AC outlet. American Audio and Pioneer use detachable power cords. Denon uses built-in power cords, which are ungrounded. The American Audio units and the CDJ-1000 can switch to 220v European current; the Denon decks and the CDJ-800 are for 120v North American current only.

Pioneer CDJ-800 rear panel. Photo courtesy of Pioneer.

Analog Audio Output – Stereo RCA jacks provide unbalanced, line-level signals for connection to a mixer. The Denon DN-D9000 has both monitor and main outputs; the DN-S5000 has a separate set of outputs for its alpha channel.

Digital Audio Output – All the units we looked at provide S/PDIF digital output through an RCA-type output jack. Digital mixers are a rarity on the DJ scene; these digital outputs are more frequently used to connect the deck to a digital recorder or computer sound card. The original Pioneer CDJ-1000 only provided "archival" digital output, meaning normal full-speed CD playback was supported, but no pitch changing or scratching. The new Pioneer CDJ-1000MK2 and all of the other decks covered in this chapter have full-function digital ouputs that will support scratching, varispeed and all other types of playback.

Remote Cueing – All the CD players in this chapter include support for remote cueing, which means cueing the decks with crossfader movements. When the crossfader is moved all the way to the left, CD deck 1 (channel 1) will begin playing from the cue point. Moving the crossfader to the right starts CD deck 2 playing, and returns deck 1 to its cue point.

American Audio calls it Q-start, Denon calls it fader control, Pioneer calls it fader start but the jack is labeled "control". In all cases, a one-eighth inch mono mini-jack is provided, which accepts a control signal from any compatible mixer.

American Audio Pro-Scratch 2 rear panel. Photo: Linda Monson

American Audio Velocity rear panel. Photo: Linda Monson

American Audio decks include a flash control input, which lets the crossfader start and stop any sample. Denon DN-S5000 and DND-9000 users who have the Denon DN-X800 mixer can use the similar X-effect function to control cue points, samples and the alpha track.

We tested remote cueing using the American Audio Q-D5 mixer. It controlled the Denon and Pioneer CD players just as well as it handled the American Audio decks. We encountered no problems cueing between two different make/model decks.

CD Transport – The Denon DN-D9000 has drawer mechanisms, which extend and retract a tray when ejecting discs. All the other players we looked at are self-loading, the disc is passed through a thin slot in the front of the player. Self-loading is preferable; extended trays are easily broken.

The rest of the transport mechanism in any pro CD player is completely hidden from view. Small servo-motors maneuver the disc into position, move the sled, and spin the CD.

Be nice to your CD transport! Don't try to pull out discs that are being inserted, or push back discs as they eject; such actions could damage the loading mechanism. Use only standard-sized CDs, because these decks can't handle CD singles, "business card" discs or other oddly shaped discs.

Pioneer CDJ-1000 front panel; note the memory card to the left of the CD slot. Photo courtesy of Pioneer.

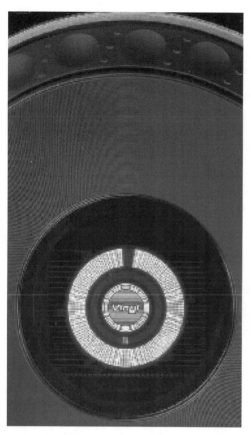

The Pioneer CDJ-800 jog wheel display is one of the features that distinguish it and the CDJ-1000, Photo courtesy of Pioneer.

Top Panel Controls and Player Functions

Display – Pro CD decks use a liquid crystal display, or LCD, to show time, transport states, player modes, and other information. Displays vary from model to model; time is usually the most prominent field. Elapsed time or remaining time can be shown.

The Pioneer models have an additional LCD in the center of the jog wheel, which gives a cool graphic representation of the CD's play state, cue point, and position. It's easy to lose your place when scratching on a jog wheel; only the Pioneer decks provide this kind of handy visual reference. The Pioneer CDJ-1000 includes a simple waveform display in the main LCD that helps visualize the breaks in a song.

Eject – The eject button opens the CD drive tray or passes the CD through the slot so that it may be removed. The Denon DN-S5000 Hot Disc feature can store about a half-minute of audio, so an ejected disc may continue playing while a second disc is loaded and cued. The Pioneer CDJ-1000 has a unique eject lock switch, which can be thrown into lock to prevent accidental disc ejection.

Play/Pause Button – One of the two largest buttons on any pro CD deck, the play/pause button is used to start and suspend playback. This button is typically lit with a solid green (or white) light when playing and with a flashing light when paused. Press the play/pause button to play the current CD track; press it again to pause the playback. Then press play/pause a third time to resume playback from the current time/ location.

Pro CD decks don't have stop buttons; both play/pause and cue will suspend playback. The play/pause button stops and resumes playback at the current time/location, whereas the cue button stops playback and returns to the current cue point.

Cue Button – Like the play/pause button, the Cue button has two functions. Pressing the cue button during playback will stop playback and return to the last cue point. This is called "back cue." When playback is stopped, holding down the cue button will begin playback from the last cue point. Press the cue button repeatedly to "stutter" the cue.

Methods of setting cue points vary between the manufacturers. In all cases a cue can be set by default at the beginning of the current CD track. On the American Audio and Pioneer decks, press the in button to set a new cue point. You can press the in button on-the-fly, while play-ing the music, or press it while paused after locating a cue with the jog wheel. On the Denon and Pioneer machines, go into search mode, turn the jog wheel until you reach a cue point, then press the cue button.

Denon machines allow you to set a cue (while playing in search mode) by pressing the play/pause button. Likewise, you can set a cue while paused in scratch mode by turning the jog wheel, then pressing the play/ pause button.

The Pioneer models also allow you to simply pause playback, (with either the play/pause button or the touch-sensitive jog wheel surface) then push the cue button to set a new cue point.

Denon's cue setting has some modalities; it may be difficult to remember whether you're supposed to press the cue or play button while in a particular mode. The Pioneer and American Audio implementations are much more consistent and straightforward – just press the in button (or the cue button, on Pioneer decks.)[1]

Denon DN-D9000 dual CD deck control panel. Photo: Linda Monson

The cue button is usually illuminated with a solid light when cued (meaning the CD is at the beginning of the cue). The cue light typically goes dark (or flashes) when the disc is playing or the deck is paused.

The American Audio Velocity and Pro-Scratch 2 players include a variant cue button, called a bop button. Like the cue button, the bop button returns playback to the current cue point. But whereas the cue button back cues and pauses, the bop button back cues and plays, returning to the cue point and keeping the music going.

---

1 The American Audio Velocity and Pro-Scratch 2 Reference Manuals incorrectly state that cue points can be set by pressing the play button, while in pause or cue mode. We found that is not the case with either machine; only the in button will set a cue on the American Audio decks.

Track Select – The track select feature is usually labeled with double forward and backward arrows as on any CD player. Track select steps through the tracks on the disc. A cue will be set at the beginning of the selected track by default if the auto-cue feature is on.

This feature is called track search on the Pioneer decks; hold down either of the Pioneer track search buttons while turning the jog wheel to scroll quickly through the tracks.

Search – The search feature lets you scroll through the audio and hear it in short, full-speed segments. Although it's somewhat like scratching with the jog wheel, search is intended for previewing and locating within the track. Search plays audio frames, short segments of the music (1/75th of a second) that are always heard in real-time at play speed. Search frames are always played forward, even when searching backwards through a file.

On the American Audio Pro-Scratch 2 and Velocity players, you can search while in pause by turning the jog wheel by its outside edge. This feature duplicates the functionality of the search knob.

The Denon DN-D9000 is in search mode by default on startup; twirl the jog wheel to scroll through the track. The Denon DN-S5000 has a

Denon DN-D9000 drives. Photo: Linda Monson.

four-position knob, select search and turn the scratch disc (jog wheel) to scan through the track. The S5000 also has a fast search lever that steps through by larger increments.

The Pioneer CDJ-800 and CDJ-1000 have forward and backward search buttons. To frame search with the jog wheel, turn off the vinyl jog mode (on the 1000, select "CDJ" mode.) For super-fast searching, hold down either search button while turning the jog wheel.

Jog Wheel – The jog wheel is the largest dial or knob on any pro CD deck. Jog wheels are implemented differently on various models. In general, they can be used to search through the track, speed up or slow down playback, scratch the audio, cue up tracks, or adjust other parameters such as effects.

Search feature implementations were discussed in the preceding section, and scratching is covered in the next section. Jog wheels can be used to locate cue and set points, which may be done in either scratch or search mode. Varispeed, meaning temporarily speeding up or slowing down playback, is another typical mode. All the models surveyed here, except the Denon DN-S5000, can momentarily increase or decrease the pitch (playback speed) when the jog wheel is spun forward or backward. Spinning backward rapidly may slow playback to a near-standstill.

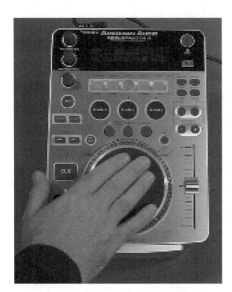

The American Audio Pro-Scratch 2 (above) and Velocity (not shown) both have four-and-a-half-inch diameter jog wheels. That works out to about three or four inches of scratch room. Photo: Linda Monson

The Pioneer CDJ-800 and CDJ-1000 can varispeed in vinyl mode; spin only the outer ring of the jog wheel. On the Denon DN-S5000 one can drag or push the spinning jog wheel much like a turntable, which may be slightly more intuitive.

The size of the jog wheel determines the physical range of scratch movements and to a great degree, the accuracy and level of control. The easiest movement and hence most of the action, is a 45-degree arc between nine and twelve o'clock (on the left; between twelve and three on the right). On a twelve-inch vinyl LP, there's roughly eight inches of hand room between nine and twelve. Compare that to the Denon DN-D9000's two-and-a-half-inch diameter jog wheel; it essentially provides a two-inch range of movement.

The Pioneer decks have the largest jog wheels among the machines we surveyed, eight inches in diameter. The Denon DN-S5000's scratch disc measures seven-and-five-eighths-inches in diameter. American Audio Velocity and Pro-Scratch 2 jog wheels are about four-and-three-quarters inches. To summarize, big dials are good, small dials are bad.

None of the decks we looked at have any provision for recalibrating the jog wheel's mapping, so that one might change the amount of audio time per inch of movement.

The Denon DN-D9000 jog wheels are simply multifunction dials. The jog wheels on the American Audio Pro-Scratch 2 and Velocity players have touch-sensitive top surfaces, with a non-sensitive outer ring; CD playback will pause whenever this surface is touched (in skid or scratch mode). The Pioneer CDJ-800 and CDJ-1000 operate in a similar manner, albeit with a pressure switch under the wheel that pauses playback when pushed in Vinyl mode. The Pioneer jog wheels respond to pressure, instead of capacitance, as found in the American Audio decks. As a result one can lightly touch the wheel without pausing play.

The Pioneer CDJ-800 has a feature called quick return, which is not found on its predecessor the CDJ-1000. When quick return is on, pressing the jog wheel's top surface will stop playback and return to the cue point; taking the hand off the jog wheel resumes playback from the cue point.

The Pioneer CDJ-1000 and CDJ-800 jog wheels have a large LCD in the middle that shows play state, cue point, and position, providing a helpful visual reference. The outer edge of the Pioneer jog wheel is ringed with little pits and bumps that make it very easy to hold on to. We really like this design, which helps maintain a reliable grip on the wheel that won't slip when scratching.

The Denon DN-S5000 features a motor driven, spinning jog wheel; it has two parts, a metal platter and a plastic "record" called the scratch disc. The platter is turned by a servo-motor whenever the CD is playing. Atop the platter is a slip mat and the permanently attached, grooved plastic scratch disc. The disc can be held, released, and scratched much like any vinyl record. It's a fairly reasonable emulation of a turntable's behavior and allows certain traditional DJ moves to be applied to a CD.

When it comes to scratching CDs, the jog wheel is the only point of contact. On some of these machines scratching means simply turning a big knob; the feel is far different from vinyl. The Pioneer machines, and the Denon DN-S5000, offer the greatest degree of control, the best visual feedback, the most satisfying touch, and the most vinyl-like experience.

Scratch Mode – In our evaluation of pro CD decks, scratching is the acid test. Ease of use, sound quality, and realism (similarity to vinyl scratching) are all factors to consider.

On the Pioneer CDJ-1000 and CDJ-800, set the jog mode button to vinyl. The word vinyl will appear in the jog wheel display. Pressing the top surface of the jog wheel will pause playback; moving the wheel back and forth will scratch the audio.

The America Audio Pro-Scratch 2 and Velocity decks power up in scratch mode by default. When scratch is enabled, the scratch/skid button will be amber on the Velocity, and green on the Pro-Scratch 2. Touching the black surface of the jog wheel will pause playback; moving the wheel back and forth will scratch the audio.

On the Denon DN-D9000 press the scratch button to enter scratch mode. Either the CD or a sampler sound can be scratched. The Denon DN-S5000 will scratch the main CD playback channel, the alpha track, or the sample; use the four-position scratch mode dial to select the jog wheel's target. The DN-S5000's scratch disc can be held and moved as the platter spins, or scratched with a stationary platter.

American Audio Velocity dual deck, control panel top, drives below. Photo courtesy of American Audio.

The Denon DN-D9000 and DN-S5000 have a cool additional feature, scratch direction. On the S5000 look for the toggle switch next to the scratch mode dial. Settings are FWD (forward), wherein backward movements are silenced, and BOTH, meaning both backward and forward movements are heard. It's a neat option; it means perfect stabs every time, no fader required. The D9000 has an extra wrinkle here, the RVS setting, providing reverse scratching (forward movements are silenced). Hold down the D9000's scratch/dir button to enter the direction mode and turn the parameter knob to select a setting.

In terms of physical responsiveness, the latency (or time lag between movement and result) is very low, practically imperceptible on all the models surveyed. They all react quickly and predictably to jog wheel movements. As mentioned in the previous section, the size of the jog wheel is a central consideration in terms of physical control and playability. The mass and resistance of the wheel may also be a factor.

All of the decks covered in this chapter sounded pretty good during our subjective listening tests. Any differences in scratch sound quality are comparatively minor and really only noticeable during a direct, head-to-head comparison:

- American Audio Pro-Scratch 2 – Scratches have slightly less high end than competing brands, but lots of beef.
- American Audio Velocity – Scratching sounds somewhat muted, slightly muddy.
- Denon DN-D9000 – Slightly raw, unfiltered scratch sound, may strike some as harsh, tinny.

- Denon DN-S5000 – Scratching sounds bright, but not harsh like the D9000. Slightly thin, not as much presence in the low and midrange as other brands.
- Pioneer CDJ-1000 – Bright, clear high-end, punchy midrange and full-sounding low end, plus the best audio specs of any deck reviewed here.
- Pioneer CDJ-800 – Sonically indistinguishable from the CDJ-1000, which means it sounds great.

In terms of sheer sonic quality, we'd choose either of the Pioneer CDJ units. Other users may prefer the high, bright scratch sound of the Denon DN-S5000, or the more mellow tones of the Pro-Scratch 2. In the end it's a matter of taste and budget.

Reverse Play – All of the machines surveyed have reverse play, wherein the CD will start playing in reverse from the current point. Other controls, including varispeed and pitch bend, continue to work as normal during reverse playback.

The Pioneer CDJ-1000 direction toggle switch is the most fun way to control this feature. The Pioneer CDJ-800 and the American Audio units have a REV button on their top panels, not quite as cool. The Denon players slightly bury the feature; on the DN-D9000 it's accessed through the platter modes button, on the DN-S5000 use the dump/RVS button.

Denon machines have an additional reverse mode, called dump, which plays the audio in reverse then returns to forward playback at the appropriate elapsed time. For example, if it played in reverse for one measure, dump would return to forward play at a point one measure later in the song, whereas reverse simply resumes forward play from the current position.

Start/Brake Time – All the machines we looked at have adjustable start and brake times. These features control the amount of time required for the deck to get up to full speed or to slow to zero when pushing the play/pause button or pausing with the jog wheel.

Each model implements this feature in a different way; the Pioneer CDJ-800 has a single knob controlling touch/release. On the Pioneer CDJ-1000, touch (brake) and release (start) are separate knobs.

On the Denon DN-D9000 the start and break times are found under the platter mode button; press it repeatedly to step through each mode. The Denon DN-S5000 has separate platter mode buttons, controlling drag (start) and brake as well as reverse.

American Audio start/brake times are packaged as the skid effect. Turn on skid, press the hold button (so changes take effect) and use the parameter knobs to adjust. The parameter time knob controls start time, and the parameter ratio knob controls the brake time.

Pitch Slider – All pro DJ CD decks have pitch sliders, much like the pitch controls on Technics SL-1200s, or any other professional turntables.[2] Like their analog forbearers, CD pitch controls speed up or slow down playback. And just like a record, speeding up playback raises the pitch or key of the music, slowing playback lowers the pitch.

But unlike any analog turntable, a pro CD deck can also adjust the speed of playback while leaving the pitch (key) unchanged. Manufacturers refer to this capability by various confusing names; we call it time shifting. On the American Audio units press the tempo lock button to hold the pitch constant; on the Denon models press the pitch/key button. On the Pioneer machines press the Master Tempo button so it glows red. In all

2 The "Pitch" slider is labeled "Tempo" on the Pioneer CDJ units; the purpose is the same.

cases the effect is the same: speed (tempo) can be changed by moving the pitch slider, while maintaining the original key. Time shifting is an awesome feature, although it does color the sound of the track, most noticeably when shifting down to a slower speed.

All the machines surveyed allow the user to adjust the range of the pitch slider, from single digits to as much as +/- 100% (except the Pioneer CDJ-1000 which goes from +/- 6% to 24%; 100% is allowed in the CDJ-1000MK2). On Pioneer decks, press the tempo button to step through the slider range settings. For American Audio Pro-Scratch 2 and Velocity decks, hold down the pitch % select (on/off) button, while pressing the + pitch bend button, to step through pitch slider resolutions. Pitch slider values on the Denon models are adjusted by holding down the pitch/key button (to enter the range function) then turning the parameter knob to select the percentage.

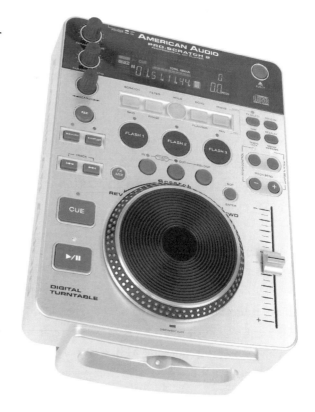

Pulling the pitch slider down to −100% gives a great digital drag effect, a signature sound you could never get with vinyl. And try going down to −100% while in time shift mode, for some truly adverse sounds.

American Audio Pro-Scratch 2. We like the way it handles cue and sample memory. Photo courtesy of American Audio.

The Pioneer CDJ-1000 has a unique tempo reset feature; pressing the tempo reset button defeats the pitch slider and returns the pitch to 0%. The pitch sliders on the Pioneer CDJ-800, the American Audio decks, and the Denon DN-D9000 have detents at their zero points, so they're easy to center.

Cue Points – A cue point is a time/location in the music at which playback can begin. Pressing and holding the cue button while playback is paused will start playback from the current cue point. Pressing the cue button during playback will stop playback, and return the CD to the current cue point; this is called back cueing. Cue points can be saved to memory, and recalled by the touch of a button. Several different cue points might be utilized within a particular song. Make sure to check out the section on the cue button (earlier in this chapter) and cue memory (next) for more information about using cue points.

All the decks covered here can set a cue point at the beginning of the current track. On the Denon and American Audio machines, it's done by default. On the Pioneer machines you have to be in auto cue mode; press and hold the time mode/auto cue button until the auto cue indicator appears in the LCD.

Naturally the cue point can be changed, check out the cue button section (earlier in this chapter) for instructions. Cue points can be saved to, and recalled from, any number of buttons on the player. The American Audio decks have three flash buttons, and a bop button, all of which will trigger a cue. Denon players have four hot start buttons; Pioneer CDJ-1000 has three hot cue buttons. And don't overlook the reloop button, which replays the last loop.

Cue Memory – All of the CD decks covered here have the ability to save and recall cue (or loop) points. Several different cue points can be selected and stored for a particular song, so that the song can be cut simply by pressing the memory buttons. There are two levels to cue memory: current (or volatile) cues, which can be accessed from buttons on the top panel, and long-term (non-volatile) cues, which are saved and recalled using the player's internal or external memory.

Each manufacturer implements current (volatile) cue memory in a different way. On the American Audio decks, once you've set a cue point or a loop, press the memory button, then press any of the flash buttons to store the cue or loop. On the Denon machines press any one of the four hot start buttons (A1 through A4); you can also set cue points for the alpha channel and main channel. On the Pioneer CDJ-1000, press the rec mode button, then press any one of the three hot cue buttons (A through C) to set cue points while the CD plays; press the rec mode button again for hot cue playback. The Pioneer CDJ-800 omits the hot cue feature; it only works with one cue (and one loop) at a time.

As for non-volatile (long-term) memory, the Pioneer CDJ-1000 can save 10 cue and loop points per CD in the deck's internal memory, up to a maximum of 100 CDs. And that's expandable, because the CDJ-1000 includes support for removable memory cards. As many as 100 cue and loop points per CD may be stored, up to a maximum of 10,000 CDs on a 16MB multimedia card. The Pioneer CDJ-800 is more limited, allowing one cue and loop to be saved for each disc, up to a maximum of 500 CDs. On Pioneer machines press the memory button to store the current cue or loop points.

The American Audio Velocity and Pro-Scratch 2 decks can save three cue points per disc, up to a maximum of 128 CDs. No special steps are necessary; flash points are saved to non-volatile memory as soon as they're set.

The Denon DN-S5000 and DN-D9000 can store up to six cue points plus other information for each track on a CD, up to a maximum of 5000 CD tracks. Press the Memo button to enter the memory set function, and push the parameter button to confirm the save.

The Denon DN-S5000 has a rotating platter and scratch disc instead of the usual jog wheel. Photo: Linda Monson

Recalling stored cue points from non-volatile memory is quite simple. First insert the CD. The American Audio decks will load the cue (or loop) points for that CD automatically. On Pioneer decks press the call button(s) to access any saved cues or loops; the CDJ-800 saves one cue and loop per CD, while the CDJ-1000 allows many different cue setups for each disc. On the Denon machines press the memo button to enter the memory call function, then push the parameter button to load the settings.

One might well ask: "How do the players recognize which CD is loaded, and call up the right cue points for each disc?" *Red Book* audio CDs do not contain any title or artist information within the disc itself. So a pro CD deck looks at the number of tracks on a disc and the number of bytes (the amount of data) on the disc. The deck stores that information along with the cue point memory. In this way the player can recognize any CD by its track-and-byte count, and calls up the appropriate cue memory settings whenever it sees each disc.

Loop In/Out Buttons – Looping is another fantastic feature of pro DJ CD decks. Looping means repeatedly playing a segment of audio in a seamless manner. All the players in this chapter can create loops "on the fly" while the music is playing without interrupting the flow of the beats.

On the American Audio decks the feature is called seamless loop and is embodied by in and out buttons. The Pioneer models likewise have in and out loop buttons. The Denon machines have four different in buttons, labeled A1 through A4, and two different out buttons, both labeled B.

In all cases, while the music is playing press the in button to set the beginning of a loop. The in point is usually the first beat of a measure. When the end of the loop is reached, press the out button. The loop will begin repeating, playing start-to-end, over and over. If the loop does not sound smooth and seamless, you blew it. Restart the music and grab the loop again. Staying in time with the music by tapping your foot or banging your head will help set the in and out points accurately.

American Audio decks and the CDJ-800 can change an out point by catching a new out point on the fly; in points can't be altered and must be redone. Denon decks and the CDJ-1000 allow adjustments to both the in and out points, but frankly it's too much work. It's much faster and more effective to just grab the loop again, as opposed to twiddling with the in and out times.

To exit a loop and resume the continuous flow of music, press the out button on the American Audio decks, or the exit button on the Denon and Pioneer machines.[3]

American Audio Pro-Scratch 2 and Velocity decks allow loops lasting 6.5 seconds or less to be saved to any of the three flash buttons as samples; if the loop is longer than 6.5 seconds only the in point is saved (the loop becomes a cue). Loops are stored to the non-volatile long-term memory automatically.

The Denon players allow up to four loops to be defined, on the A1 through A4 buttons. Loops can be saved to long-term, non-volatile memory by pressing the memo button and entering the memory set feature. Denon has their alpha track concept, providing a second playback channel so that loops and cues can be layered over the main CD. Denon machines also have a splice feature, which removes the audio between the in and out points.

The Denon hot start buttons have different modes, which can be confusing. The A1 and A2 buttons are either cue points, or loop in points, depending on the B button and exit/reloop status. The A3 and A4 buttons are assignable; on the DN-S5000 and DN-D9000 they can be used as two additional hot start (cue/loop) buttons, as sampler buttons (meaning a superimposed loop,) or as hot start buttons for the alpha track. Press the A3/4 button and turn the parameter knob to select their mode. In order to really use the Denon machines one needs to understand this modality and the fact that sampling and alpha track cannot work at the same time.

---

3 It's labeled reloop/exit on the Pioneer machines, exit/reloop on the Denon decks. Their functions are identical.

The Pioneer CDJ models are a model of sheer simplicity in comparison, supporting just one loop at a time. The loop can be of any length, and can be saved by pressing the memory button during loop playback. Naturally loops can be recalled on all these machines; refer to the cue memory section earlier in this chapter for details.

Reloop – The reloop function works along with the loop feature (described in the previous section.) Pressing reloop during regular CD play will restart the most recent loop. Reloop is a simple and very useful feature.

On the Denon and Pioneer units the reloop button also acts as the loop exit button.[4] Pressing reloop/exit during loop playback discontinues the loop, resuming the normal, continuous flow of music. Pressing reloop/exit again will take it back to the loop.

Tempo Detection – All of the machines discussed here, except the American Audio Pro-Scratch 2, include automatic tempo calculation. The tempo is shown in the liquid crystal display, as BPM (beats per minute).

All of the machines that have a BPM read-out will calculate the tempo automatically; this works best on musical passages that have a prominent, steady beat. In some cases the machine-derived tempo reading may not be accurate. The American Audio Velocity and the Denon DN-D9000 and DN-S5000 have tap buttons that allow tempo to be entered by hand. The Pioneer decks omit the tap tempo feature; they're auto-BPM only.

The fact that the American Audio Pro-Scratch 2 has no tempo calculation is one of the few strikes against that machine. Pitch changing and time shifting on the Pro-Scratch 2 is calibrated in percentages, which is rather counterintuitive.

---

4 See footnote 3, on page 248.

Relay – All of the decks examined have relay playback. In relay play two CD decks will alternately play tracks, one after the other. American Audio calls this flip-flop, Pioneer and Denon call it relay. In all cases, CD player 1 will play, then pause at the end of the track or disc, and CD deck 2 will begin playing. CD 2 pauses when it reaches the end of its track (or disc), and CD 1 begins playing again.

Relay play features take advantage of the fader control jack on the rear panel of the CD deck. Connect a one-eighth inch (mono) mini cable between the control jacks of the two decks. (It's called the fader jack on Denon units, and the cue jack on American audio models.)

Denon and American Audio have single and continuous relay modes. In single mode, the decks take turns after every track; continuous mode allows each CD to be played all the way through before switching.

The Pioneer CDJ-800 won't relay in the vinyl jog mode, although the CDJ-1000 will relay in both vinyl and CDJ jog modes.

We tested relay interoperability between the different decks with limited success. Although the Denon DN-S5000 can be started by a control signal from a Pioneer CDJ unit or the American

Pioneer CDJ-800 professional CD player. Photo courtesy of Pioneer

Audio Pro-Scratch 2, the Pioneer and American Audio units will not respond to signals from the Denon machine, or each other. The upshot is two same-make units are required for relay play with this generation of decks.

Other Distinguishing Characteristics

Now that we've covered controls and behaviors that are universal among pro DJ CD players, let's look at some of the aspects that set these machines apart from each other.

Continuous/Single Play – The American Audio and Denon decks have the option of playing one track at a time, or playing a CD straight through. In single mode, the deck goes into pause at the end of each track. In continuous play the deck will play the CD tracks in series, just like any consumer CD player. The Pioneer decks have a similar capability, but it's not packaged as a feature per se—turning auto cue off gives continuous play.

Pitch Bend – The Denon and American Audio models we looked at have pitch bend, which momentarily speeds up or slows down playback. The effect is comparable to pushing or dragging a vinyl record. In both cases, there are two pitch bend buttons, labeled + and − (plus and minus). The pitch bend occurs when either button is pressed and returns to normal when the button is released. The Pioneer decks omit this feature, although jog wheel varispeed is supported as on other decks.

Sampling – Denon and American Audio players have limited sampling features. These sampling functions save and play back audio clips. The sampled loop can be layered and mixed with the main CD audio, and the sample's pitch and volume may be adjusted.

The Denon DN-D9000 and DN-S5000 can store two samples (per deck) at the A3 and A4 buttons. Samples can be up to fifteen seconds long. Press the A3/4 button and turn the parameter knob to select sampler mode, then use the A3 or A4 button and the B button to set the beginning and ending of the sample. Press the stop (alpha cue) button to stop sample recording or playback; note that the exit/reloop button can be used to pass beyond or return to the looped sample.

American Audio Velocity and Pro-Scratch 2 players can store three samples of up to six-and-a-half-seconds long. After defining a loop, press the memory button and any of the three flash buttons, to store the sample. To play back a sample, press the sample button, then any flash button. If the sample is more than six-and-a-half-seconds long, or if you've forgotten to turn on the sample button, the flash button will play as a cue with no end point. For more regarding sampling, see Chapter 5.

Effects – The American Audio and Denon decks used in this chapter have some built-in audio effects that can be applied to CD and sample playback. The effects are all fairly simple and the degree of user control over them is limited.

The Denon DN-S5000 has an echo effect that can be added to the end of a cut; it's one of the platter modes. The Denon DN-D9000 has a slightly more extensive selection, including filter, delay, flanger and transform, an imitation crossfade effect. Each effect has one or two parameters that are controlled by the parameters knob and jog wheel. The Denon decks don't include any factory presets or any way to save user settings.

The America Audio Velocity and Pro-Scratch 2 units have filter, echo, phaser, flanger, pan and transform effects, and like the Denon units offer a maximum of two user-adjustable parameters per effect. The American audio machines include an FX mix function that drops in effects when transitioning between different tracks, cues, or samples. The bop button fires the FX mix. A handful of effect presets are provided, which can be accessed by pressing the PSP button. The Velocity has the ability to save one user preset for each effect.

The Pioneer decks we looked at don't include built-in effects, and that's no strike against them. Many professionals would prefer to use a high-quality rack-mounted effect or a software plug-in instead of a rudimentary built-in effect. That's not meant as a knock against decks that do include effects; they're certainly useful, they provide a few more sound choices, and permit a few more moves. For more on effects check out the last part of Chapter 5.

Data Entry Knobs – When adding things like effects, more knobs are needed. American Audio decks include parameter time and parameter ratio data entry knobs, which control all the user-adjustable effect settings. Denon decks have a single parameter knob, which likewise is used in a number of situations.

Parameter knobs on these units can be pushed as well as turned, but such push-button functionality is by no means a prerequisite for a data entry knob. The player's jog wheel is the biggest data entry knob of all.

Secondary Audio Channels – The Denon DN-D9000 and DN-S5000 have a second audio channel, called the alpha (α) track. Much like the sampler mode, the alpha track is an independent audio channel that can be mixed and layered with the main CD playback. The alpha track can be playing another cut from the same disc, and the playback can be sent to its own mixer channel through the monitor or alpha output jacks.

Denon's alpha track implementation allows separate cueing, pitch, and volume control for the second audio channel on both of the machines we examined. The Denon DN-S5000 goes a bit further by allowing scratching of the alpha track. Neater still, the S5000 has a hot disc function that provides 35 seconds of alpha track memory, so that CDs can be ejected, loaded, and cued without interrupting alpha track playback.

The alpha track is not compatible with the Denon players' sampling functions; you can't have alpha track and sample playback at the same time. To really take advantage of the alpha track, hook the main output channels to your mixer's channel 1 and connect the alpha or monitor output channels to the mixer's channel 2, so that you can preview and crossfade the main and alpha channels.

Program and Random Playback – Programmed and random playback modes are much like those found on consumer decks; they're a type of DJ autopilot. The DJ can set up some musical selections, then walk away from the decks. Denon has support for both random and programmed play, found under the program button on the D9000, and under the memo/ preset button on the S5000.

Headphone Output – Surprisingly, only the American Audio Pro-Scratch 2 includes a headphone jack, allowing stand-alone listening. The other decks covered here omit that feature, assuming a mixer will be used.

Control Unit cable (for dual decks) – The American Audio Velocity and the Denon DN-D9000 dual decks have separate control panels and disc drives. A cable connects the drives to the control units. The Velocity uses two cables, the DN-D9000 uses just a single cable. In both cases the cables are rather short, which limits installation options.

Other Features – It's natural for manufacturers to include unique or exclusive features that distinguish their products from the competition. The Pioneer CDJ-800 has two such features, the auto beat and quick return functions. Auto beat controls the loop end point, and will play just the first half, quarter or eighth of a loop. Each loop fraction is fired from a dedicated button. The CDJ-800 quick return function makes the jog wheel behave like a cue button. Pressing the jog wheel stops playback and returns to the cue point; releasing it unpauses the playback.

Quick return is a somewhat similar to the American Audio bop button feature, mentioned earlier, which behaves as an unpaused cue. Pushing the bop button on the Velocity or Pro-Scratch 2 players immediately begins playback from the cue point.

Another view of the Pioneer CDJ-1000. Photo courtesy of Pioneer.

Audio Specifications – The possible specs for all of these devices are constrained to a degree by the limits of the CD format. In general practice 20,000Hz is the upper limit for frequency reproduction, because that's the most that can be achieved with an audio CD's 44.1kHz sampling rate; higher frequencies are filtered out. All the decks surveyed have a search precision of 1/75 of a second, which is the length of one CD subcode frame.

The Denon and American Audio units reviewed here all claim to have a signal-to-noise ratio of 90dB or greater, except the Velocity which has an S/N ratio of 86dB. They claim to reproduce frequencies as low as 20Hz, and have a total harmonic distortion of 0.01% or less.

The Pioneer units claim significantly better performance, offering a signal-to-noise ratio of 115dB or greater, and reproducing frequencies as low as 4Hz. The total harmonic distortion in the Pioneer decks is rated at 0.006%, almost half that of the other brands.

Although it's not quantified, the Pioneer machines also put out significantly more gain than competing models – they're just louder than the other decks we evaluated.

Pioneer has a technology called Legato Link Conversion, or LLC, which is "supposed to take out the digital harshness and put in some analog warmth" according to Pioneer marketing coordinator Nick Hahn. LLC is a proprietary process and we couldn't get a definitive tech briefing on it. It's believed that LLC converts sixteen-bit audio up to a higher bit depth, then smoothes the values between the samples, so that the original waveform path (and possible audio content above 20kHz) is replicated. The resultant sound would presumably be output using high-resolution (20 or 24-bit) digital-to-analog converters. In any event, the decks sound terrific.

This concludes our coverage of pro DJ CD decks. CD players for pro DJs are a relatively new development and have become a surprisingly crowded and mature field in a very short time. While some vinyl purists may scoff, this crop of CD scratching decks are serious, expressive musical instruments. We offer a few comments and predictions about the next stages of CD player development in the Conclusion of this book. First let's make a quick survey of computer DJ gear in the next chapter.

Chapter 7

Computer
DJ Tools

Computer software and hardware tools for professional DJs are a new product category. While digital audio production became feasible on personal computers in the early 1990s, most of the tools were very general-purpose, modeled on familiar gear from the analog production world. DJ-specific computer products are a much more recent development.

There are two basic varieties of audio software: stand-alone applications, and plug-ins. Stand-alone applications are self-contained programs, that don't require any additional software. Plug-ins are programs that can be added to certain stand-alone applications. Plug-ins always require a host program, they don't just run on their own.

While computers can do many useful and impressive things, they also have obvious disadvantages. The main shortcoming is reliability, computers are notoriously unstable, they all crash occasionally. While one can take steps to minimize crashing, you'll never be entirely safe. Computers are complex systems in which any number of things can go wrong resulting in a freeze or sudden program termination. Computer software is also far from perfect; all programs have bugs, usually non-fatal, but occasionally one encounters a real showstopper.

The upshot is that computers can be risky for on-stage use. Dedicated hardware such as mixers, turntables, and CD decks, are more reliable. Computers are also fragile, expensive, and ill-suited to nightclub or party environments. While many mixers will survive a spilled drink, that same beverage could instantly ruin a $3,000 laptop.

Yet in spite of the risks DJs are dragging computers out of the studio and into the nightclub or concert hall. Hundreds, possibly thousands of intrepid DJs and other performers routinely use computers onstage. Reliability, feature sets, and computing horsepower have all come a long way, and will only continue to improve. Without a doubt the computer will be a permanent part of DJing henceforth.

DJ-relevant computer tools encompass a broad range of products with a diverse array of features and capabilities. It's also a fairly immature market, some of the most exiting products are in their first versions at the time of this writing, and they're all being upgraded and improved. A detailed documentation of comparative feature sets is beyond the scope of this book. The intention in this chapter is to give an overview of the market, an orientation to the main product categories and applications.

Most of the software products mentioned in this chapter have free demo versions available, which can be downloaded and tried out on any compatible computer with an Internet connection.

Generic Music Software and Hardware

The first professional music software tools were called MIDI sequencers. MIDI sequencers do not record or play back digital audio. Instead, they send a stream of control messages to synthesizers, drum machines, samplers, or other hardware or software instruments. The control scheme is called the musical instrument digital interface; MIDI gear uses a distinctive five-pin socket; the MIDI jacks are always labeled in, out, or thru.

MIDI sequencing made it possible to create realistic multitrack performances very inexpensively. It became a central tool for dance music production and got the whole computer music field rolling. MIDI came to be associated with a robotic, sterile, repetitive style of music and it also had some natural limitations. The biggest limitation is that MIDI doesn't record audio.

As computers got more powerful, it became feasible to cheaply record digital audio to a computer's hard drive. Sound editing programs were the first popular digital audio applications, they generally will record, modify, and save a stereo audio file. Bias Peak and Sonic Foundry Sound Forge are among the top sound editing programs for Mac and Windows, respectively.

Next came multitrackers, also called digital audio sequencers, which can record, layer, and mix many different sound files much like an analog tape deck and console. The big advantage over analog tape is that the audio waveforms are represented onscreen where they can be easily edited, looped, or processed. Graphic waveform editing is a powerful thing and became a dominant mode of music production. Digidesign Pro Tools is the defacto standard in professional studios, but lots of records get made with programs like MOTU Digital Performer for the Mac, Sonic Foundry Vegas for Windows, or Steinberg's cross-platform Cubase.

All of these programs can scale, meaning they can work with a cheap, basic sound card, or with fancy professional interfaces. Audio input/output hardware often comes in the form of an add-in card for a computer's card slot. An audio interface may also be a box that plugs into a USB or Firewire port. In all cases sound adaptors are evaluated according to the number of analog input and output channels provided, the type(s) of digital input and output, and the sound quality.

While all *Red Book* audio CDs are 16-bit recordings sampled at 44.1kHz, sound cards and audio software can work at much higher bit depths and sample rates. 24-bit sound cards, with rates of 96kHz and higher, have become very common. Higher resolution systems have a lower noise floor, and allow engineers to more faithfully preserve the signal throughout the production process. Although some of that sound quality gets lost when it's down-sampled for audio CD, high-resolution consumer formats such as DVD and DVD-Audio are already in place.

Looping Programs

One of the advantages of using multitrack software is that it's really easy to loop sections of audio. While any sampling keyboard can loop a beat, their waveform displays are limited at best. Multitrack recording software can edit, fine-tune and layer loops through a simple visual interface, much like any graphic layout program.

Although looping a section of audio in a digital audio sequencer is very simple, layering two or more loops can be problematic. Unless those loops are at the same tempo, with the same length and number of beats (or an even multiple thereof), the loops won't lock. Getting two slightly different loops to play in sync initially required a lot of tedious editing to make the beats align. Eventually, software tools evolved that automatically changed the time base of loops by slicing and shifting the beats.

Propellerhead Software ReCycle (Mac and Windows) established the slicing and time-shifting paradigm. Sonic Foundry Acid (Windows) was the first multi-track looping program, and many others, including Ableton Live (Mac and Windows) have followed in its wake. Looping is so popular that most professional audio sequencers, such as Cakewalk Sonar and Digidesign Pro Tools, offer built-in or plug-in looping capabilities.

In all cases these programs reduce each loop into a series of slices, which can be played faster or slower. Hence the loop can be time-shifted with little or no effect on the sound of the recording. This is in contrast to DSP time-stretching algorithms, which almost always color the sound.

Multitrack looping tools provide a lot of freedom, practically anything can be mixed and matched. Take clips from any number of records, open them in the loop sequencer, and start mixing and layering – all tempos are adjusted to the master session tempo automatically. Loop sequencing lets one take a building-block approach to composing and arranging music.

In recent upgrades both Live and Acid Pro have improved the way they handle long files (such as an entire song). Pitch shifting is another DJ-relevant feature commonly found in these tools, allowing the keys of melodic passages to be matched. Ableton Live has a crossfader and headphone cueing.

Loop sequencers and looping features within other programs like Pro Tools have really come to the fore in the last few years. Although many DJs, producers, and remixers use looping tools, they're essentially general-purpose applications. They're not particularly differentiated or optimized for DJ work.[1]

---

1 For the full skinny on software looping tools, see the author's previous book *Loops and Grooves: The Musician's Guide to Groove Machines and Loop Sequencers*, 2003, Hal Leonard Corporation.

DJ Plug-ins

Most professional audio software supports plug-ins, which are smaller special-purpose software programs that can be added to a sound editor or multitracker. Many audio plug-ins are DSP audio effects, such as reverb or delay, which modify the sound of an audio file or track. (For more about DSP effects see Chapter 5.) There are also instrument plug-ins, which add synthesizer or sampler voices to compatible recording software.

Our emphasis is on DJ plug-ins that mimic the turntable experience in various ways. The Fruity Scratcher plug-in, part of the Image-Line FruityLoops dance music production package, is a simple example.

The Fruity Scratcher will scratch any audio file. A waveform display helps you locate within the file and an onscreen turntable is used to rock the sound back and forth. This turntable can be moved by a MIDI controller, such the pitch bend lever or modulation wheel on any MIDI keyboard, or by clicking and dragging with the mouse. Scratch movements can be automated, meaning the movements can be recorded and played back. The Arturia Storm software music studio has a comparable double deck display, allowing crossfading, scratching, and pitch control over any sample. All such onscreen scratching features suffer from the same shortcoming: scratching with a mouse is lame.

Serato Scratch, a plug-in for Digidesign Pro Tools, addresses that problem using real turntables as the scratch controllers. The Scratch software package includes two special vinyl records. Instead of music, the records contain an audio control signal. Turntable audio outputs are connected to the Pro Tools audio inputs. The Scratch software listens to the control signals, detects the turntable speeds and directions, and applies those movements to any audio files. The output can be routed to a DJ mixer and sent back to the computer to record a new track.

Although Scratch won't handle needle dropping, it provides the authentic physical experience (and much of the sound quality) of vinyl scratching and works with any turntable. Serato announced that they're cooking up Scratch Live, a stand-alone program (that doesn't require Pro Tools) aimed at the gigging DJ; it should be available by the time you read this.

Serato Scratch plug-in software for Pro Tools.

In addition to such professional tools, there is also an array of consumer-grade mixing and beat matching plug-ins available for the Nullsoft Winamp MP3 player, many of them free. Nullsoft (a division of AOL) also makes the Shoutcast software, a free Winamp plug-in that turns any PC into an Internet radio station. It's worth checking out.

Stand-Alone DJ Applications

Most DJ software programs are toy ware, inexpensive and entertaining, but unsuitable for rigorous professional work. Mixman set the pace for that class of product, offering simple mixing/scratching studio software as well as a dedicated hardware control panel that plugged into the computer.

There is a large group of consumer or semi-professional mixing and beat matching programs, many of them supporting the MP3 file format. Most have a CD player onscreen metaphor, a playlist display, and some degree of control over crossfading and pitch. It's all very nice, but rudimentary, and the sound quality is usually marginal.

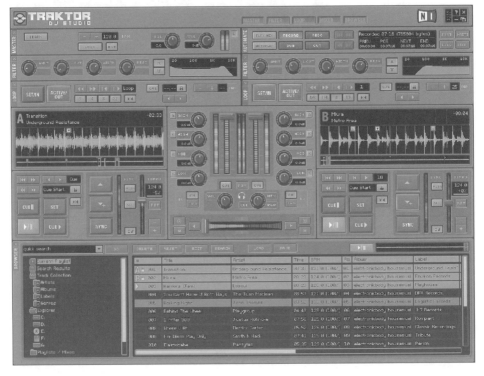

Traktor DJ Studio software, from Native Instruments can time shift and synchronize entire tracks.

The best of the stand-alone mixing/beat matching programs is Traktor DJ Studio, from Native Instruments. Although it has a slightly complicated onscreen interface, Traktor is a pro-quality solution for beat matching, mixing, looping, and cueing audio files.

Like the loop sequencers mentioned earlier, Traktor uses a slicing technique. It looks at the audio file as a series of one-beat segments, then manipulates the playback speed of those slices to match any tempo. Unlike the loop sequencers, Traktor is optimized for full-length songs (as opposed to small loops). The application looks and operates much differently from any conventional audio sequencer or sound editor. Traktor uses a two-decks-plus-mixer visual metaphor; arrangements are created from playlists and by recording real-time mix moves and manipulations.

Onscreen controls such as the crossfader and filter knobs can be mapped to external MIDI devices for easier performance. Traktor will even scratch, and it sounds pretty good, although scratching through a mouse or MIDI controller is a long way from turntablism.

That vinyl gap is bridged by Stanton Final Scratch, the most well-known pro DJ computer program. Like the Serato Scratch plug-in, Final Scratch makes use of any turntable. It includes three vinyl records that contain audio control signals (instead of music). It also comes with the ScratchAmp, a hardware break-out box that allows you to connect two turntables and a two-channel DJ mixer to the computer's USB port.

The first release of Final Scratch ran on the BeOS, a promising operating system that didn't make it. After the demise of Be, Inc. and the acquisition of Final Scratch by Stanton, it was ported to a Linux operating system, which likewise has limited mainstream appeal. Stanton subsequently teamed up with software firm Native Instruments, makers of the aforementioned Traktor. The resultant Traktor-powered Final Scratch runs on Mac OS X; PC users still need to install the Linux-based operating system that is included with the product.

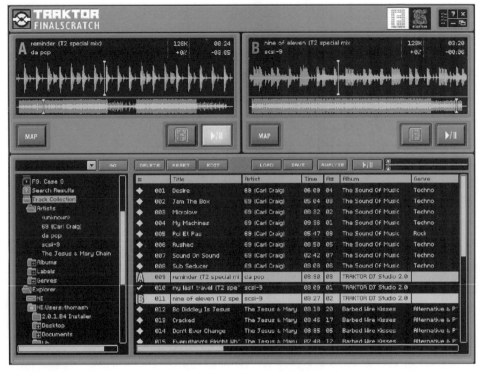

The software half of Stanton's Final Scratch product is based on the Native Instruments Traktor program.

Like Traktor, Final Scratch will mix and scratch any WAV, AIFF, MP3 or CD audio file. DJs can record vinyl collections to a digital file format, put away the records, then play the audio files. There's less to carry around – the time code records are all the vinyl that's needed – and the audio never deteriorates when it's in a digital format.

Many great songs are long out of print and hard to find on vinyl or CD. With the advent of Internet file sharing, a lot of music has become available as MP3 files from any number of licensed or unauthorized sources. When one can scratch and mix any MP3 track, it removes the record collecting imperative. It's not necessary to search through bins of vinyl or CDs digging for artifacts. Practically any desired track is just a download away on peer-to-peer networks such as Kazaa and Gnutella.

No longer bound to the vinyl embodiment the DJ's potential catalog is dramatically expanded, while the tribal practice of record hunting is de-emphasized. You can't beat the Internet for selection and convenience, but one hopes the DJ's traditional competitive scavenging is never totally abandoned.

Other DJ Software

Vinyl restoration software can take away pops, clicks, hiss, and other surface noise, removing it from the digital recording while leaving the music intact. Audio restoration professionals use systems such as Sonic Solutions, Cube-Tec and Cedar, which cost many thousands of dollars. Fortunately there are also serviceable semi-pro editions, such as Arboretum Ray Gun, Dartech Dart XP, and Steinberg Clean, which cost less than a hundred bucks.

Pro audio tools are cool to the point of seeming magical, yet there are other types of DJ software, equally useful, but much less glamorous.

Station automation software, which compiles and executes playlists of music, advertisements and announcements, has been around for years. It's used by radio broadcasters in place of live DJs. Internet DJs can get the same effect by using Winamp with any crossfading/mixing plug-in.

Music library software, which catalogs and organizes a record or CD collection, is another old school application. Today most software players, including Winamp, iTunes and the Windows Media Player, have full-featured library or jukebox displays that organize the music on your hard drive.

We've also seen a variety of customized business applications meant to streamline the daily operations of a music office, radio station, or mobile DJ business. While there is certainly great value in having specialized databases and workflows, it may be overkill. Standard-issue business software like Microsoft Access and Excel can easily be adapted for the simple invoicing and record keeping most DJs require.

Any DJ – indeed, anybody at all – can benefit from using a contact and time management system. It doesn't matter whether it's on paper, like a Franklin Quest organizer, on the computer in Microsoft Outlook, or on a handheld device like a Palm or Blackberry. If you can get your schedule, phone numbers, and to-do list all in one place, keep it updated, and keep it by your side, you'll be way ahead of the curve.

DJ-Specific Computer Hardware

We've seen some fancy toy-ware for aspiring DJs, such as the Mixman control surface mentioned earlier. A more current example is the Yamaha DJX-IIB, a high-end audio toy that combines scratching, loop playback and effects. It has seven hundred preset audio loops, seventy scratchable sounds, a crossfader, a jog wheel, two sets of filters, and ten other effects.

The DJX-IIB has MIDI in and out ports, and includes software that allows user loops to be loaded into the machine. The DJX-IIB is a fun unit, kids love it, and it can even be worn on a guitar strap. But we don't expect to see many people stepping on stage wielding a DJX-IIB. It's just not a professional tool, and it's just barely a computer peripheral.

Yamaha DJX-IIB, a DJ toy for grown-
ups, includes a software utility for load-
ing custom sounds.
Photo: Linda Monson

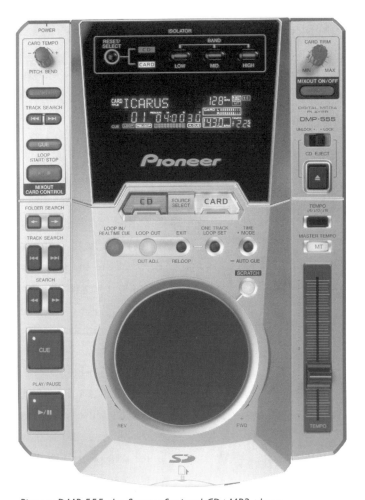

Pioneer DMP-555, the first professional CD+MP3 player.
Photo courtesy of Pioneer.

Professionals should have a look at Pioneer's CD + MP3 players, the
DMP-555. The DMP-555 includes software for loop editing, CD ripping,
and sound library management, and will attach to a computer by a USB
connector. The unit has lots of internal memory, plus support for remove-
able memory cards. The real selling point is MP3 support; the DMP will
tempo sync MP3 loops, and works with essentially any MP3 file pulled
down from the Internet. It's a flexible, multi-format DJ machine and computer sound peripheral. We consider this the shape of things to come.

Sadly, more pro DJ computer peripherals haven't been available. Up until now one needed a sound card with four analog audio outputs and a separate DJ mixer to have a cue channel. But as we went to press, sound card manufacturer Echo Digital Audio announced the availability of a DJ sound card called Indigo DJ.

The Echo Indigo DJ's key feature is a headphone cue channel. The card, compatible with Mac and Windows laptop computers, has separate line level (master) and headphone (preview) outputs. The Echo Indigo DJ is a high-resolution audio interface, capable of playing back 24-bit, 96kHz audio. Up to eight channels of audio can be mixed in the Indigo DJ's software control panel. While the separate monitor/preview channel seems like a simple thing, no previous audio card offered that capability. It simplifies setup and improves portability for computer DJs who use applications such as Native Instruments Traktor or Ableton Live. We expect to see more cards like it in the future.

The Indigo DJ sound card includes a special headphone cue channel, designed for DJs. Photo courtesy of Echo.

Interview:

The Freelance
Hellraiser

A British DJ and remixer, The Freelance Hellraiser is the first real star of the mash-up scene.

What does your live performance setup consist of?

I don't have a live performance setup as such. When I started doing remixes and bootlegs I would take out a Roland SP-808 'Groove Sampler' for live work. Now I do everything at home and burn onto a CD-R before I leave the house.

In the U.K. most venues have a set of Technics 1200's (or equivalent) and a generic mixer so there's no need to carry anything for DJing. I'm not one of these DJ's that has to take his own cartridges/needles. I don't scratch so there's no real need.

Most places now have a set of CD decks, too. If they don't, I have a pair of Pioneer CDJ-1000's and a Numark Axis 8 that I can take to a venue. I also take out my own set of Pioneer headphones.

What does your studio setup consist of?

Here's a full list of my studio at present:

Apple Macintosh G4

Mark Of The Unicorn MOTU 828 audio interface

Emagic AMT8 MIDI interface

Emagic Logic Platinum recording software

Native Instruments Reaktor software synthesizer

Mackie VLZ-1402 14-channel mixer.

Korg MS2000 synthesizer

Korg Microkorg synthesizer

EMU Proteus 2000 sound module

Alesis M1a powered near-field monitors

Numark turntable

Numark Axis 8 CD player

Pioneer CDJ-1000 CD players (two)

What should people look for (or avoid) when putting together their first DJ or computer sound systems?

Avoid spending months reading magazines dreaming of all the really expensive top-end gear that's totally out of your range. Just go out right now with whatever money you have and get the very best your budget will allow. I know it's a cliché but ideas are a million times more important than equipment. I did my first remix on a Yamaha DJX home keyboard that had about 6 seconds of sampling time and cost £150. The band I did the remix for loved it and it ended up being played on radio. That exposure was worth much more than £150.

Before I could afford my current computer system I bought a Roland SP-808 Groove Sampler. It had everything in one box: Sequencer, sampler, synthesizer, digital recording and ran everything off of cheap ZIP disks. It was about £700. Although the magazine write-ups were not entirely flattering (don't always believe what they say) it was perfect for my needs. I got several remixes/bootlegs completed on it that were played on radio.

When the time was right and I had a bit more cash I 'graduated' to a computer-based system. I'm still building my system now.

How did you acquire DJ and production skills, and how would you suggest a youngster approach it?

Practice. Play stuff to your friends. They'll be your harshest critics—even if they're being polite you'll know when they think something stinks. They're also your best form of encouragement. It's where much of your self-belief comes from.

Put on parties at home/school/clubs. Any excuse will do. Also go to clubs where others are DJing and observe what gets the crowd going. Listen to mix tapes by other DJ's and listen to the themes running through their sets. There's often a common thread that links their tunes together.

Be a bit boring, kiss your social life goodbye for a bit and practice loads in your bedroom. All these DJ's with seemingly effortless skills have gone through thousands of hours practicing in their rooms.

Do you practice mixing?

I've always been more concerned with tune selection than getting a perfect mix. I'll sometimes practice a set before I go out to work, but generally I do most of my practicing when I'm out.

What's the relationship between your live performances and your recordings? Do you consider yourself primarily a producer, a DJ, or both?

My recordings are divided between:
A) Would this work on a dance-floor? or B) Would I enjoy sitting at home and listening to this ?

Most of my bootlegs are created with the dance-floor in mind. I like the idea of messing with people's pre-conceptions of a song/genre/artist. A bootleg is best served once—after a few plays they can become a bit tedious.

My original material is more about creating a song that will sound good indefinitely.

I consider myself to be a producer first. I've been writing songs and learning production techniques much longer than DJing. I also enjoy producing more than DJing—you're not nearly as exposed sitting in front of your computer in the comfort of a studio.

DJing serves two main purposes: to pay the rent, and to test out the songs I like (including my own productions) on an audience that will not have heard them before. I suppose there's also a certain amount of musical evangelism involved. "I love this record so much, you have to listen to it!"

We think "Stroke of Genie-us" is an amazing mash-up, far better than either of the original songs. What can you tell us about the creative process on that track, and about the technical process?

I'd had the Christina a cappella for some time and knew that I could do something great with it. She has a superb voice and it's unusual to get a pop a cappella. Most of them are hip-hop or R&B. The 'Genie...' track is really slow (about 75 beats per minute) so I knew it would work well as a 'skank' (a 150BPM double-time rhythm track.)

The Freelance Hellraiser. Photo courtesy of Nick DeCosemo.

It's purely by luck that the Strokes song worked so well. I knew the tempo was good, but the pitch was a gamble that paid off. You have a certain amount of control over pitch and tempo but any significant changes usually result in a serious deterioration in the sound quality. The other great thing about "Hard To Explain" is that virtually the whole song is played out during the intro, prior to Julian's first verse. I had several interesting chord-changes and guitar flourishes to work with.

Finally you have the rhythm track. I thought for ages that it was a drum machine—it was only later when I read an interview with their producer that I discovered it was Fab Moretti playing a live kit. The producer recorded several small bursts on the kit and tracked them to deliberately make them sound like a lo-tech 1980s drum machine. It meant the drums were really tight. I put a bit of overdrive on them using one of my standard Logic effects plug-ins.

I deliberately stayed away from using too many effects because I did want it to sound like a duet, rather than a mash-up. Too much tampering would have detracted from the 'live' feel of the song. The only other change was a bit of phasing on the guitars on the last chorus and a little chop-up of her voice near the end of the track.

I originally did the track having come home drunk one night and did it for a bit of a laugh. To me it was one of many bootlegs I had done at that time. I wasn't even sure if it worked at first and my friends' reactions won me over. The first cut was just shy of five minutes (too long) so I cut it down to three minutes in the hope it would get a couple of plays on radio.

"Last Night Ice Baby" is another favorite track...

I didn't make this track. I don't know who did it.

The other one I'm often wrongly credited with is "Smells Like Teen Booty." That was the fault of *The Best Bootlegs...* compiler. It's actually Soulwax.

What attracts you to a track, what do you look for in remix material?

A bootleg plays on the familiarity of a song, so you tend to stay clear of obscure samples. This is the opposite for my original compositions or a remix.

The most important thing is getting two songs that work well together sonically. Once that comes together it's easier for the listener to apply an intellectual argument to it. I get the most excited when I'm placing a strong vocal track (such as an R&B vocal) over a rock instrumental with interesting chord changes. If all the changes work harmonically there really is nothing like it. To me it's the musical equivalent of striking gold. Achieving this involves hours of listening and no small amount of luck.

How do you get isolated vocals? Do you find a cappella versions, or do you filter out the accompaniment?

I search for a cappellas.

We heard that you received a cease and desist letter. Tell us about your encounters with the record business.

XFM actually received the cease and desist letter for playing "A Stroke..." Eddy Temple-Morris (an XFM DJ) passed on a copy to me to frame and hang in my toilet. No labels have contacted me (yet) to complain about any of my bootlegs.

I've since read interviews with Christina and The Strokes where they've been asked about "A Stroke..." She's on record as liking it ("It's how it should have sounded all along") whereas Julian from The Strokes was less flattering ("I was expecting more").

Are you strictly underground at this point? Will there be mainstream, licensed Freelance Hellraiser releases?

I never set out to be underground. Due to the spread of my bootlegs on the Internet, a lot of people thought of me as some kind of musical anarchist/copyright freedom fighter. I've quite enjoyed the notoriety (who wouldn't?!) but that was never really my aim. There are no intentional political statements in any of my bootlegs. What people read into them is up to them.

Releasing mainstream/licensed music was always my first aim. There will be a few of these coming out this year, along with several legitimate remixes and maybe the odd cheeky bootleg.

What's your goal with DJing and remixing? What are you trying to achieve?

With my DJing/remixes/bootlegs/original songs I want to go out to as many people as possible and show them there is another way. I've never subscribed to the notion that you can only stay true to one genre, either as a DJ or a recording artist. My goal is try and break down those barriers. The blinkered marketing policies of the record labels (both major and independent) should shoulder much of the blame for this.

At what age did you start DJing and how long have you been doing it professionally?

I started DJing when I was 15—just doing parties in and around my home town of South Woodham Ferrers in Essex. I started getting paid at 18. My friends and I ran our own clubs while at university in Dundee, Scotland. We'd make money by charging a small 'tax' on the door to cover our costs.

What DJs, producers, or other artists influenced you as an artist?

My predominant influences are: Prince Paul, The Dust Brothers, Prince, Stevie Wonder, Terminator X, Kraftwerk, Art of Noise, A Tribe Called Quest, Giorgio Moroder, James Brown, Elvis Presley, Norman Cook, James Lavelle, DJ Premier, Primal Scream, Lalo Schiffrin, Ice-T, William Orbit, John Williams, Eric B & Rakim, Bruno Martelli, Pete Rock and CL Smooth, The Rolling Stones, DJ Shadow, The Chemical Brothers, Tom Jones, Jimi Hendrix, Harold Faltermeyer, NWA and Andy Wetherall.

Who do you listen to now?

My current favorites are: Soulwax, The Neptunes, Freeform Five, David Holmes, Snow Patrol, Felix Da Housecat and Tommie Sunshine, Jay-Z, Osymyso, Sugababes, Radio 4, Miss Dynamite, The White Stripes, Soulchild, The Datsuns, Nas, The Faint, The White Sport, DFA, Cosmos, Arthur Argent, Jacknife Lee, and Dr. Dre.

Are there other people who helped you get going as a professional, assisted with your career?

Too many to mention them all. I've been blessed with amazing friends and family who have worked tirelessly for the past few years to encourage me, promote me, and put me in the position I'm currently in.

In terms of the music itself, Gary Lightbody from Snow Patrol/The Reindeer Section. The first remix I completed was of Snow Patrol—it got me my first radio play. Gary and myself are currently recording original material for my debut album. The man is a genius.

Anu Pillai—the creative mastermind behind Freeform Five—has been a big inspiration. He's one of the best producers I've ever heard, and my current studio was built largely on his advice and recommendations.

The Dewaele brothers (Soulwax) have been really helpful to me. I've always admired their production values, and they advised me on how to improve the sound of a lot of my tunes.

Eddy Temple-Morris is a DJ at London-based radio station, XFM. He played out my first Snow Patrol remix (one year prior to any of my bootlegs) and was the first DJ anywhere in the world to play "A Stroke Of Genius." His partner in crime and another huge help has been James "The Rinse" Hyman.

We got your tracks from Kazaa—what are your thoughts on peer-to-peer file sharing networks?

To be honest I don't use any of them. I come from the old school, and although I purchase a lot of music from online stores, I really enjoy going out to record shops and rooting through the racks.

I don't think P2P harms the music industry as much as they (the industry) would have us believe but I do accept the fact that it's illegal and, to a certain extent, morally wrong. I certainly do not believe that music is there to be 'liberated' from its owners. It's easy to forget that someone, somewhere along the musical chain (be it the trainee engineer/tea-boy in the studio, to the band, to the multi-million selling record producer, to the junior office clerk mailing out 10,000 promos, etc.) put a lot of effort into making that track and somebody, somewhere paid them for that work. Simple. Just like any other job. Somebody paid for it and they want to keep ownership of it. This is why most "law-abiding" people don't liberate cars from their owners, or believe all homes should be shared by everyone.

Let's not pretend that this dilemma is anything new. Just within my lifetime I remember the "Home Taping Is Killing Music" campaign of the 1970s and '80s. The labels tried to convince us they would become bankrupt within a couple of years if Maxell, BASF, and TDK had their evil way. And yet we still got to a point recently where a major record label was able to offer Robbie Williams £80 million ($120 million U.S.) to sign-on and £20 million ($30 million U.S.) to Mariah Carey to sign-off! In the meantime millions and millions of C60s and C90s clutter up the attics and garages of houses around the world.

The real problem at the heart of this argument is that the music industry and the music retailers have been operating as a cartel for years and have been artificially sustaining the high price of their products. The prices they are charging today are not fair and cannot be justified. Once this is properly tackled and CDs are offered at realistic, fair prices (I don't think any single CD album should cost any more than £9.99/$9.99) the peer-to-peer "problem" will disappear. To me, paying £14.99/$17.99 for an Eminem album is morally wrong, though not because of his lyrics.

As I mentioned I'm a strong believer in music copyright and a strong believer that someone should get paid fairly for the work they do. People who steal music and "bootleg" it are breaking the law, pure and simple, and I agree with that.

I might argue that me pressing up 500 copies of a song on seven-inch vinyl is unlikely to dent the pockets of RCA Records or Christina Aguilera, or indeed The Strokes. It's still wrong though, and I did it knowing the possible consequences. There's no "gray area" or blurring of lines. There are laws out there whether people agree with them or not. You can live by them, live outside them, or swim happily around in the middle of them getting the best of both!

Do you foresee a day when the record industry will sanction and encourage your type of work?

It's already happening. I've been commissioned by two of the world's biggest record labels to do "legitimate bootlegs" and have been given access to their entire back-catalogues. It's not just me; Soulwax, Osymyso, Richard X, Jacknife Lee, Kurtis Rush and The Cartel Communique have all been offered similar projects.

The DJ
Tomorrow

The Technology Forecast

One of the nice things about turntables is they are a mature technology. Indeed, the vinyl formats that turntables serve are solidly obsolete. The LP, seven-inch, and twelve-inch single are frozen in time, they will evolve no more. As for turntables, their fundamentals haven't changed since stereo came along. But as we noted in Chapter 3, demand from DJs breathed a second life into the turntable and caused it to morph from a consumer entertainment system into a professional music production tool.

The classic Technics SL-1200 embodiment hasn't been – and shouldn't be – significantly altered. Like Coca-Cola, or a Gibson Les Paul, it's an immortal cultural icon. But other fine turntable brands abound and digital features such as BPM counters, time shifting, and S/PDIF outputs are all points on which these decks compete. Future turntables may include cueing and looping features much like a CD deck with many minutes of sample memory.

It's certain that digital technology will continue to crop up at every point along the signal chain. Digital input and output channels will appear on more mixers, turntables, and amplifiers, allowing DJs to have an all-digital audio path. Audio CDs are always recorded and played back as 16-bit audio at a sampling rate of 44.1kHz, but larger bit depths and faster sampling rates are commonly found in pro recording gear. High-resolution mixers, decks, and power amps, all digitally linked, will become commonplace.

Delivery formats and players will continue to evolve. Pioneer is already making the first professional CD + MP3 player, the DMP-555. It includes computer software for loop editing, CD ripping, and sound library management. You can plan on seeing more multiformat players, and more software front-ends to professional DJ gear as time moves forward.

Vinyl will probably never completely go away, thanks to demand from DJs, but the audio CD is next in line for obsolescence. DVD audio, or some other format like it, will take the CD's place, providing high-resolution audio, surround sound, and any number of other digital extras.

One of the most important extras will be copy protection, so content owners can restrict the copying or distribution of the audio/video content. Audio CDs have no copy protection or digital rights management (DRM). Attempts to add copy protection to Audio CDs violate the *Red Book* specification and cause compatibility problems. The recording industry wants a purpose-built secure disc format and had hoped to piggyback on DVD's consumer acceptance.

Those plans were scratched when the DVD's content scrambling system, or CSS, was defeated in a couple of ways. These vulnerabilities are not fixable. Software programs such as DeCSS and DVD X Copy, that allow individuals to make backup copies of DVDs, are now widely distributed. The recording industry sensibly deferred any mass migration to DVD audio when it witnessed the film industry's massive security failure. The record industry is in the midst of a multiyear experiment with secure CD variants, trying copy protection solutions from a host of vendors. It's anybody's guess as to whether one of these, or some entirely different format, will be the one to replace the *Red Book* audio CD. All we know is that a better-sounding, more-secure premium release format is inevitable.

As surround sound becomes a routine consideration in the studio and home, nightclub sound systems will follow the same trend. Mixing in a 2-D space leads to controllers like joysticks, or the Korg Kaoss Pad.

Certain DJ CD decks and mixers have sampling functions, allowing an audio clip to be saved in memory and played on demand, layered over the main CD sound. We were struck by the comparative stinginess of the implementations: these decks can only save a few samples, each sample must be brief, and changing the pitch or volume involves button pushing and knob turning.

Watch for manufacturers to add more megabytes of memory for longer samples, and additional buttons (or pressure-sensitive "pads") so that more samples can be played. Adding sampling, plus cue and loop features to a turntable would permit certain CD techniques within a vinyl context. As sampling support improves, a natural progression might be to add MIDI in jacks, so that sampled loops could be triggered, pitch- or time-shifted, and volume-controlled from any MIDI keyboard or controller. Better waveform displays that show more detail will appear on high-end decks.

Another thing that surprised us while researching this book was the absence of control over grain (a.k.a. frame or window) size, meaning the length of the audio segments used when scratching and searching. None of the CD players we looked at had any support for changing the grain size. Because it can have a dramatic effect on the sound and tone, and lead to unique effects, we hope that some deck maker will eventually add grain control.

Built-in effects are a natural way to differentiate pro audio devices, and DJ equipment manufacturers are already going down that path. The variety of effects, the degree of parameter control available to the user, the configuration (patching) of multieffect chains, and the types of physical interfaces that control the effects will all surely continue to develop.

It seems very likely that turntables, CD players, and mixers will begin to look more like computer peripherals. Adding a MIDI out, USB or Firewire jack to any of these devices so that the platter, jog wheel, sliders or buttons could control onscreen samples would be a good start. Then add a big hard drive to the turntable, player, or mixer, so that entire LPs or CDs could be saved to, and played from, internal memory. Naturally you'd want support for MP3, WMA and other audio file formats, and the ability to transfer files with any computer.

We're already seeing CD decks that can play back multiple sound sources so one can hear two different tracks at the same time. We figure this will continue; a player could have any number of virtual internal decks or sound channels. The jog wheel and other controls would be assignable to any or all of the channels.

The logical conclusion of such a progression would be the stand-alone digital DJ workstation. You'd combine the functions of the turntable and CD player, add a mixer channel strip and crossfader to the top panel, plus a headphone jack for previewing the cue channel. One could scratch and mix any number of channels and sound sources from a single device, and record those mixes on the unit's internal hard drive.

You'd want a software front end, for editing and jukebox loading as well as some degree of compatibility with popular DJ or remix software, so one might use familiar programs in conjunction with the unit.

CD drives should be CD/DVD burners as well as players, and easily replaceable, to facilitate repairs and upgrades. As for jog wheels, we'd propose a radical step into the past: Use a real turntable with a platter and tonearm. One should be able to scratch a vinyl LP, or a time code record (a la Final Scratch), a CD, a sample, or any audio file, all from the same physical interface. For jog wheel action, remove the record and slip mat and move the platter. Or mix and scratch with real records, backed up by the ability to sample, layer, and record everything all within the same device.

Competition is intense in the pro audio industry, and the best way to compete is through innovation. We hope that digital crossbreed devices will never fully replace real vinyl and turntables, but they're already becoming a factor in the marketplace. Hybrid devices such as the Pioneer DMP-555, the Numark TT-X1 turntable, and the Korg Kaoss Mixer are steps along that evolutionary path.

Trend Lines

The fact that DJs use other people's recordings has put DJs at the center of a long series of hassles over property rights. Digital sampling and Webcasting have returned DJs to the intellectual property crossfire. With the advent of Internet music and film piracy, copyright has become a hot-button issue for people of all walks of life. DJs as a class have nearly a century of experience in these battles.

The record industry built fences around digital sampling controlling it like prescription medicine. Today sampling is allowed, even encouraged, but only with a license from the copyright owner, who may refuse to grant it and may demand any level of fee. As with most prohibitions, certain people get rich from it, while circumvention becomes the norm for many. The end result is an unmistakable chilling effect, as licensing makes multisourced sound collages commercially unviable.

As we noted earlier in the book, the sampling problem faced by DJs, remixers, producers, and musicians is a problem shared by society in general. We're promised freedom of speech. But when we really quote someone they gain veto over our expression and acquire vast powers of taxation. The limited, ineffective doctrine of fair use is able to occasion-ally shield teachers and parodists, but is powerless within the commercial arena of music production.

In the 1970s some FM stations would broadcast entire albums, expressly so that their listeners could tape record the music. It was quite common, some of the biggest stations did it. The record industry leaned on the FCC to ban the practice. Today radio DJs can play no more than three songs in a row by a single artist, no more than two songs from the same album, and pre-announcing artist blocks is prohibited.

Putting handcuffs on DJs wasn't enough; Congress eventually passed the Audio Home Recording Act of 1992, which placed a tax on every blank tape sold. That tax money, millions of dollars each year, is given to the largest record labels and music publishers; it's a form of corporate welfare.

The Audio Home Recording Act operates on the assumption that every-one buying blank cassettes or DATs is pirating music. The presumption of criminality is an ironic trend in a country where one is supposedly innocent until proven guilty. Many people buy blank tapes for office use, to record their own compositions, or to save non-copyrighted audio. Unfortunately non-infringers are penalized right along with the pirates; no one's exempt from the blank tape tax.

The Home Recording Act was a landmark example of cooperation between industry and government. They've nominally legitimized a fair use practice that could never be policed if outlawed. And they've established a nice little shakedown racket for the benefit of the alleged victims, which include some of the world's biggest corporations. Media businesses would like to extend this pattern on a grander scale to the Internet and beyond.

When Internet audio streaming became feasible, veteran broadcasters and hordes of Web newbies began DJing on the net. The record industry scrambled to erect walls around Webcasting and other Internet music activities. They've been very successful. A U.S. performance right for sound recordings on the Internet is now the law, a feat the record industry failed to achieve with radio. The industry's trade group then "negotiated" royalty rates for Internet music streams and appointed themselves to collect and disburse the revenues. That series of events is thought to have settled the issue over Internet radio. However, as we go to press, a group of small Webcasters are preparing an anti-trust lawsuit against the Recording Industry Association of American (RIAA) over this set of issues.

Technology progresses faster than business models, case law, or legislation, and unlicensed music distribution is growing at an exponential rate. Music piracy occurs in a variety of ways on the Internet; the peer-to-peer (P2P) file sharing systems, which descended from Napster, are the most well-known and trafficked venues at this time.

P2P file sharing is a boon for DJs. Programs including Kazaa, Blubster, Shareaza, and dozens of others, provide convenient access to vast music libraries. Most shared audio files are in the MP3 file format, and can easily be burned to an audio CD. P2P is more than just a musical pig trough, it's also a distribution system. Mix tapes and mash-ups that can't be commercially replicated are disseminated worldwide through the file sharing networks.

Researchers say as many as fifty million Americans download music from the Internet; one in five computer users share files with others. The criminalization of that entire class is becoming a generational issue for this era. Radio DJs trained people to expect free music. That expectation didn't evaporate when the Internet came along; it expanded.

As these words are being written, the controversy over Internet music has reached the point where the RIAA is now subpoenaing hundreds of file sharers every week. Unable to compete online, the record business has resorted to suing music lovers. It's a sign of an industry in crisis.

The battle over online music has led some to question the underpinnings of copyright and intellectual property. As for the media companies, they're striving to expand copyright through legislation and through technological means such as DRM. All forms of media, including films, television, books, and software applications, will face erosion of their business models, due to the Internet. The music industry was simply the first sector to really get hammered, and to strike back.

We don't foresee any quick conclusion to this battle for control over media. In fact, we believe the key participants benefit from escalating the hassle. The dangers are that build-ups of copy protection technology hamper people's access to information, and anti-piracy efforts, along with the war against terrorism, could provide a platform for a police state.

DJs have as much experience on the borders of copyright, commerce, and technology as any class of citizen. Their history shows that these market issues can be resolved to the benefit of most participants, although it's usually a painful, costly process. One way DJs survived is by generally ignoring authority figures, keeping the music playing, and keeping the party rolling. Why would the next century be any different?

The Musical Implications

At the end of the day, it's all about the music. DJs helped nurture and popularize most of the significant musical trends during the Twentieth Century. By the second half of the century, DJs evolved from musical scholars and record announcers into creators in their own right. Dub, hip-hop, and every flavor of contemporary dance music owe their very existence to DJs.

Dancing and music enjoyment are archetypal human activities, which seem to exist in all cultures. Technology disembodied music from the musician and instrument; it became possible, even preferable, to have dances without bands. DJs sprang up in that vacuum, providing the selecting, emceeing, and show directing that were previously handled by bandleaders or conductors.

It should come as no surprise that the class of music selectors began to have tremendous influence over the music from which they chose. What's surprising is the double standard that DJs are held to: the idea that DJing is sacrosanct and must not be profaned by commerce. Broadcasters can take money for playing obnoxious ads, but it's an ethical issue if the money is for playing a new song. That's a strange attitude for a capitalist society.

DJ influence over music extends beyond mere hit picking and song pushing. The way music is recorded has evolved in large part to fit DJ requirements. Prominent drums, and a big low end, are the foundation for almost all popular music of the last fifty years, because DJs and dancers want a good beat. The sonic profile associated with the dance and hip-hop genres comes directly from the dub godfathers, Jamaican DJs-turned-producers.

Jamaicans came up with a significant name for DJs, they called them selectors. To acknowledge that disk jockeying is an art form is to accept that an act of selection, a decision, can be an artistic statement. This broader understanding of selection began informing the visual arts, courtesy of Marcel Duchamp and some others, around the same time that radio disk jockeys were getting rolling, right after World War I.

Although there are all kinds of DJs, covering every possible musical genre, DJs as a group have a special occupational relationship to dance music. As dance floor gatekeepers transitioned into remixing and production, DJs exploded the framework of song construction, and dispensed with the idea of the immutable sonic artifact. When sampling became pervasive, DJs challenged the very notion of authorship (and lost).

It became routine for records to be constructed from recycled parts; at that point, the primacy of musicianship and the lingering cult of musical virtuosity went out the window. DJs with no formal training and no instrument but a record player could sculpt sound like a Hendrix and be taken seriously.

While there will always be the verse/chorus archetype, a less structured, more linear approach to record making has come about, particularly evident in electronic music that grew out of emulating DJ mixing styles.

Before the innovations of the dub and disco pioneers, there was no such thing as a remix. Each recording had exactly one mix; an artist released a song once, and moved on. Thanks to the DJ-driven practice of remixing, recordings are now understood to have a more fluid character. Any release is just one of an infinite number of possible versions.

Moreover, it was DJs who established the recombinant mode of music production, building new tracks out of breaks and samples lifted from other records. The watershed event of pop cannibalism was "The Adventures of Grandmaster Flash on the Wheels of Steel." In the wake of that single, looping became a predominant means of record making. Sampling's success is due in large part to its cost-effectiveness and ability to stimulate an instant familiar response in the listener.

DJs have become agents of change in a Darwinian cultural ecosystem. Musicians had been stealing from each other since time began, but always indirectly, through the filter of a physical performance. It was probably inevitable that hits would be made by directly grafting together the best bits of other records. But it took DJs to bring it about, birthing this powerful hybrid called the derivative composition.

DJs are groove liaisons, conduits between label and dance floor, between producer and consumer. Over the course of time DJs have come to resemble the musicians and bandleaders they essentially replaced. They have taken on the shamanic cultural role, and are accorded much the same respect (or lack thereof) as any artist.

In fact, some DJs have become musicians, using the turntable as a musical instrument. The turntable metamorphosis, from consumer device to analog sampler, is a unique event in musical history. For almost a hundred years, no one would dream of scratching a record – interrupting playback was to be avoided. One teenager turned that whole idea of record handling on its head, and established the turntable scratch as one of the most distinctive sounds in the world.

When the record industry ordered an upgrade, DJs pulled the turntable off the scrap heap of obsolescence. They rounded up records that nobody else wanted, and used these cast-off parts to create things that were truly beautiful, challenging, lasting, and important.

Where all of this is going is hard to predict. We believe that the erosion of song structure, originality, and authorship will continue, perhaps accelerate. Expect to hear more experiments with noise and dissonance, the last sonic frontiers. And expect technology to make new sounds possible.

Plan on seeing more video DJs, meaning artists who do visual mixing, looping, and scratching in addition to cutting sound. Emergency Broadcast Network, a political-minded industrial band, went the furthest in this direction to date, producing entire concerts (and CDs) from film and TV actualities. The group built their own video sampler and toured in the mid-1990s but didn't sustain their career. Video sampling is going to become more accessible and more prevalent as digital video technology matures. Some video jockeys will be glorified lighting directors, others will become true audio/video artists.

The hardware business depends on an annual upgrade cycle. Manufacturers put new competitive features in each successive generation. Likewise the music business has come to depend on seasonal changes in youth culture to keep the merchandise fresh. The various arms of the music/media complex labor mightily to maintain an endless parade of consumer trends. In the rare occasion that any actual subculture or grass-roots movement arises, the industry moves quickly to co-opt and dissipate the scene. Anti-materialist tendencies especially need to be squelched and converted into consumable goods, lest they threaten the whole setup.

That culture machine's not going away, at least not without a hellish fight. But as long as DJs are out there, keeping things stirred up, keeping it real, and keeping the party rolling, the machine will have to struggle to stay on top. The DJ has historically been an unpredictable factor in an otherwise tightly controlled media business food chain. DJing attracts mavericks, music lovers, and other dangerous sorts – that's not likely to change.

Teen rebel subculture is thoroughly commoditized, has been since Elvis. Yet every so often a breach develops, and a little light shines through. In a great many cases, it was DJs who kicked open the hole.

We trust that disruptive tradition will continue. We think DJs will never be fully assimilated by the media business. We believe DJs will continue to be an engine in the ongoing mutation of musical forms. We hope that DJs will always have the potential to confound and perplex the establishment, to astound and delight the crowd, and to take the party higher.

Now that you've read this book, if you're a dancer or listener, give the DJ some love. If you're a DJ, get down with your bad self.

And go wild,

TJS

Cueing

Cueing is the DJ technique of starting a record at a particular point. The cue point may be the first note or beat of the song, the first beat of a drum break, or any other position in the track. No one's sure who invented cueing; radio DJs have been backspinning and cueing records for many years; nightclub DJs picked up on the practice in the late 1960s as discotheques first proliferated.

These lessons require two turntables or two professional CD decks, plus a DJ mixer, monitors (either a PA system, an amplifier and speakers, or self-powered speakers), headphones, and any two records or CDs.

Slip-Cueing

A basic DJ workflow entails playing a record on turntable 1. While the audience is listening to that record, the DJ cues up the next record on turntable 2. Turntable 2 is monitored through the mixer's cue channel, which can be heard on headphones but is not in the master (house) mix. By using the cue channel, the DJ can find and practice the cue point without the audience hearing.

- Play a record on turntable 1.
- Move the mixer's crossfader to the left, so channel 1 is heard in the master mix, and channel 2 is silenced.
- Assign turntable 2 (channel 2) to the cue channel.
- While listening in the headphones to the cue channel, play the record on turntable 2.
- When you reach the point where you want to cue, lightly touch the record so that the vinyl stops spinning. The platter and slip mat should continue rotating below the record as you hold it in place.
- Rotate the record counter-clockwise under the needle to locate the cue point. This is called backspinning. You can move the record back and forth, like scratching, to find the exact spot. When doing this, continue to hold the record lightly so that the platter can keep rotating.
- When you've found the right spot, practice the cue by releasing the record.
- The record does not reach playing speed instantly, there is a lag as the vinyl gets up to speed. You can reduce this lag and help the record get up to speed by releasing the vinyl with a slight forward movement of the fingertips.
- Once you're happy with the cue point, and able to perform the cue satisfactorily, locate the cue point once more, and again hold the record.
- Move the mixer's crossfader to the center, so that channel 2 comes into the master mix.
- Release the record to perform the cue.
- Move the mixer's crossfader to the right, to remove channel 1 from the master mix.

CD Cueing

Since there is no physical contact with the disc, and no speed issue, CD cueing is much easier than vinyl cueing. Professional CD decks allow you to set and recall cue points. The cue button works in conjunction with the play/pause button.

- Play a CD on CD player 1.
- Move the mixer's crossfader to the left, so channel 1 is heard in the master mix, and channel 2 is silenced.
- Assign CD player 2 (channel 2) to the mixer's cue channel.
- While listening in the headphones to the cue channel, select any CD track on player 2, using the FWD, track, or search function.
- Press the play/pause button to start playback at the beginning of the track.
- A cue point is automatically set at the start of the track. Press the cue button to stop playback and return to that cue point.
- Press and hold the cue button to hear playback from the cue point. Playback stops when you release the cue button.
- Move the mixer's crossfader to the center so that channel 2 comes into the master mix.
- Press the play/pause button, or hold down the cue button, to perform the cue.
- Move the mixer's crossfader to the right to remove channel 1 from the master mix.

Cueing In Time

Once you have the knack of finding and performing a cue, the next step is to release the cue in time with the music. The next series of steps applies to both turntables and CD players.

• Play a record on turntable 1.

• Move the mixer's crossfader to the left so channel 1 is heard in the master mix and channel 2 is silenced.

• Assign turntable 2 (channel 2) to the mixer's cue channel.

• While listening in the headphones to the cue channel, find and hold your cue point on turntable 2. (CD player users, set this point as a cue. Press the in button or the play/pause button to set the cue. Pioneer owners press the cue button.)

• Move the mixer's crossfader to the center so both channels can be heard in the master mix.

• Tap your foot or bang your head in time with the beat of turntable 1.

• While holding the record on turntable 2, count with the beat from turntable 1: one, two, three, four.

• Release the record on turntable 2 slightly before the next one so that the cue starts in time with the first record. (CD decks: press the play/pause button or hold down the cue button to play the current cue.)

• Move the mixer's crossfader to the right, to remove turntable 1 from the mix.

If the two records aren't at the exact same tempo, there will be a noticeable shift in the beat during this segue. That's okay, the point of this exercise is to get a clean start on the one. To create smooth rhythmic transitions and tempo-synchronized layers, check out the beat matching instructions in Appendix B.

Beat
Matching

Beat matching, also called beat mixing, is the technique of smoothly layering records with no interruption or variance in the beat. It entails adjusting a turntable's speed (the pitch control) so that the tempo of one record matches another. It also entails accurate cueing, so that each new cut begins in sync with the ongoing music.

Appendix A has instructions for slip-cueing and cueing in time. Beat matching builds on those skills. Beat matching can be used to extend the length of any record by cutting between two copies of the same song. The technique can also be used to segue smoothly between two different records. New York DJ Francis Grasso is credited with inventing and popularizing beat matching. Grandmaster Flash supercharged the technique within a hip-hop context, he perfected ultra-fast breakbeat matching and called it the Quick-Mix Theory. There's more about both DJs in Chapter 4.

Beat matching requires two turntables and a mixer, monitors, headphones, and some records. You'll want to have two copies of the same record (practically any record will do, just have two copies of it) for the first part of this lesson.

Matching Identical Records

First, let's get two copies of the same record to match. This is easiest to learn with records that have long drum beat introductions.

- Set the pitch slider of both turntables to the center (zero) point, so that both decks are theoretically at the same speed.
- Play one copy of the record on turntable 1.
- Move the mixer's crossfader to the left, so that only channel 1 (turntable 1) is heard in the master mix.
- Listen to the beat of the record; make sure you can identify the kick drum and snare drum.
- Count along with the beat of the song and identify the drum sound of the one, the first beat in each measure.
- Assign channel 2 to the mixer's cue channel; you'll listen to turntable 2 through headphones.
- Play the second copy of the record on turntable 2, and find a good cue point. The first one beat of the song's introduction, or the first one beat of a drum break would be typical choices.
- Once you've located the cue, hold the vinyl still while the platter spins below (as discussed in Appendix A). We're going to practice the cue in the headphones.
- Tap your foot and count-in to the beat of the record on turntable 1: one, two, three four.
- Release the record on turntable 2 slightly ahead of the next one beat.
- You should now hear the two turntables playing at the same time and they should be more or less in sync.
- If the records are slightly out of sync, you can lightly tap, push, or drag either record to get the beats closer together.
- If the two records grow more out of sync over time then the turntable speed needs to be adjusted:
  - Try to determine whether turntable 2 is running faster or slower than turntable 1. Use the mixer's crossfader to isolate and compare the two turntables.

- o With your left hand, push or drag the record on turntable 2 to re-align the beats
- o With your right hand, make a slight increase or decrease to the pitch setting by moving the pitch slider.
- o If the beats continue to drift apart, repeat the two previous steps until they lock.
- Once you've finished adjusting the pitch so that the two records will synchronize, find and hold the cue point on turntable 2 again.
- Move the mixer's crossfader to the center so that both channels can be heard.
- Release the record to perform the cue.

When two identical records are close to being synchronized, they'll sound phased or flanged. Once you're able to get the two records to play in sync, you can cut between the two copies, alternately lining-up and performing cues on each turntable without interrupting the beat. This is not an easy technique, don't expect to master it on your first session. It may take weeks or months of diligent practice to get consistent, seamless matches. Start with long breakbeats; as you progress you'll be able to increase your speed and mix shorter segments.

Matching Different Records

Creating smooth segues between two different records is much like matching identical records, but with two complicating factors: First, you'll almost always have to adjust the pitch (speed) of the new record. Second, there are many different beats and rhythmic patterns, and not all of them sound great together, even when played at the same tempo. So selection is always a factor.

For starters, find two records that have very simple beats, preferably with long drum breaks or introductions, and which are already fairly close in tempo. A lot of slow jams are around 90 to 100BPM, many disco favorites are in the 110 to 120BPM range, and speeds of 130 to 140BPM or higher are common in latter-day club music styles. You don't have to know the tempos, just have a sense that they're in the same ballpark.

- Set the pitch slider of both turntables to the center (zero) point, so that both decks are theoretically at the same speed.
- Play the first record on turntable 1.
- Move the crossfader to the left so that only channel 1 (turntable 1) is heard in the master mix.
- Listen to the beat of the record; make sure you can identify the one, the first beat in the measure.
- Assign channel 2 to the mixer's cue channel; you'll listen to turntable 2 through headphones.
- Play the second record on turntable 2, and find a good cue point. The first one beat of the song's introduction, or the first one beat of a drum break would be typical choices.
- Once you've located the cue, hold the vinyl still while the platter spins below.
- Tap your foot and count-in to the beat of the record on turntable 1: one, two, three four.
- Release the record on turntable 2 slightly ahead of the next one beat.

- You should now hear the two turntables playing at the same time, and they are probably somewhat out of sync.
  - o Try to determine whether the record on turntable 2 is at a faster or slower tempo than the first record. Move the crossfader to isolate and compare the two records.
  - o With your left hand, push or drag the record on turntable 2 so that the one beats are re-aligned.
  - o With your right hand, make a slight increase or decrease to the pitch setting of turntable 2.
  - o If the beats continue to drift apart, repeat the two previous steps until they lock.
- Once you've finished adjusting the pitch so that the two tempos will match, find and hold the cue point on turntable 2 again.
- Move the crossfader to the center so that both channels can be heard.
- Release the record to perform the cue.

Note the two-handed approach, adjusting the record's position with the left hand, while making small changes to the pitch slider with the right.

Once you're able to get the two records to play in sync, make note of the songs you just matched and the amount of pitch adjustment applied to record 2. You may want to use a notebook or a computer spreadsheet to keep track of your beat matches. Or just write on the record sleeves. Retaining and using this information will help you increase your speed as you learn to mix.

If you know the tempos of the songs you're working with, it can save a lot of guesswork. Digital turntables such as the Numark TT-X1 have BPM counters built-in, which makes pitch setting a snap. Some mixers, such as the Korg Kaoss Mixer, include BPM counters, as do certain CD decks, or you can get an outboard counter.

We've seen simple hand-held tap counters, such as the Behringer Beatcounter BC100, selling for as little as five bucks. And check out the professional options, such as the Gemini BPM-1, a rack-mounted dual counter that will handle two turntables and two line inputs. The BPM-1 lists for around two hundred dollars, and streets as low as seventy bucks.

CD Beat Matching

Since most professional CD players include a BPM counter and don't require physical cueing, the task of matching beats and mixing different tracks is much easier.

- Set the pitch slider of both CD players to the center (zero) point so that both decks are theoretically at the same speed.
- Move the mixer's crossfader to the left, so that only channel 1 (turntable 1) is heard in the master mix.
- Play a CD on deck 1 and note its BPM (tempo) display.
- Listen to the beat of the record; make sure you can identify the one, the first beat in the measure.
- Assign channel 2 to the mixer's cue channel; you'll listen to CD deck 2 through headphones as you practice the cue.
- Play the second CD on CD deck 2 and note the track's tempo (BPM value).
- Adjust the pitch slider on deck 2 to match the BPM setting of the CD on deck 1.
- Find a good cue point on the second CD (deck 2). The first one beat of the song's introduction or the first one beat of a drum break would be typical choices. Set the cue for this point.
- Tap your foot and count-in with the beat of the song on CD deck 1: one, two, three four.
- Play the cue on CD deck 2 exactly on the next one.
- You should now hear the two CDs playing at the same time.

- They may be slightly out of sync. If so, trigger the cue on the one a few times, while making slight adjustments to the pitch slider, until the tracks lock.
- Once you've finished adjusting the pitch so that the two tempos match, return to the cue point on deck 2 again.
- Move the mixer's crossfader to the center, so that both channels can be heard.
- Press the play/pause button on CD deck 2 or hold down the cue button to perform the cue.

Even with all this great technology, it still takes considerable practice, skill, and listening ability to beat match CDs. It doesn't happen instantly, but you will get better over time, so keep at it!

Scratching

Beat matching and cueing are basic parts of the DJ's craft. They're techniques, skills that can be developed and measured with varying degrees of precision. It's pretty cut-and-dried: two beats are either locked in-sync, or they're not.

Scratching is much more than just a craft or technique, it's an instrumental skill and an art form. Unlike a beat match, there's no simple way to measure the success or failure of a scratch, since it's a purely aesthetic consideration.

No book can truly teach you how to scratch, because there's no simple formula. The best we can do is get your hands on the decks and orient you to the task. It takes months and years of dedicated effort to develop true skills and style.

Stationary Platter

The first two exercises will acquaint you with the basic scratch, or baby scratch. We'll focus just on the turntable and record and leave mixer moves until later.

- Put a record on turntable 1.
- Move the crossfader to the left, so that channel 1 can be heard in the master mix.
- Place the needle on one of the tracks, but leave the turntable motor off (don't press the play button).
- With your left hand place your fingertips on the record, touching the vinyl at about ten o'clock.
- Gently move your hand so that the record turns back and forth, moving the groove underneath the needle.
- You should be able to hear the track as you move the record back and forth.
- Try to locate a kick drum or snare sound.
- When you've found a drum hit, move back and forth over the sound a number of times. Listen to how it sounds as it's played forward and backward.
- Get a feeling for the drum hit's envelope, meaning the note's volume characteristics. Kick and snare sounds usually have a short, fast attack, and a tapered release or fade-out.
- Try varying the speed of your hand movements, notice how a quicker scratch will be higher-pitched, while slower scratches are low-pitched. Faster scratches are also louder than slow scratches.
- Move the needle to another part of the record and find some different sounds, such as a guitar power chord, vocals, or a synth part. Try scratching each sound you encounter, and notice the differences in envelopes, volumes and tones.

Seems pretty easy, right? In a sense, it is. Try moving the record with either hand, keeping a relaxed wrist and arm, making smooth, fluid movements. If the needle skips out of the groove you're probably pressing too hard, bouncing the record. A light touch, applying slight, constant pressure is all that's required.

Spinning Platter

In this section we'll learn to cut, and add that to the basic scratch.

* Press the play/pause button on turntable 1 to start the platter spinning.
* Move the crossfader to the left so only channel 1 is heard.
* Lightly hold the record so that the platter continues rotating freely beneath the vinyl disc and slip mat.
* Move the record to find the sound you wish to scratch. A vocal or horn segment is suggested.
* Release the record with a slight push or throw from the fingertips so that it gets up to play speed almost immediately.
* When you reach the end of the sound, touch the record again to stop it.

This is what's called a cut, it's not much different from the idea of cueing in time as discussed in Appendix A, except that it's in the service of scratching. Use this technique to scratch in a sample from any recording; with a little help the turntable can quickly get up to playing speed.

Now, let's get turntable 2 going and scratch to a beat.

* Put a record on turntable 2 and press the play/pause button to start it playing.
* Move the crossfader to the center, so you can hear both channels in the master mix.

- While listening to the music on turntable 2, scratch on turntable 1.
- Think of the scratch sound as a percussion instrument. Try just scratching in single hits, on every one beat, with silence in between.
- Next, try scratching in two hits per measure, a forward scratch on the one and a backward scratch on the three.
- Then, step up to scratching quarter or eighth notes (four or eight beats per measure), just moving the record back and forth.
- Once you're able to cleanly accompany the beat, start adding accents, playing some notes louder and others softer. The speed of each scratch movement determines its volume and pitch; vary the speed of your scratching motions to create accents.
- Think of the scratch as a percussion instrument; use it to create rhythmic patterns that play with, or against, the beat from turntable 2.
- Now alternate between cutting and scratching. Drop a cue on the first measure, then scratch it on the second measure, then drop it again, and so forth.

CD Scratching

The needs of professional DJs drove the recent advances in CD player design. All of the CD decks mentioned in this book have scratch features, which emulate the behavior of vinyl scratching to various degrees. The jog wheel is the largest knob on any pro CD player, rocking it back and forth lets you scratch the track.

- Put a CD into player 1 and select any track.
- Select the CD player's scratch mode, if it's not already on by default. (Pioneer decks: use vinyl mode.)
- Move the crossfader to the left so that channel 1 can be heard in the master mix.
- Press the play/pause button to play the track until you hear a sound you want to scratch.
- Press the play/pause button to pause the track when you find a sound you want to scratch.

- With your left hand, place your fingertips on the jog wheel, touching the edge of the wheel at about ten o'clock.
- Gently move your hand so that the jog wheel turns back and forth. This will play the audio samples forward and backward.
- Try to locate a kick drum or snare sound.
- When you've found a drum hit, move back and forth over the sound a number of times. Listen to how it sounds as it's played forward and backward.
- Get a feeling for the drum hit's envelope, meaning the shape of the note's volume. Drum sounds usually have a fast, loud attack, and a quick tapered release.
- Try varying the speed of your hand movements, notice how quicker scratches are higher pitched, while slower scratches are lower-pitched. Faster scratches are also louder than slow scratches.
- Set a cue point at the beginning of the current scratch sound. Now play around with the cue, alternate between scratching and cue triggering.
- Move to another part of the track and find some different sounds, such as a guitar power chord, vocals, or a synth part. Try scratching each sound you encounter and notice the differences in envelopes, volumes and tones.

Now, let's get the other deck going, and scratch to a beat.

- Put a CD in player 2 and press the play/pause button to start it playing.
- Move the crossfader to the center so you can hear both channels in the master mix.
- While listening to the music on deck 2, scratch on deck 1.
- Think of the scratch sound as a percussion instrument. Try just scratching in single hits on every one beat, with silence in between.

- Next, try scratching in two hits per measure, a forward scratch on the one and a backward scratch on the three.
- Then, step up to scratching quarter or eighth notes (four or eight beats per measure), smoothly moving the jog wheel back and forth.
- Once you're able to cleanly accompany the beat, start adding accents, playing some notes louder and others softer. The speed of each scratch movement determines its volume and pitch; vary the speed of your scratching motions to create accents.
- Think of the scratch as a percussion instrument; use it to create rhythmic patterns that play with, or against, the beat from CD player 2.
- Now alternate between cutting and scratching. Drop a cue on the first measure, then scratch it on the second measure, then drop it again, and so forth.

Rudimentary Mixer Moves

Although it may appear to casual onlookers that all of the action is on the turntables, half of the art of DJing is mixer control. The channel volume fader, the crossfader, and the input selector toggle switch can all be used to control the envelope, or volume characteristics, of each scratch. This set of instructions applies equally to both phonographs and CD players; we'll use the terms record and turntable for convenience.

- Place your left hand on the record on turntable 1 (the record we're using for scratching).
- Place your right hand on the mixer's channel 1 volume fader.
- First we'll practice forward scratching, also called a stab; start by finding a good scratch sound on turntable 1, then:
  - o Lower the channel 1 volume fader to 0 (off).
  - o Push the record so that a forward scratch is heard, while simultaneously raising the channel 1 volume fader.

o Lower the channel I volume fader, while simultaneously pulling the record backward to return to the beginning of the scratch.

o Work on moving the turntable and volume fader at the same time until you can make clean stabs, silencing the back spinning.

- Next, let's reverse the technique and practice backward scratching, also called a back stab. Locate your scratch sound and position the record so that the stylus is located at the end of the sound since you're playing this sound in reverse.

o Lower the channel I volume fader to 0 (off).

o Pull the record in reverse, so that a backward scratch is heard, while simultaneously raising the channel I volume fader.

o Lower the channel I volume fader, while simultaneously pushing the record forward to return to the end of the sound.

o Work on raising the fader in conjunction with the backspin until you can make clean back stabs, silencing the forward motion.

- Now let's do some work on the crossfader. Raise the channel I volume fader so that turntable I can be heard and play the record.

- Play a record on turntable 2 and raise the channel 2 volume fader so that it, too, can be heard.

- Place your right hand to the mixer's crossfader.

- With two records playing, slowly move the crossfader back and forth, and listen closely for where each channel fades in and out. Look at the crossfader and make note of its position at these cut-in points, where the opposite channel becomes audible.

- The cut-in point is your baseline for crossfader mixing; it determines the range of motion needed to add and silence the scratching.

- Now put your left hand on turntable 1 and your right hand on the crossfader.
- Practice forward and backward stabs, using the crossfader to mute the sounds of the return motions. The goal is to learn the crossfader's range so that you can drop in a sound from turntable 1 without interrupting or muting the beats from turntable 2.
- Next, set the mixer's crossfader at the center point, raise both channel faders so that both turntables can be heard, and place your hand on the input selector toggle switch for mixer channel 1.
- Again, practice forward and backward scratches, but this time use the input selector toggle switch to mute the sounds of the return motions.
  - o Place the channel 1 input switch on phono.
  - o Push the record so that a forward scratch is heard, while flipping the input selector switch to line.
  - o Then quickly pull the record backward to return to the beginning of the scratch, while flipping the input selector switch to phono.
  - o Do lots of forward scratches, as in the two steps above, then switch to backward scratches. In both cases, use the switch to cut off the tail of the return stroke.
- Next, try dropping some cuts, using the input selector switch to mute the sound of the backspin.
- Move over to scratch on turntable 2 and practice with your left hand on the mixer and your right hand on the record.

These exercises are obviously just a starting point. The practices of turntablism have broadened the turntable's expressive range with idiomatic moves such as the transformer scratch, the crab scratch, and beat juggling. You'll learn these as you develop. There are a number of scratch how-to videos and that are a terrific resource for picking up new moves. Better still, once you've mastered the basic motions, you'll start thinking up your own scratches and combinations.

Index